Investment finance in economic development

As a result of the liberalisation of the 1980s, the financial system has acquired a prominent role in developing economies. It is now conventional wisdom that 'financial liberalisation' is *the* means to stimulate economic development.

Investment Finance in Economic Development challenges this assumption and offers an alternative view. The book presents a post-Keynesian approach to the role of banks, financial markets and savings in economic development. It departs from the conventional belief that financial institutions are mere intermediaries between savers and investors, to show that banks have a key, active role in the process of investment finance and growth. Further, financial markets, as the *loci* of allocation of financial savings, are shown to have an important role in supporting financial stability during the process of growth.

Rogério Studart is Associate Professor of Economics and Tutor of Undergraduate Studies at the Federal University of Rio de Janeiro.

Investment finance in economic development

Rogério Studart

ROUTLEDGE

London and New York

First published 1995
by Routledge
11 New Fetter Lane, London EC4P 4EE

Simultaneously published in the USA and Canada
by Routledge
29 West 35th Street, New York, NY 10001

Typeset in Times by Solidus (Bristol) Limited
Printed and bound in Great Britain by
Biddles Ltd, Guildford and King's Lynn

British Library Cataloguing in Publication Data
A catalogue record for this book is available from the British Library

Library of Congress Cataloguing in Publication Data
A catalogue record for this book has been requested

ISBN 0-415-10866-7

To Christine, Rafaella, Camila and Marlene

Contents

Foreword

Victoria Chick

Rogério Studart worked out the ideas in this book as a PhD student at University College London from 1988 to 1992. It was great fun watching the thesis develop through many intense discussions, seminars and summer barbecue parties. While these ideas were developing Rogério's wife Christine was pursuing a Masters degree and they had two lovely daughters. Their time in London was fruitful indeed.

The feature which has long served as the core for development economics as a separate subject is surely the recognition of the specific circumstances of individual countries, yet the mainstream analysis of the financial problems of developing countries is characterised by a proposition long left behind by the institutional structure of most of those countries: that the main inhibitor of investment is insufficient saving. This proposition was valid in eighteenth and even early nineteenth century Britain, where the development of financial institutions lagged behind the needs of the transforming economy; but it is no longer valid in countries with developed banking and financial systems of their own or access to the international financial markets.

Rogério Studart takes this proposition as his starting point and shows that it is the foundation of two of Keynes's propositions: that investment precedes and causes changes in saving, and that finance is independent of saving. Studart uses these propositions to provide a thorough critique of two-gap analysis and the potent modern panacea of financial liberalisation. He substitutes for these conceptions an analysis which develops the institutional foundation of Keynes's distinction between finance and saving, finding a role for saving in the funding, rather than the financing, of investment.

Funding is shown to be important as a means by which the liquidity of the banking system is perpetually restored, thus mitigating the danger of yet further investment: it is essential to find finance, but it is equally essential to fund, that is, to find a permanent home for investment in stable portfolios.

Studart draws a lesson from the now advanced countries during their stage of early development. The Industrial Revolution was, by contrast to today's development ambitions, a very gradual affair, in which financial institutions were growing up along with forms of corporate ownership and capitalist organisation. In this climate of gradual growth, it was possible to imagine steady, stable growth, though in fact the process was punctuated by crises. Why then should we be surprised to find modern development, where both the rate of growth of the economy and its structural transformation is expected to proceed so much more rapidly, devoid of difficulty?

Studart's framework unifies the experience not only of modern and early development but of developed and underdeveloped countries, for it fully acknowledges the influence of institutions, real and financial, on the process of growth and development. The unifying principle which he proposes, as a replacement for the institution-free notion of efficiency, is functionality: a financial system is deemed functional when it is able to provide finance and funding in a way which supports development without substantially increasing the fragility or illiquidity of the financial system.

The theoretical framework is then applied to the Brazilian experience from 1947 to 1983. Detailed examination of the institutional structure – the interrelations between the banks, foreign lending, the central bank, and government – exposes the shifting sources of stress in the system. He particularly demonstrates that the reforms of 1964–5 were a mixed blessing. After 1983 currency reform plans were attempted at frequent intervals. Under these circumstances there was not sufficient stability in the institutional structure to permit the application of a theoretical framework without getting into great detail with little prospect of deriving general results. In any case the basic point has been made: the development of the Brazilian banking system and access to the international system is such that finance is not the operative constraint on growth and development in Brazil. The problem lies in the real investment decisions perhaps, but also, unambiguously, in an underdeveloped and flawed mechanism for funding investment and controlling the liquidity pressure of rapid development. The liquidity pressure has, in various ways which are documented here, been taken on by Government rather than the private sector. Thus the experience does not mirror the crises and bankruptcies of the early British experience; it has, rather, resulted in inflation of staggering proportions.

Rogério Studart presents in this book an integrated approach to the financial preconditions for growth and development, with applicability to any country, advanced or developing. Simultaneously he shows that the general principles here developed manifest themselves differently according to the different institutional structures prevailing. The theory is general; the application is necessarily specific. There is great scope for further applications.

The thesis on which this book is based won the Sayers prize for the best thesis on a topic of monetary theory or monetary history in the University of London. Richard Sayers would have been pleased, and I am very proud.

Victoria Chick
University College London

Preface

One common assumption in models of finance and economic development is that saving is a precondition to investment and economic growth – an assumption which we call hereafter the 'prior-saving' argument. The two-gap models, for instance, claim that external saving is required for development if both the investment–saving and the import–export gaps are to be overcome. The prior-saving argument is also present in the financial liberalisation models, which maintain that internal saving/investment can be increased by stimulating savings with positive interest rates and by enhancing the competition between financial institutions through financial deregulation.

The mention of these two models in this preface is not random, as they have been influential for policy purposes in multilateral agencies as much as in less developed countries' (LDCs') governments. For instance, the two-gap models were fashionable in the 1970s, and were to a great extent used to support the mounting of foreign debt by LDCs. When the debt crisis began in 1982 and voluntary capital inflows rapidly declined, the financial liberalisation models became the main theoretical foundation behind the financial policies advocated by multilateral development agencies such as the World Bank and the International Monetary Fund to LDCs.

This book fully accepts the importance for economic development of efficiency of the allocation of real *and* financial resources, and subscribes the view that financial development is an important facet of the process of development. However, it also claims that the prior-saving argument is a fallacious foundation to understand the problems concerning the financing of growth and is misleading as the basis for a policy towards financially sustainable development.

That the prior-saving argument is a pre-Keynesian concept is recognised by many post-Keynesians. Notwithstanding, few have explicitly acknowledged the full consequence for the analysis of finance and growth, let alone of finance and economic development, of the reversal of causality between investment and saving proposed by Keynes. This reversal in turn relies on a sharp distinction between finance and saving. In this book, this distinction is used in search for an alternative approach to the role of banks, saving and financial markets in the process of development, along post-Keynesian lines.

Our adherence to post-Keynesian theory does not mean, though, that this theory can be straightforwardly used to analyse problems concerning the financing of economic development. Post-Keynesian theory is based on a specific type of financial system, with well-developed banking and non-banking financial institutions and markets for a diversified range of financial assets. Most developing countries, in contrast, do not have developed financial markets, and growth has to depend heavily on bank credit. Such credit-based financial structures need to develop alternative institutions to finance – and, especially, fund – long-term investment, to avoid the risk of financial instability and other possible adverse side-effects of growth. Therefore, the theoretical modifications to post-Keynesian theory, necessary in applications to developing countries, are discussed in this book in the context of the Brazilian case.

Acknowledgements

This book was developed out of my Ph.D. dissertation at the University of London and therefore represents the final stage of a long trajectory which began in January 1989. I cannot thank by name all those who, at different points of this trajectory, inspired my ideas and gave me support to continue. Among the people I want to single out the first is Professor Victoria Chick, my former supervisor, to whom I am intellectually indebted and who discussed substantial matters relating to this book, always providing brilliant comments and suggestions on how to proceed with my research.

I also wish to thank Professor Fernando Cardim de Carvalho, now a friend and a colleague at the Universidade Federal do Rio de Janeiro, who patiently read several draft versions of this study, contributing substantially to it. It was under Professor Carvalho's influence that I began studying post-Keynesian economics and to a great extent it was thanks to his unwavering support and encouragement ever since we first met in 1988 that this book became a reality.

Thanks are also due to Dr Sheila Dow and Rogério Sobreira Bezerra, who read parts of my dissertation and provided me with insightful comments; and to Professors Philip Arestis and Laurence Harris, who gave detailed comments on earlier versions of this study.

I also need to mention the late Professor George Shackle and his most kind wife, Mrs Catherine Shackle. I met Professor Shackle in a conference in Great Malvern, England, in 1988, and was later his and Mrs Shackle's guest for a memorable lunch at his home in Aldeburgh. Even though I was only beginning my postgraduate research, Professor Shackle carefully discussed my ideas, providing me with lessons which I shall never forget. Even now, it is difficult to express in a few words how honoured I feel to have met, to have discussed my ideas with and to have been encouraged by a brilliant academic of the stature of Professor Shackle.

Christine, my wife, has been more than just an 'understanding' partner of this enterprise. She has read, re-read and edited drafts of several versions of this study. In addition, her support and tender comradeship made it possible for me to bear the most difficult times during which this book was written. My family, and especially my mother and my sister Carla, always stood by me, creating an enabling environment for writing this book. Adhemar Mineiro offered his wholehearted friendship when I needed it most. I sincerely thank all these people.

Finally, the financial support received from the National Research Council of Brazil (CNP_q) is thankfully acknowledged.

List of abbreviations

BCB	Banco Central do Brasil (Central Bank of Brazil)
BB	Banco do Brasil S.A. (Bank of Brazil)
BNCC	Banco Nacional de Crédito Cooperativo (National Bank of Cooperative Credit)
BNDE(S)	Banco Nacional de Desenvolvimento Econômico e Social (National Economic and Social Development Bank)
BNH	Banco Nacional da Habitação (National Housing Bank)
CDB	Certificados de Depósitos Bancários (certificates of bank deposit)
CDC	Crédito Direto ao Consumidor (direct consumer credit)
CEF	Caixa Econômica Federal (Federal Savings Bank)
CMN	Conselho Monetário Nacional (National Monetary Council)
FGTS	Fundo de Garantia de Tempo de Serviço (Job Tenure Guarantee Fund)
FGV	Fundação Getúlio Vargas (Getúlio Vargas Foundation)
FINAME	Agência Especial de Financiamento Industrial (Special Agency for Industrial Financing)
Financeiras	Sociedades de Crédito e Financiamento (finance companies)
FINSOCIAL	Fundo de Investimento Social (Fund for Social Investment)
GDP	Gross domestic product
IBGE	Instituto Brasileiro de Geografia e Estatística (Brazilian Institute of Geography and Statistics)
IPEA	Instituto de Pesquisas Econômicas Aplicadas (Institute of Applied Economic Research)
LDC(s)	Less developed country(ies)

LIBOR	London interbank offer rate
LTN	Letras do Tesouro National (National Treasury Bill)
ORTN	Obrigação Reajustável do Tesouro Nacional (Readjustable Treasury Bond)
OTN	Obrigação do Tesouro Nacional (National Treasury Bond)
PAEG	Programa de Ação do Governo (Government's Action Plan)
PASEP	Program do Patrimônio do Trabalhador do Setor Público (Asset Accumulation Program for Public Servants)
PIS	Programa de Integração Social (Program for Social Integration)
SFH	Sistema Financeiro de Habitação (Housing Finance System)
SNCR	Sistema Nacional de Crédito Rural (National Agriculture Credit System)
SUMOC	Superintendência da Moeda e do Crédito (Superintendence of Money and Credit)

Chapter 1

Introduction

In the preface to this book, we expressed our dissatisfaction with the conventional, prior-saving view on finance and economic development. This book, in effect, should be seen as a long essay in persuasion of the need to pursue alternatives to such an established view. The post-Keynesian theory is used as 'large shoulders' in this search for *one possible* theoretical alternative.

In contemporary post-Keynesian theory, finance in a monetary production economy is sharply distinguished from saving – which is said to *derive* from, rather than be a pre-condition for, growth. Investment is the motor of accumulation and finance is what permits investment decisions to materialise. The supply of finance is *causally* determined by banks: it is banks, and not savers, who hold a key position in the process of growth. Only if they share the optimism of entrepreneurs in periods of growth or are led, for any other reason, to accommodate the demand for investment finance, can the monetary production economy grow. This conclusion would appear to leave no role for savings and, hence, for capital markets, but such is far from being the case. Saving, which funds (but does not finance) capital accumulation, has an important role, as we shall see, in maintaining the financial stability of the growing economy.

Keynes's monetary production economy may represent a paradigm on which an alternative view on finance and growth can be built. Nevertheless such a view is based on a specific type of financial system, with well-developed banking and non-banking financial institutions and markets for a diversified range of financial assets. Most developing countries, in contrast, do not have developed financial markets, and growth has to depend heavily on bank credit. Such credit-based financial structures need to develop alternative institutions to finance – and, especially, fund – long-term investment, to avoid the risk of financial instability and other possible adverse side-effects of growth. The theoretical modifications to post-Keynesian theory, necessary in applications to developing countries, are also discussed in this book, especially in the context of the Brazilian case.

As regards its organisation, this book is set out as follows. Chapter 2 surveys the economic literature on finance and economic development. This aims at establishing the theoretical foundations of the prior-saving argument and at determining how such a unifying principle has been used for policy purposes. As illustrations of the use of the prior-saving argument in models of finance and economic development, the two-gap and the financial liberalisation models are appraised. The choice of these two models was not random, as they have been influential for policy purposes in multilateral agencies as much as in less developed country (LDC) governments, as noted earlier in the preface.

Chapter 3 presents the post-Keynesian foundations for the critical appraisal of the prior-saving argument and for the alternative view on finance and economic development proposed in this book. This is done by discussing three common assumptions in most post-Keynesian analyses of finance and growth. These are: (1) finance, and not saving, is the pre-condition to investment; (2) banks, and not savers, play the most fundamental role in the process of finance; and (3) saving *funds* but does not finance accumulation.

In Chapter 4, using the Minskian financial fragility hypothesis, we built on the above-mentioned assumptions in order to complete our post-Keynesian approach to finance and growth with the following complementary assumptions: (4) growth increases the economy's financial fragility; (5) this financial fragility can be mitigated by active *funding*, i.e. the issue of long-term securities by the investing firms to consolidate their short-term liabilities; (6) well-structured and well-functioning financial markets may play a fundamental role in a financially stable process of growth/development, a role which is nevertheless ambiguous because of the inherent volatility of those markets.

The book is mainly concerned with the internal mechanisms to finance accumulation. Nevertheless, given the importance of the external debt problem in many LDCs, the role of foreign debt in development is also addressed. The main conclusion that we want to establish here, which is soundly based on a post-Keynesian perspective, is that foreign capital inflows as sources of finance are only functional to the process of development if they finance transfers of real resources from abroad, which can complement internal accumulation.

Post-Keynesian theory emphasises the role of institutions and conventions in mitigating the uncertainties of decision making in market economies. But most post-Keynesian models implicitly assume a specific institutional background – i.e. one with a developed banking system and organised financial markets. In the context of LDCs, therefore, a post-Keynesian alternative to the 'prior-saving argument' must attempt to generalise its conclusions to other types of financial structures.

Hence Chapter 5 concludes the theoretical part of the book by applying the model of finance and growth (established in the previous two chapters) to the context of development. It begins by distinguishing between credit-based and capital market-based financial structures in the context of the post-Keynesian theoretical framework developed in Chapters 3 and 4. It also shows that the pace and the path of financial development is not independent of the historic circumstances in which development takes place, and it points out the reasons why most 'late-coming' industrialising economies tended to start with bank-dominated financial structures and to develop credit-based systems. Further, this chapter formalises the concept of *functionality*, which is the counterpart from our post-Keynesian perspective of the concept of efficient capital markets. A functional financial system is defined as one which, irrespective of its stage of development or institutional fabric, finances accumulation with the least increase of financial fragility through the process of growth.

Once the post-Keynesian view on finance and economic development is discussed, Chapter 6 establishes a transition between theory and application. This justifies concentrating the case study on the period 1947–83; and presents the method to be used in the analysis and the main hypothesis that we want to analyse in the case study.

In the empirical part of the book (Chapters 7–9), the Brazilian experience of financial and economic development between 1947 and 1983 is analysed. The period is divided into two distinct phases of Brazil's development. The first one (1947–66) was characterised by the import-substitution of durable consumption goods and of a substantial part of light capital goods (1947–61), followed by a recession between 1962 and 1966. The second phase (1967–83) marks the resumption of growth (1967–73) and industrialisation (1974–80) with the Second National Development Plan which promoted the import-substitution of heavier capital goods and chemicals.

As regards the financial structure, the two phases are also divided by the 1964–6 financial reform, which transformed the bank-dominated system into a more complex and segmented structure. The relevance of the Brazilian experience lies in the fact that the reform, at least as regards the provisions for the development of mechanisms to finance long-term investment, was guided by what was previously called the prior-saving argument. This reform attempted to enhance the country's internal saving, and at the same time creating a mechanism to increase the absorption of external saving. This was done by a mixture of institutional reforms (creation of investment banks and incentives to acquire stocks), indexation of financial assets and other measures which were viewed as stimuli to saving. We claim that the misleading theoretical foundations of the 1964–6 reform created a financial system which was even less functional to Brazil's economic development than the one which existed before the reform. In addition, it is claimed that much of the financial chaos which the country increasingly had to face in the 1980s – i.e. internal and external debt, severe financial instability and the highly speculative character of the financial system – can be partly blamed on the 1964–5 financial reform.

Chapter 10 summarises the findings of this book and then presents the conclusions.

Chapter 2

Finance and economic development

The dominance of the prior-saving argument

INTRODUCTION

One common assumption of the models concerned with finance and development is that saving is a pre-condition to investment and economic growth – a view which was called the prior-saving (PS) argument in the introduction to this book. The PS argument has had both theoretical and policy consequences for development economics. From the theoretical perspective, it implies a hierarchy in the dynamics of a capitalist economy: savers, as suppliers of saving/capital, ultimately determine the pace of accumulation.[1]

In what concerns policy-making, the need to increase the availability of either internal or external saving is normally implicit in models attached to the PS argument. Thus policy recommendations have stressed the need to create internal institutional mechanisms to stimulate saving; to attract foreign saving by opening the internal financial system to foreign capital inflows; and to eliminate 'financial repression' and to correct other constraints to the functioning of the market-clearing mechanisms.

This chapter aims at discussing the origins of the PS argument and its consequences to economic development models. The relevance of this discussion will become evident in the next chapters, when Keynes's disputing assumption (that finance and investment precede saving) is used to build an alternative view of finance in economic development.

The chapter is set out as follows. First, we discuss the theoretical foundations of the view that identifies finance with saving. Second, we describe how macroeconomic/financial theories have converged towards the implicit acceptance of this view. Third, the relevance of the above-cited identification to economic development models (the two-gap model and the financial liberalisation model are specifically discussed) is assessed – in view of their relevance in policy recommendation for developing countries in the last thirty years.

THE ORIGINS OF THE 'PRIOR-SAVING' ARGUMENT

Even though it is difficult to trace the origins of any established view in social science, one may at least conclude from reading Schumpeter's *History of Economic Analysis* that the identification of finance and saving has been present in the economic theory every since its founding pillars were laid.[2] For instance, Adam Smith stressed that 'parsimony, and not industry, is the immediate cause of the increase of capital' (op.cit.: 301; as quoted in Schumpeter 1954: 193). Indeed, Smith's influence on this topic of economic theory, as in many others, was crucial: as Schumpeter points out, Smith's position on the macroeconomic virtues of thrift 'marks the victory for more than 150 years to come of a pro-saving theory' (ibid.).

In modern economic theory, the PS argument is in fact a legacy of the classical theory, which, as Chick (1983: 184) correctly reminds us, 'had its beginnings in the setting of an agricultural economy, where the archetypal form of saving was the seed-corn: production not consumed, a real resource.' In such an agricultural economy, income – the harvest – is predetermined; hence the only source of investment is the corn-seed saved, which must logically exist previously to the act of investing.

If the PS argument is a reasonable working assumption in the analysis of an agricultural, barter economy, it is much less acceptable in an industrial economy, where significant part of the means of production are produced for order, thus *after*, and *pour cause*, the act of investing. The question of investment finance is not so much how to allocate a predetermined output between consumption and investment, but to define how much of the *current* output will be made available to investment.

Further, in a monetary economy, the only possible association between the finance and saving is the use of accumulated stocks of money to finance investment, rather than consumption. However, in an economy which has moved beyond metallic money to the use of credit and loans – and this is the case in England since, at least, the seventh century[3] – investment can be financed by 'new money' as much as by the transfer of existing money savings.

Thus, the view that saving is the motor of accumulation – or the creator of 'capital' – contrasts with both 'real' and financial evolutions of capitalism. Paradoxically, this view represents one of the important pillars of mainstream economics. The persistence of such a paradigm can only be explained by other non-economic reasons. For instance, Chick sees the persistence of the principle in the Anglo-Saxon economic in association with the principle of the 'virtue of the thrift':

> [T]hat Victorian principle was urged in that subliminal way that societies find their way to, because its basic aim was industrialisation, and the banks, in the 19th century stage of development, were not adequate to cope with the needs of the rapidly-expanding industry. Most borrowing had to be direct, and that meant prior saving.
>
> (Chick 1983: 191)[4]

Chick's hypothesis is corroborated by the fact that the fast development of the banking system at the end of the nineteenth century did inspire a revision of this view in economic theory. Indeed, the denial of the identification between finance and saving was a central feature of both Keynes's macroeconomics (e.g. Keynes 1936: 178; 1937a: 249) and Schumpeter's (1934) theory of economic development.

Nevertheless, and despite these authors' emphasis that this identification was fallacious as the theoretical foundation of macroeconomics, the pre-Keynesian view became one of the fundamental aspects of 'modern' macroeconomic theory. How this theoretical tendency evolved and how it affected development economic models is assessed below.

Neutral money, neutral credit and the loanable funds theory

As argued above, the 'prior-argument' is only conceivable for the analysis of a barter economy, or if the analyst assumes that the capitalist economy behaves *fundamentally* as a barter economy. A barter economy is one where output and income are predetermined and hence the process of exchange – rather than production – is the main concern of economic analysis.

To picture an industrial economy as a barter economy is thus to assume that, given the state of technique, income is predetermined and, for the purpose of analysis, may be assumed to be unchanging. Indeed, it is one of the principal results of neoclassical theory that full-employment equilibrium is a natural outcome of a competitive economy. Two assumptions are crucial to such a result: first, that techniques and prices are flexible and the latter contain all information required for agents to trade; second, that Say's law – namely that output always creates equal demand – prevails. Price flexibility entails that market-clearing equilibrium is incompatible with the existence of involuntary idle resources. Say's law guarantees that aggregate demand will always correspond to aggregate supply: any discrepancy between individual supply and demand will generate the migration of resources towards the more profitable sectors.

In such a market-clearing competitive economy, money plays two distinct roles: a medium of exchange and the unit of account. Once money is a non-interest-bearing asset, holding money as a store of value can only be justified in the interval between the receipt of income and the acquisition of a good. In the long term, money is necessarily neutral. In this case, the quantity theory of money cannot be disputed: changes of money supply cannot affect real variables, but only money variables.

The postulate of long-term neutrality of money is one of the fundamental principles of classical and neoclassical economics. This postulate has permitted the mainstream economist to distinguish short-term monetary phenomena from long-term equilibrium values, so that all the fundamental theorems can be established in real terms – by the direct consideration of goods, preferences and technical constraints (Carvalho 1992: 32).[5] In Schumpeter's words:

> Real analysis proceeds from the principle that all the essential phenomena of economic life are capable of being described in terms of goods and services, of decisions about them, and of relations between them. Money enters the picture only in the modest role of a technical device that has been adopted in order to facilitate transactions . . . it does not affect the economic process, which behaves in the same way as it would in a barter economy: this is essentially what the concept of Neutral Money implies.
>
> (1954: 277)

Even though constructed for the analysis of an economy where metallic money prevails, the evolution of bank money does not change this postulate as long as banks as well as other financial institutions are pictured as mere intermediaries between saving and investment. That is, as long as credit is also *neutral*, in the sense that it does not interfere with the real forces behind accumulation (thrift and productivity). This has been the role of the loanable funds theory (LFT) in monetary economics (Rogers 1989: ch. 2).

In LFT models, output is 'neoclassically' determined in the labour market. Equilibrium is only achieved when all factors are remunerated according to their productivity.[6] For the purpose of analysis of the 'capital' (saving) market, income can be assumed to be predetermined. In other words, there is no fallacy in the passage from the microeconomic to the macroeconomic level. Consequently, the supply of 'real' saving/capital (S) is seen as determined according to households' inter-temporal preferences (and is inversely related to the interest rate r). In turn, the demand for capital (investment) (I) is a direct function of the return on capital (or the marginal productivity of capital, mpc). Hence the equilibrium (or 'natural') rate of interest (r_n) is the rate which equilibrates the quantity of capital saved (saving) and of capital invested (investment), thrift and productivity.

Now, assume that some technical innovation is introduced into our LFT economy, so that the marginal productivity of investment rises – which is illustrated in Figure 2.1 as a rightward shift of the demand for loanable funds schedule (I). If the savers' intertemporal preferences do not change, this would normally imply an increase in the *natural* rate of interest, causing a decrease in consumption symmetrical to the increase of investment. The banking system *may* decide to maintain the market rate of interest below the natural one, but this can only be achieved in the LFT if the banks accommodate the increase in the demand for loanable funds by creating deposits *ex nihilo* (ΔM^s).

For identical reasons, an increase in the supply of bank money may provoke a departure from equilibrium by reducing the market rate of interest. However, if full employment is assumed and consumers'

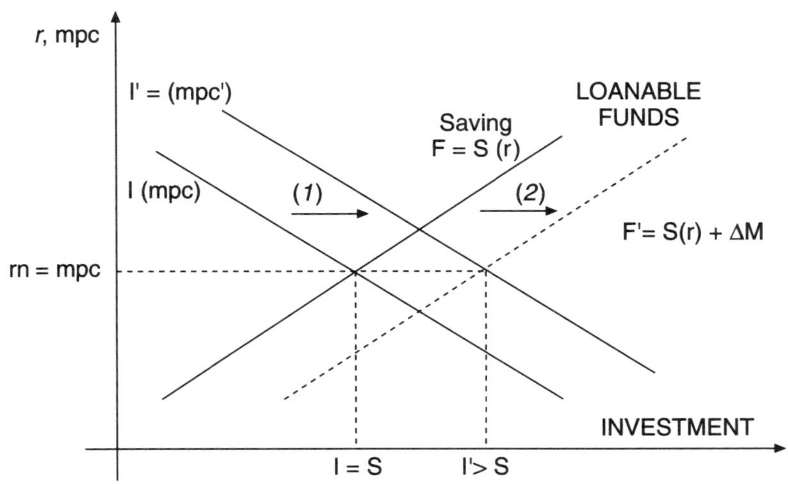

Figure 2.1 The saving and investment schedules in a simplified loanable funds model

preferences are unchanging, this disequilibrium in the money and saving–investment markets will set off a cumulative inflationary process.[7] This is the logic behind the 'forced-saving' hypothesis, which has been, from Wicksell to Robertson, from Pigou to Friedman, a main pillar of monetary economics.

To sum up the argument thus far, the first pillar of the PS argument is the view that 'savings' are the main source of supply of real 'capital'. The second theoretical basis of identification of finance with saving is the application of the perfect market paradigm to monetary economics. This application has been put forth by Lewis (1992: 204) as follows:

> In an ideal world of complete and perfect capital markets, with full and symmetric information amongst all market participants, economic decisions do not depend in any way upon the financial structure. All the potential gains from adding banks are assumed away because every transactor is completely informed and honest about the environment, and frictions and indivisibilities do not exist. If banks do operate, they do so as traders or equity-financed mutual funds . . . since households and firms have the information to arrange their own risk diversification.

The perfect market paradigm establishes that in the long run, if competition prevails in the financial system, the real interest rate will equate saving and investment optimally. For the purposes of this chapter the application of this paradigm to monetary economics has one important outcome: it makes the financial system, including banks, a neutral intermediary between savers and investors. There are, however, two other consequences which are worth remembering.

First, the above-cited application determines that, in equilibrium, there will be no mismatch between investment and saving – hence between aggregate supply and aggregate demand. This is an important hypothesis to sustain Say's Law.[8] Second, the application of the perfect market paradigm is important for policy reasons. If the competitive capital market becomes the standard of efficiency of financial intermediation, inefficiency is associated with anything outside that paradigm.[9] This permits the analyst to view a 'disequilibrium' in the optimal allocation of capital as the result of constraints on the functioning of the capital markets: lack of perfect competition or asymmetric distribution of information become 'distortions' in relation to the optimal, idealised structure. The role of analysis is thus to spot such imperfections and, perhaps, to point ways of re-establishing the sovereignty of the market-clearing forces (e.g. financial liberalisation).

From Hicks and Tobin to the monetarists

The convergence of monetary economics back to the PS argument has followed the track of the 'neoclassicisation' of macroeconomics after Keynes.[10] This theoretical convergence was achieved by the almost universal acceptance by monetary theorists of the Hicksian neoclassical synthesis (Hicks 1937) and the portfolio balance analysis (e.g. Tobin 1958; 1965). Already in Hicks's (1937) 'Mr. Keynes and the classics' Keynes's denial of the identification of saving and finance was played down, as aggregate saving is determined by the rate of interest (and hence is dependent on individual saving decisions):[11]

> As against the three equations of the classical theory,
>
> $$M = k.I,\ I_x = C(i), I_x = S(i,I)$$
>
> Mr. Keynes begins with three equations,
>
> $$M = L(i),\ I_x = C(i),\ I_x = S(I)$$
>
> These differ from the classical equations in two ways. On the one hand, the demand for money is conceived as depending upon the rate of interest (Liquidity Preference). On the other hand, any possible influence of the rate of interest on the amount saved out of a given income is neglected. Although it means that the third equation becomes the multiplier equation, which performs such queer tricks, nevertheless this second amendment is a mere simplification, and ultimately insignificant. It is the liquidity preference doctrine which is vital.
>
> (Hicks 1937: 132–3)

Later Hicks will point out that:

> Mathematical elegance would suggest that we ought to have *I* and *i* in all three equations, if theory is to be really General. Why not have them like this:
>
> $$M = L(I,i),\ I_x = C(I,i),\ I_x = S(I,i)?$$
>
> (ibid.: 138)

The second logical step towards the re-establishment of the pre-Keynesian view on finance/saving is Tobin's (1958) reinterpretation of Keynes's liquidity preference theory. Keynes's liquidity preference theory maintains that the interest rate is mainly a *monetary phenomenon*, determined by supply and demand for money. Especially, he emphasised the role of uncertainty in provoking changes in the demand for money as a store of value. In his framework, money was *not* hoarded for saving purposes, but as a means of postponing the decision (to spend) when the uncertainty of the future changed substantially. This implies that individual saving decisions have little, if any, important effect over the level of interest rates.[12]

The portfolio-balance analysis reinterprets Keynes's liquidity preference theory within a general equilibrium framework, substituting Keynes's concept of uncertainty (as affecting the allocation of financial wealth and its relation to money interest rate) by the one of risk (see Pettenati 1977; and Chick 1983). Risk here is defined as the variance of the return of an asset, which is assumed to be known by all agents. Once the risk preference is established and agents allocate their savings accordingly, the aggregate portfolio of financial assets is determined (Tobin 1958). Variation within the portfolio of assets can only be achieved by changes in interest rates.[13]

The acceptance of the portfolio-choice analysis by Keynesians opened one front of the Keynesians/Monetarists debate, focusing on the period of expectation adjustment and substitutability between assets.[14] This debate can be summarised as follows. In equilibrium savers choose their portfolios according to their preferences and the relative remuneration of different assets. However, in the short run their choice can suffer from monetary illusion and credit can 'force saving' and thus finance levels of investment which are higher than the equilibrium one: monetary phenomena can affect the real forces of thrift.[15]

The convergence towards the view that saving is independently determined from investment partly explains why Keynesian and the Monetarist visions only differ in the short-term analysis (see, for instance, Goodhart 1975: 219–21). For, in the long run, when all monetary illusions disappear, the balance between investment and saving must be re-established. If investment exceeds *ex ante* saving, either the propensity to save rises or saving will have to be 'forced' through inflation. Thus, if the question of the relation between saving and investment became more subtle in the Keynesians/Monetarists than in the Keynes/Classics debate, it is because of the common theoretical background of the former.

From rational expectations to asymmetric information

The rational expectations revolution represented a frontal attack on both the Monetarist and the Keynesian positions.[16] If agents form rational expectations then the possibility of monetary illusion is limited to the very short term. If a strong form of rational expectations is used then money is neutral both in the short and in the long term: any anticipated increase of money supply would just affect prices leaving the level of investment and output intact.

By incorporating rational expectations, neoclassical monetary economics finally abandoned the Wicksellian connection (Leijonhufvud 1981: 131–202) for neo-Walrasian 'monetary theory'. This conversion, however, had a high cost: as Rogers (1989: 3) rightly put it, 'one horn of a dilemma facing neoclassical monetary theorists' is the inessentiality of money in 'modern' neoclassical theory (see also Hahn 1981).

Furthermore, another interrelated horn exists: in neo-Walrasian monetary economics the distinctions between credit, saving, capital and investment, which so much concerned monetary economists since Wicksell, became irrelevant. This has allowed mainstream economics to address saving without even mentioning the mechanisms by which it is transformed into investment – i.e. the financial system. For instance, this is the case of the long survey on saving and development by Gersovitz, which is introduced by the following statement:

> *Saving, a sacrifice of current consumption, provides for the accumulation of capital which, in turn, produces additional output that can be used for consumption in the future.* The process is thus inherently intertemporal. Its presumed operation makes the saving behavior of citizens and their governments central to the development of poor countries. Moreover, threats of expropriation, repudiation and other hostile acts against foreign suppliers of capital, and donor resistance to significant increases in aid, mean that domestic savings is likely to remain the predominant source of capital accumulation in developing countries.
>
> (Gersovitz 1988–9: 382; my emphasis)

If the neo-Walrasian economics renders no role for the financial system, the question of finance also becomes useless. The only way that financial analysis becomes relevant is when the strong assumptions behind the perfect-market paradigm are criticised. That is, the only way out from the straight-jacket of the 'sound microfoundations' of new-Walrasian economics is to point to market failures which inhibit the achievement of the equilibrium results of such economics. This has been the core of the so-called New Keynesian economics.[17]

As regards the role of financial markets as efficient (neutral) intermediaries between savers and investors, New Keynesian models have focused on heroic assumptions about the availability and distribution of information between borrowers, lenders and financial institutions.[18] The relaxation of the perfect information hypothesis permitted these models to explain the role for financial intermediaries in a competitive economy: the lack of costless information gives financial intermediaries the role of assessing the credit-worthiness of borrowers.[19]

A common theme in this new line of thought in financial economics is, in a nutshell, that 'informational asymmetries may introduce inefficiencies in financial markets which may have *quantitatively* significant real effects'.[20] Furthermore, the growing literature on information and incentives information also points to two problems in financial intermediation which can jeopardise the allocative role played by intermediation: adverse selection, where trading parties have asymmetric information prior to contracting, and moral hazard, where the asymmetries arise after contracting.[21] *Asymmetric information* occurs when lenders have trouble determining whether a borrower is a good risk (i.e. good investment projects with low default risk) or a bad risk (bad investment projects with high default risk). Because of this lack of information, lenders will desire to pay for a security that reflects the average quality of firms issuing the securities – a price which is higher than the market value for high quality firms and too high for the low quality ones – a classic case of 'the lemons problem' proposed by Akerlof (1970). Hence, only low quality firms will be willing to sell their securities.

Stiglitz and Weiss (1981) also demonstrated, using a loanable funds framework, that adverse selection would generate credit rationing because low quality firms with riskier projects will be the ones willing to pay the highest interest rates. If lenders cannot identify the riskiest projects, then the supply of loanable funds will shrink when interest rates increase, exactly the opposite result from that theoretically expected. The danger of *moral hazard* may prevent lenders from extending credit, if the interest rate makes it very attractive to do so. In other words, lending would be at sub-optimal levels.

The two cases just point to the possibility that, due to asymmetric information, the financial system may not play its role as broker in the saving–investment process efficiently. In other words, in these cases loanable funds to investment will be lower than potential and allocation of resources will be distorted. This literature presents an embarrassing challenge to the view that financial markets are efficient allocators of capital. But, in reality, it does not seem to advance much from the neoclassical perspective: the role of the financial system is still to be an intermediary between saving and investment;[22] what is at stake is how well this role is performed. This type of argument leads to the view that, were it not for the problems generated by imperfect information distribution or other market failures, then that role would be fully restored and allocative efficiency of capital would prevail.

To sum up, these recent developments explore deviations from the perfect markets paradigm as regards the optimal allocation of the *assets* of financial intermediaries. As far as the theory is concerned, the *liabilities* side is an exogenous variable, determined by the preferences of consumers/savers. The identification of finance and saving is still sovereign.

THE IDENTIFICATION OF FINANCE AND SAVING IN GROWTH MODELS

In growth theory the question of finance has traditionally been seen as one of availability and allocation of saving, normally denoted by the marginal propensity to save s. This is surprising given the Keynesian credentials of one of the founders of modern growth theory: Harrod. Again, this paradox has to do with the convergence towards the PS argument of the models which followed Harrod's.

Harrod's (1939) model is concerned with establishing the level of investment throughout time that will maintain a dynamic equilibrium, i.e. that will continuously fulfil expectations of previously made investments. The fulfilment of such expectations depends on the current level of expected demand in relation to the level of output capacity created by previous investment projects. Thus the model can be built on key variables determining the two outcomes of investment undertakings: namely, income creation (and thus the level of saving) and additional productive capacity (and thus the resulting aggregate production function). The result of Harrod's model is the well-known warranted growth rate which is defined as follows:

$$G_{\mathrm{w}} = \frac{\Delta x}{x} = \frac{\Delta I}{I} = \frac{s}{C} \tag{2.1}$$

where x is output, I is investment, s is the marginal propensity to save and C is the capital–output ratio.

It is important to stress that in Harrod's equation the marginal propensity to save (s) only expresses the gap between income created by a certain level of investment and consumption. Hence, Harrod's perspective is very Keynesian: effective demand must be maintained at a level that satisfies producers. The lower the level of saving, the higher the multiplier and the lower the level of investment required to fill the gap. Or, what is the same, if growth is to be maintained this would require increasing levels of investment in order to compensate for a marginal propensity to consume which is normally lower than 1. Nothing, in Harrod's model, refers to the question of the financing of growth in market economies, and it may be said that financing is implicitly assumed to be always forthcoming.

Already in Domar's version of Harrod's dynamic model, the causality between the marginal propensity to save and the rate of growth is blurred. Harrod's equation was reinterpreted in order to show that the balanced growth would require an improbable co-ordination of the saving ratio, of the capital–output ratio and of the natural rate on a sharp knife edge. If capital is assumed to be scarce, however, saving can constrain growth.[23]

As a matter of fact, after Solow's (1956) interpretation of the Harrod–Domar model, very little remained even of the saving side of the growth model.[24] Solow reinterpreted Harrod's Y as a result of a production function $Y = f\ (K,L)$ homogeneous of the first degree and with substitution elasticities lower than 1. With that reinterpretation he was able to prove that, in the long run, the real product growth rate depended only on the rate of growth of labour supply, and not on the rate of savings. Suddenly, even the saving 'constraint', together with the question of finance, disappeared from the theoretical concern of growth models.[25]

THE PRIOR-SAVING ARGUMENT IN DEVELOPMENT ECONOMICS

The identification of saving with finance in mainstream economics has had a direct consequence on models concerned with finance and development. Capital is commonly assumed to be the scarce factor in less developed countries (LDCs), so saving becomes a constraint to growth (see, for example, Todaro 1981: 58–63; Simonsen 1991): *in development economics, the identification between saving and investment becomes the prior-saving argument.* This is confirmed by a extensive survey on saving and economic development found in the *Handbook of Development Economics*, which begins by the statement by Gersovitz already quoted above (p. 13). That statement is an extreme representation of the view that has permeated the discussion of the question about finance and development ever since Gurley and Shaw attempted (and did not manage) to emphasize the 'financial aspects of growth'. Below we briefly describe this theoretical trajectory.

The Gurley and Shaw heritage

The mainstream literature on finance and economic development owes much to the seminal works of Gurley and Shaw (1955; 1960). For these authors:

> Development is associated with debt issue at some points in the economic system and corresponding accretion of financial assets elsewhere. It is accompanied, too, by the *institutionalization of saving and investment* that diversifies the channels for the flow of loanable funds and multiplies varieties of financial claims. Development also implies, as cause and effect, change in market prices of financial claims and in other terms of trading in loanable funds.
>
> (Gurley and Shaw 1955: 515; their emphasis)

Gurley's and Shaw's debt-intermediation view established a clear interrelation between financial and economic development. First, economic development would be associated with financial development because financial intermediation (external indirect finance) provides potential surplus units with the capacity to spend beyond their earnings. Second, growth would stimulate and be stimulated by the 'institutionalization of saving and investment': income grows, richer wealth-holders will increase their desire to diversify their asset portfolio; if financial innovation is such as to accommodate this 'diversification demand', financial institutions can enhance their lending capacity and thus boost growth; the process becomes then a benign circle.

To sum up, for Gurley and Shaw financial development enhances the intermediation of loanable funds and therefore growth could be stimulated. Nevertheless they also warned of the dangers of financial development. In their view, the separation between the acts of investment and saving meant that financial development would permit higher levels of indebtedness and growth; but this would be closely followed by the deterioration of debt profiles, which would result in higher interest rates.[26] Hence financial development widens the scope for regulatory management.

Notwithstanding the innovative aspect of the debt-intermediation view the prior-saving argument was still the basic tenet: by putting the banking system with the rest of financial institutions in the passive role of mere brokers, Gurley and Shaw denied their capacity to influence the growth path:

> Neither banks nor other intermediaries create loanable funds. That is the prerogative of spending units with surpluses on income and product account. Both banks and other intermediaries have the capacity to create special forms of financial assets that surplus units may accumulate as the reward for restraint on current or capital account. Banks alone have the capacity to create demand deposits and currency, to be sure, but only savings and loans associations can create savings and loans shares: both 'create credit', both transmit loanable funds, both enable spending units to diversify their portfolios.
>
> (1955: 521–2)

At the end of the day, it is the forces of productivity and thrift which matter in the financing of development. The financial dimension only matters if it is underdeveloped.

Gurley and Shaw's failure to present a fundamentally different approach seemingly had a high cost: some of their ideas seemed to have been forgotten by the mainstream economics.[27] Indeed development finance has for the last thirty years been mainly treated by development economics as a problem of availability and allocation of internal and external saving. Two models have dominated the literature: the two-gap model and the Shaw–McKinnon financial liberalisation model.

The two models have different emphases: the two-gap model is concerned with the *external* finance for resources to support development and with development planning; whereas the Shaw–McKinnon model deals with the increase and mobilisation of *internal* resources, mainly through the liberalisation and deregulation of internal saving. Both approaches are based on the PS argument. In the subsequent subsections we describe these models, establish comparisons between the two and seek for the common aspects which ultimately link them to the same theoretical roots.

The role of external saving: the two-gap model

The identification of finance with saving is as much rooted in closed-economy macroeconomics as it is in open-economy macroeconomics. For instance, the saving–investment approach to the balance of payments defines 'external saving' as the difference between internal investment and internal saving, which is identical to the result in the current account of the balance of payments:

$$Y \equiv C + I + G + (X - M) \tag{2.2}$$

$$S_e \equiv I - S \equiv M - X \tag{2.3}$$

where Y is income, C is consumption, I is investment, S is internal saving, S_e is external saving, G is government expenditure and $(X - M)$ is the deficit/surplus of the current transactions of the balance of payments (see, for example, Dismoor 1990: 3–4n).

The identification of external finance with external saving may seem inconsequential. However, when it comes to policy it shows its importance. For instance, if a continuous balance-of-payments deficit problem is interpreted as scarcity of internal saving, then the solution is to increase internal saving. Finally, if the PS argument is carried out consistently, interest rates must be raised and internal absorption must be reduced in order to re-establish the external sector equilibrium. This was, for instance, the line followed by the International Monetary Fund (IMF) and the World Bank to the debt crisis in the 1980s (see FitzGerald and Vos 1989; Felix and Caskey 1990).[28]

An application of the PS argument to the analysis of the role of 'external saving' in the context of an open developing economy is the two-gap model. Two-gap models (TGMs) are based on the idea that the lack of internal saving can posit a constraint on economic development.[29] External saving is thus required in two initial stages of development: first, to overcome the difference between planned investment and saving; second, to finance the increasing gap between planned imports and exports. The two gaps are expressed *ex post* by the national account identity

$$I - S \equiv M - X \tag{2.4}$$

where the left-hand side of the equation represents the investment–saving gap and the right-hand side the import–export gap. By definition, equation (2.1) is concerned with *ex post* concepts, whereas the TGMs are concerned with the relation of the two gaps with economic growth and with the means to overcome them. The model can be summarised as follows:

The investment–saving gap

$$Y_t = Y_0 e^{rt} \tag{2.5}$$

$$I_t = \frac{\mathrm{d}K}{\mathrm{d}t} = \frac{\mathrm{d}(kY)}{\mathrm{d}t} \tag{2.6}$$

$$S_t = \alpha Y_0 \mathrm{e}^{rt} \tag{2.7}$$

$$I_t - S_t = (kr-\alpha) Y_0 \mathrm{e}^{rt} \tag{2.8}$$

The import–export gap

$$X_t = X_0 \mathrm{e}^{xt} \tag{2.9}$$

$$M_t = mY_0 \mathrm{e}^{rt} \tag{2.10}$$

$$M_t - X_t = mY_0 \mathrm{e}^{rt} - X_0 \mathrm{e}^{rt} \tag{2.11}$$

where r represents the target rate of growth, k is the constant capital output ratio ($Y = kK$), α is the marginal propensity to save, m is the marginal propensity to import and x is the expected rate of growth of exports (determined by the conditions of world trade).

The condition for balanced growth is (i) that the economy starts off from balanced trade, (ii) that $r = x$ and (iii) that $kr = m$.[30] Since there is no automatic mechanism that will guarantee any of these three conditions, the TGMs conclude that development will be a disequilibrium process. Such a state of disequilibrium cannot be held forever: the continuance of growth depends on the LDC's capacity to raise internal saving or on the supply of external saving. Furthermore, since the saving capacity of LDCs is assumed to be limited because of the low *per capita* income, foreign aid is desirable in the starting-up of the growth process (Chenery and Strout 1966; 1968).

The short-term disequilibrium between internal saving and investment will, according to the above-cited authors, be overcome in the long run: it is assumed that once the developing economy has sufficiently increased its per capita income (which allows for a higher propensity to save) and its export capacity (by improving productivity in export sectors), it can finally achieve self-sustaining growth and even repay the debt acquired in complement of financial aid (Chenery and Strout 1968: 913).

Many Latin American countries launched growth-cum-debt development strategies in the 1970s using as theoretical guidance views which were very similar to the two-gap model. This took the form of proposals to open the countries financially in order to profit from the excess of liquidity of the international financial market of the 1970s (Felix and

Caskey 1990). The main idea behind this view has neoclassical roots: since the return on capital had to be higher in the underdeveloped countries than in the developed economies (due to the former's lower capital intensity), international interest rates would be lower then the prospective returns of investment made in LDCs.

If the observation made in the paragraph above is accepted, it is easy to understand the development within the mainstream view after the so-called debt crisis of the 1980s. For, after the interest rate shock of 1979 and the Mexican *de facto* moratorium in 1982 led to a fast contraction of credit to the highly indebted LDCs, the growth-cum-debt strategy was completely discredited.

Indeed the model has been abandoned in the 1980s, and substituted by the financial liberalisation models, which emphasise the need for LDCs to increase internal saving rather than counting on external saving.[31] The PS argument remained; it was only the historical circumstances that changed.

The financial liberalisation models

The financial liberalisation model (FLM), developed after Shaw's (1973) and McKinnon's (1973) classics, has exerted considerable influence on macroeconomic policy in developing countries in the 1970s and 1980s, particularly through the recommendations of the IMF and the World Bank.[32] The analysis is based on the idea that many developing economies suffer from *financial repression*, a 'misguided' development strategy of low interest rate ceilings and selective credit policies. It is argued that financial repression inhibits saving by deliberately maintaining interest rates below their natural level. With financial repression, the argument goes, even though investment opportunities abound, growth is kept below its potential (e.g. Fry 1989: 19; McKinnon 1973: 59–61; Shaw 1973: 8).[33]

Perhaps the most interesting aspect about most FLMs is that they are completely devoid of institutional content; they completely disregard the institutional aspects of LDC's financial systems.[34] Thus, within its rationale, solutions to problems related to the financing of development need only consider re-adjusting relative prices. For instance, the lifting of deposit ceilings is pictured as a panacea that would lead to the establishment of a superior equilibrium position with higher levels of savings, investment and growth. It is also assumed that a less regulated and less 'repressed' financial market would equilibrate saving and investment optimally.

The model presented below (based on Kumar 1983) is fairly representative of FLMs developed after the original works of Shaw (1973) and McKinnon (1973).[35] First of all an unlimited supply of labour is assumed, so equilibrium output is determined not necessarily at full employment but at the point where the marginal productivity of labour equals an institutionally determined wage deflated by a price index. As usual in this type of model, output is assumed to be at its equilibrium level, so the goods equation is simply dropped, and the discussion centres on the money and saving–investment markets.

Investment is still a function of the marginal productivity of capital, but the saving function is restated. It is claimed that the lack of diversified financial markets implies no alternative for savings other than in physical capital and bank deposits. Furthermore, following McKinnon's (1973: 57–61) hypothesis of money–capital complementarity, investment is assumed to be indivisible and hence a lump-sum expenditure.[36] So individual deposits are also used for the accumulation of savings in order to finance a minimum investment level (I_{min}).

In his model, for instance, Kumar assumes that 'the net acquisition of real cash balances [$d(M/P)/dt$] by savers is channelled via bank credit to either private borrowers who wish to accumulate capital [I_b], or to government for current consumption [G]'. Investment can be either self-financed (I_s) or financed by the loanable funds intermediated through the banking system (I_b). Finally, the total supply of loanable funds available for private investment equals the newly-created money balances ($d(M/P)/dt$) minus the part appropriated by government to finance consumption (G). In algebraic terms:

$$\text{IF} = I_s + I_b = S$$

and

$$I_s = s'Y$$

$$I_b = m^* - G \qquad m^* = \frac{d(M^s/P)}{dt}$$

where Y is current income, s' is private propensity to save out of current income,[37] m^* is the additional money balances created by the banking system and held by savers, M is the nominal money balances held by savers, P is the price index, G is the increase in real cash balances appropriated by the government for current consumption purposes, S is aggregate saving[38] and IF is the aggregate supply of funds available for investment. Thus the following flow of funds equation can be written:[39]

$$S = s'Y + m^* - G. \tag{2.12}$$

Sources of finance are thus basically savings from current income and real balances accumulated in the form of bank deposits. On the demand side, government and private sectors compete for the existing loanable funds. Finally, investment is a function of the average return to physical capital (r_k) and the real deposit rate (r^*):

$$I = f(r_k, r^*) \qquad f_{rk} > 0, f_{r^*} < 0 \tag{2.13}$$

$$r^* = r - \pi^e$$

where r is the deposit interest rate and π^e is the expected rate of inflation.

In this simplified model, the banking system is simultaneously a broker of capital and a supplier of the means of payments. Deposits are demanded for saving (and investment) and transactions, and hence the real demand for money function $L(')$ – assuming it is homogeneous of degree one in Y – is as follows (after Kumar 1983: 21):

$$\frac{M^d}{P} = L\ (r^*,y) \qquad L_{r^*} > 0,\ L_y > 0 \tag{2.14}$$

where y is output and the deposit interest rate appears as a central variable. Once the money supply (M^s) is exogenously given by the monetary authorities, equilibrium in the money market is given by

$$M^s = PL(r^*,y) \tag{2.15}$$

Assuming adaptive expectations, a once-and-for-all expansion of money supply can only affect money demand during the period of adjustment of expectations. As in the loanable funds approach, any increase of money supply beyond the 'desired' level of savings (which here can only assume the form of bank deposits) would only result in inflation in the long run.

Given the above framework, the policy of 'financial repression' is described as one which seeks to promote investment by maintaining the real deposit interest rate below its (positive) equilibrium levels. Such a policy would result in the rationing (non-price allocation) of scarce saving – which is seen as a fertile ground for inefficiency and an easy source of windfall profits to the banking system (Fry 1989: 18). When associated with government deficits, it would reduce the availability of scarce resources to the private sector – and hence leave savings to be unproductively allocated by the short-sighted bureaucracy.

Hence, the argument continues, the appropriate financial policy in the context of LDCs has to focus on incentives to increase the real demand for money in the form of deposits – i.e. to raise real deposit rates. This would expand the resources (loanable funds) necessary to finance current investment, and provide 'small investors' with a way of accumulating saving for investment in a less inflationary manner. Furthermore, such a policy of financial liberalisation would unify the capital market, increase the return to domestic savers and allocate this enhanced saving to higher-return (more productive?) projects, besides eliminating other forms of fragmentation.[40]

SUMMING UP

Mainstream development economics has, in the last thirty years or so, moved from the view that external saving was required in the first stages of development (the two-gap model) to one which privileges policies towards increasing internal saving in order to achieve sustained growth (the Shaw–McKinnon liberalisation model). Even though these models present different prescriptions to the problem of financing development, both share the same unifying principle: the PS argument.

The identification of finance with saving is neither new nor unquestionable. For instance, already in 1937, Ohlin, in a well-known debate with Keynes and others on finance, investment and saving, had expressed a position identical to that of supporters of the financial liberalisation literature:

> If an authoritarian government fixes a rate of interest which is much lower than the rate which would prevail in a free market, then during any period saving and new investment *ex-post* are nevertheless equal, but the quantity of credit *offered* is found to have been smaller than the quantity *demanded*; some form of 'rationing' takes place. *The credit market reacts in the same way as the commodity market, when maximum prices are fixed.*
>
> (Ohlin 1937b: 424; my emphasis)

This view was insistently criticised by Keynes, among others, as a fallacious foundation for analysing the financial dimension of a market economy. For Keynes, individual saving was not *causally* an important variable in the determination of the supply of investment finance. Banks, and not savers, 'hold the key position in the transition from lower to a higher scale of activity ... [and] the investment market can become congested through shortage of cash ... [but] never ... through shortage of saving' (1979: 222). Banks are more than mere 'social accountants' or 'screening devices', their expectations and their 'animal spirits' are at par with other entrepreneurial expectations in the determination of the level of investment, output and employment.

In other words, Keynes's claim that finance and investment precede saving, reversing the neoclassical causality, implies a significant change in the 'hierarchy' in the determinants of the dynamics of capitalist economies. Rather than the individual saving decisions, it is the *animal spirits* of entrepreneurs and the readiness of bankers to finance investment which make the (capitalist) world go round. Keynes's critique is thus based on an alternative view of the laws of motion of a market economy (the monetary-production economy paradigm) and the finance-investment-saving-funding circuit. In the next three chapters, we build on this critique to present a post-Keynesian view of finance and development.

Chapter 3

Departing from the prior-saving argument

Finance in a monetary production economy

INTRODUCTION

In the previous chapter it was established that the unifying principle of most models of finance and development is that saving is a pre-condition for accumulation. It was also indicated that Keynes's disputing view (i.e. that finance and investment precede saving) would be used in this book as the starting point of an alternative approach.

In this chapter the foundations of Keynes's and post-Keynesians' views on finance are discussed. Initially it sets out the principles behind Keynes's paradigm of the monetary-production economy and shows why investment is the *causa causans* of output and employment in this paradigm. Further it argues the case that Keynes's view on finance is deeply rooted in his perception of the stage of development of the banking system. We then build on the Keynes's paradigm of a monetary-production economy to stress the fact that banks (and not savers) are the suppliers of finance and a simplified model of the banking firm under uncertainty is presented. Finally we address the consequences of the post-Keynesian view on finance for open-economy analysis.

THE MONETARY PRODUCTION ECONOMY

Neoclassical economics presumes that, in equilibrium, a market economy behaves as if it were what Keynes called a real-wage or co-operative economy. As the name suggests, in such an economy production is organised co-operatively and the output distributed in kind: 'the factors of production are rewarded by dividing up in agreed proportions the actual output of their co-operative efforts' (Keynes 1979: 78). In other words, in equilibrium the real income of each factor corresponds to its productivity.

If money exists in such co-operative economies, it acts as a mere medium of exchange: money can only be demanded because of the time-lags which exist in the process of trading goods. A co-operative or real-wage economy behaves like a barter economy. As stated earlier (Chapter 1), the main economic problem of such an economy is the allocation of the predetermined output. An efficient allocation of resources will be that one which, given the consumers' preference, maximises the present and future welfare of society.

In contrast, Keynes's theory is based on what he called the monetary-production economy or entrepreneur economy. In a monetary-production economy, the means of production are privately owned and production takes place through the entrepreneurs' hiring of labour. *Because in such an economy, for the reasons that we shall discuss below, full employment is not guaranteed, and because involuntary unemployment means wastage and human suffering, the main problem of Keynes's economics is to promote full employment.* The three keywords to Keynes's economics are time, uncertainty, money and irreversible time. How these words are articulated into a coherent alternative to mainstream economics is discussed below.

Time, uncertainty and non-neutral money

One of the prominent aspects of Keynes's and the post-Keynesian modelling of the economy is the use of historical rather than logical time, or, what in practice means the same, of historical analysis rather than equilibrium analysis.[1] In a nutshell the difference of approaches have been summarised as follows:

> Historical analysis is defined as the study of a series of calendar periods in which foreseen events play an important part in changing the agents' plans, and thus the path of the system over time. Equilibrium analysis is characterized by the comparison between equilibrium positions.
>
> (Amadeo 1991: 6n)

For Keynes and for the post-Keynesians, historical analysis is the appropriate way to analyse decision making in what Davidson has called a non-ergodic world. The principle of ergodicity, which is the basis of the concept of probabilistic risk, 'assumes that economic processes are basically stationary, so in the long run agents can learn how they operate and, by adapting their behaviour to the environment, long-period equilibrium positions can be attained' (Carvalho 1992: 42). In contrast, in a non-ergodic environment 'there is no basis to form calculable probabilities' so that future probabilities are 'numerically indeterminate and non-comparable'.[2]

Unlike an ergodic world, in the uncertain, non-ergodic world money is more than a convenient means to trade goods: it is also a convenient means to delay decisions.[3] This is what makes money an 'asset', despite the fact that it bears no interest. In Keynes's words:

> partly on reasonable and partly on instinctive grounds, our desire to hold money as a store of wealth is a barometer of the degree of our distrust of our own calculations and conventions concerning the future. Even though this feeling about money is itself conventional or instinctive, it operates, so to speak, at a deeper level of our motivation. It takes charge at the moments when the higher, more precautious conventions have weakened. The possession of actual money lulls our disquietude; and *the premium which we require to make us part with money is the measure of the degree of our disquietude.*
>
> (Keynes 1937a: 116, my emphasis)

The fact that money can be held as a store of wealth is the basis of Keynes's principle of the non-neutrality of money. In other words, because money is the liquid asset *par excellence*, it is a safe haven in times of uncertainty: a way of postponing expenditure when the future becomes cloudier. Its demand, that in more certain times is predominantly determined by the volume of transactions, can change abruptly in such times. This is one side of Keynes's postulate of the non-neutrality of money. The other is the supply side.

For Keynes, the supply side of money can be defined by two further characteristics of money as an asset: money has zero elasticities both of production and of substitution. This means that, on the one hand, 'money cannot be readily produced; – labour cannot be turned on at will by entrepreneurs to produce money in increasing quantities as its price rises in terms of the wage-unit' (1936: 230). On the other hand, because the utility of money is solely derived from its exchange value, 'as the exchange value of money rises there is no tendency to substitute some other factor for it'.

From the supply- and demand-side characteristics of money, as described by Keynes, emerges his and the post-Keynesians' postulate of the non-neutrality of money. In Davidson's (1988: 330) words:

> Money's non-neutrality is associated with the fact that individuals

> recognise that, in an uncertain [non-ergodic] (as opposed to statistically predicable, but risky [ergodic]) world, the possession of money provides both the flexibility which permits one to take advantage of previously unforeseeable opportunities and the self-insurance against unwelcome events.

That is, because the demand for money as a store of value can vary abruptly as uncertain expectations change, and the supply does not respond endogenously, money is non-neutral. This non-neutrality is what makes it inconceivable to analyse the laws of motions of a market economy by establishing a dichotomy between real and money variables. This is the essence behind the proposition of a different paradigm by both Keynes and the post-Keynesian: the monetary production economy. This is our next, interrelated topic.

Production and non-neutral money

Because output is not directly distributed to workers and because an entrepreneur economy is decentralised, contracts (between entrepreneurs, workers and suppliers) are essential components of this economy. These contracts must be denominated in an accepted medium of exchange. Finally, because money is at the same time a widely accepted medium of exchange and a store of value, it has the power to discharge contracts. Money allows the entrepreneur to have access to the physical resources and labour required for production –[4] thus whoever has money or the capacity to create money (for example, the State and banks) can influence the allocation of resources.

In entrepreneur economies, production is a time-consuming activity which requires that entrepreneurs commit (their own or borrowed) resources before the return on the output is known – the entrepreneur economy is essentially a forward-looking system. The law of production of an entrepreneur economy is thus defined as follows:

> [A] process of production will not be started up, unless the money proceeds expected from the sale of the output are at least equal to the money costs which could be avoided by not starting up the process.
>
> (Keynes 1979: 78)

This law is what guides Keynes's principle of effective demand. This represents, according to Keynes himself (1936: 25), the substance of his general theory of employment. Although detailed examination of this principle is beyond the scope of the present book, some analysis is nevertheless in order.[5] First, one must consider that Keynes's firms are profit-seeking entities, deciding in a non-ergodic environment. In such an environment, expectations are an inseparable part of the decision making of these entities:

> Expectation is necessary for two reasons: first, because time is in some sense irreversible; second, because there are costs associated with the use, and the transfers between uses, of resources. If it were always possible for us to retrace our steps and to put ourselves, without cost, into the most advantageous position at each moment, the need for expectation beyond the most immediate period would be removed and, thereby, uncertainty would be rendered impotent.
>
> (Dixon 1986: 586)

Unlike a barter economy, in a monetary economy a change of expectations can more easily affect production and employment because money can be used as the instrument to postpone decisions. Indeed, if the firm sees prospects of decreasing demand for its products, it is only reasonable that it will increase its demand for money in order to face its future (already contracted) financial commitments. By withdrawing money (or by not borrowing money from banks), firms obstruct the process of income creation – and thus, of aggregate-demand creation. For the firms as a whole, pessimistic expectations are a self-fulfilling prophecy.

Thus, in a nutshell, the principle of effective demand is a direct result from Keynes's depiction of market economies as monetary-production economies,[6] where money is non-neutral and expected money profits are the guide for entrepreneurial decision making. This principle maintains that output and employment will be determined at the point where the *expected* aggregate demand (D^e) curve intersects the aggregate supply curve. The D^e curve refers to the aggregate of estimates of anticipated sales (Chick 1983: 65). The distinction between *actual* and *estimated* demand is an essential feature of Keynes's analysis:

> The *expected* results are not on a par with the *realised* results in a theory of employment. The *realised* results are only relevant in so far as they influence the ensuing expectations in the next production period. This period is covered by *short-period* expectations.
>
> (Keynes 1937a: 119)

The aggregate supply curve Z represents the aggregate cost of producing an output Q, which is obtained by multiplying the marginal cost MC by the level of output. Since the cost is assumed to be composed solely of wages, then

$$MC = \frac{\mathrm{d}(wN)}{\mathrm{d}Q} = w\frac{\mathrm{d}N}{\mathrm{d}Q} = \frac{w}{Q'}$$

so that

$$Z = \frac{w}{Q'}\frac{Q}{N}N = \frac{A}{Q'}wN \tag{3.1}$$

where A stand for the average physical productivity of labour and Q' for the marginal productivity. Assuming diminishing returns, Z will increase with N, but at a faster pace (Figure 3.1).[7]

Since this is a system of simultaneous equations, the figure does not imply causality. However, for the sake of analysis we can choose one of the three quadrants to discuss the *rationale* behind the diagram.

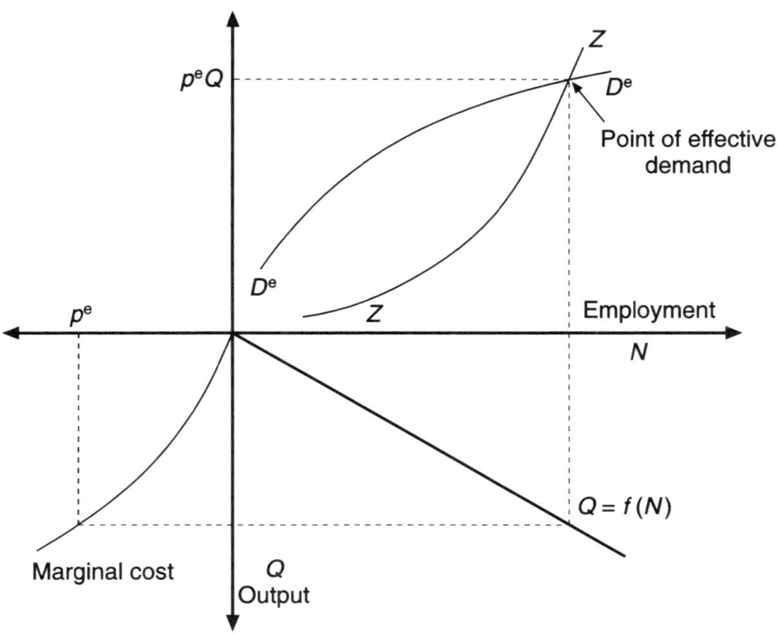

Figure 3.1

Thus, starting from the third quadrant, the marginal cost curve is drawn by assuming that the costs of production are known and returns are diminishing. The profit-maximising output is found at the point where the price entrepreneurs expect to receive from their products (p^e) equals the marginal cost of producing them.

Once the level of output is determined, the amount of employment will be determined by a function (f) associating the level of output and employment (second quadrant). The marginal cost and the level of output determine the Z curve, whereas the level of aggregate demand (D) will be partly determined by the consumption out of income corresponding to employment offered by entrepreneurs (N) (first quadrant). The point of effective demand will be that where D and Z intersect.

Keynes uses the principle of effective demand to deny the classical assumption that a market economy is a self-correcting system gravitating around full employment. He explicitly criticised the view that wage flexibility would automatically bring the economy out of a recession. On the contrary, Keynes claimed, a decline of wages would affect the aggregate supply curve as much as the aggregate demand curve, and therefore the equilibrium result was neither necessarily full employment nor stable. For Keynes, the cyclical pattern of a capitalist economy had more to do with the volatility of investment than the 'rigidities' of the labour (or indeed any other) market. This is the topic of our next section.

THE DETERMINANTS OF AGGREGATE DEMAND

Contrary to what the quotation above (p. 30) seems to imply, Keynes clearly chose not to emphasise the distinction between expected and actual aggregate demand in his *General Theory* (1937c). Instead, he proceeded to discuss, in Books III and IV of his *opus magnum*, the determinants of consumption and investment planned by consumers and entrepreneurs rather than as estimated by producers of consumer and capital goods (Chick 1983: 64). This 'tactic', however, seems consistent with Keynes's emphasis on investment – and, therefore, on the role of (inherently volatile) long-term expectations – as the *causa causans* in the determination of output and employment. That is, by assuming that short-term expectations are always fulfilled, the production of and the demand for consumption goods can be assumed stable whereas the demand for investment goods becomes the main determinant of the changes in total employment and income.[8] In more conventional (Keynesian) words, this involves redefining the aggregate demand curve (D^e), for a closed economy with a small government, as follows:

$$D = c(N,w) + I(r,E) \tag{3.2}$$

where C is consumption, N is the amount of employment, w is the average wage, I is investment, r is the rate of interest and E is the state of long-term expectations.

Having said this, it becomes clear why, after a lengthy exposition on 'definitions and ideas' (1936: 35–85), Keynes spends forty-two pages explaining the determinants of consumption and dedicates another 109 to the determinants of investment. The reason for this imbalance is well known: Keynes considered investment, of all the components of aggregate demand, to be the most volatile; whereas consumption can be assumed a stable function of income without losing much theoretically. In turn, investment is assumed to be the independent variable in (3.2) – and thus *causa causans* in the determination of employment and output. The reasons why investment is potentially more volatile than consumption are discussed below.

Long-term expectations

In the chapter of the *General Theory* dedicated to long-term expectations, Keynes attributes two sorts of uncertainties which make investment relatively more volatile than consumption. First, he emphasises the tenuity of the basis of knowledge for forecasting the yield of an asset that makes many production periods become productive.[9] The second source of instability is, according to Keynes, the close relation between stock prices and the evaluation of investment opportunities by the entrepreneurs. While the first of Keynes's assumptions is relatively straightforward, the second needs elaboration.

The financial cost of reversing an investment decision in the early stages of capitalism was normally very high, and sometimes such a reversion might not be possible. However, the evolution of organised investment markets changed the necessary long-term commitment of investment (Keynes 1936: 150–1). Because firms could be bought through mergers and take-overs, the volume of new investment became highly influenced by changes in stock prices. For,

> there is no sense in building up a new enterprise at a cost greater than that at which a similar existing enterprise can be purchased; whilst there is an inducement to spend on a new project what may be seem an extravagant sum, if it can be floated off on the Stock Exchange at an immediate profit.
>
> (ibid.: 151)

Keynes's concern with the negative role played by speculation on investment decisions is an important part of his investment theory. However, this should not shadow the basic message of this theory: that the return on any productive activity in a decentralised economy is, almost by definition, uncertain. The wider the gap between the decision to commit resources and the return on the capital used, the higher the level of uncertainty. Given the fact that investment generally involves long-lived assets, investment is thus potentially very unstable.

A further source of volatility to investment is the fact that, as a store of wealth, it competes with other assets and means to accumulate. This is where the rate of interest enters Keynes's principle of effective demand. This is our next topic.

The rate of interest

In a monetary production economy, money is demanded both as a medium of exchange and as an asset. As an asset, it provides its holders with the ability to carry wealth into the future. This, according to Keynes, is what links the rate of investment and the rate of interest. Understanding Keynes's view requires an inquiry into what that author called the attributes of money *vis* other assets in Chapter 17 of the *General Theory*.

In the above-cited chapter Keynes distinguishes assets by their 'own-rates' of return,[10] consisting of the following:

1. the rate of quasi-rents expected to be earned from its use or possession (q);
2. the ratio between the expected carrying cost (involved in holding an asset over time) and its spot price (c);
3. the expected rate of change of its expected price in relation to its spot price (a); and
4. the liquidity premium, or the implicit cost of converting the asset into a means of payment (l), both in terms of the opportunity cost involved in the time required to sell it and the transactions cost in such an operation.

The equilibrium solution in the asset market requires that all the assets' own rates be equal. That is, for every asset i or j:[11]

$$a_i + q_i - c_i - r_i = a_j + q_j - c_j - r_j. \tag{3.3}$$

Money is the liquid asset par excellence: its liquidity premium is the maximum liquidity premium – whereas all other assets share that attribute in a descending scale – and its carrying cost is negligible. If money is the nth asset, the equilibrium solution for the $n - 1$ assets existing in the economy is

$$a_i + q_i - c_i - r_i = q_n - r_n \qquad i = 1 \ldots n - 1. \qquad (3.4)$$

Assuming increasing carrying costs (c) and decreasing marginal returns (q), the own-rate of each non-monetary asset declines as its stock increases. Given that equilibrium stocks are adjusted so that all the own-rates must be equal, the asset with the most slowly declining own-rate will set the floor for expected returns: all the other own-rates will eventually have to conform with this asset's own-rate (Winnet 1992: 58). In particular, this means that the 'marginal efficiency of investment' will also have to be higher than the interest rate in order for investment to be worthwhile.

This remits us to the determinants of money's own-rate of interest, i.e. its demand and supply functions. As explained earlier in this chapter, if uncertainty could be ruled out, there would be no reason to hold money balances either for transactions purposes or as a store of value. Theoretically all transactions could be contracted in advance and delivered in the future according to those contracts. In an uncertain environment, money is demanded both as a means of payment for current and forward contracts and as an asset. Let us consider first the demand for money as a means of payment.

In an economy where both the organisation of production and the distribution of its fruits are based on contracts, money balances are held because of their power to discharge contracts (the transactions motive)[12] and/or as stores of value to be used for unexpected expenses (the precaution motive). This means that the demand for money on these accounts is determined by both the current and the expected levels of activities (Davidson 1978: chs 7 and 8).

Expectations are also an important factor in the demand for money as an asset (the speculative motive) – a demand which is guided by the perceived opportunities of capital gain in financial markets. The speculative demand for money mirrors the state of expectations of the agents in financial markets and changes with shifts in liquidity preferences.

In the *General Theory* the demand for money on transactions and precautionary accounts is assumed to be relatively stable in relation to the level of activities. In contrast, the speculative demand is deemed relatively more volatile (Keynes 1936: 172). By the method similar to that employed in his investment theory, this artifice allows Keynes to single out the speculative motive as the *causa causans* in the determination of variations in the demand for money. However, as many post-Keynesians (e.g. Davidson 1978; and Carvalho 1992) rightly point out, the liquidity preference theory should be seen in the context of a wider demand for finance.[13] At different circumstances, distinct motives behind the demand for money will predominate. But the important interrelated factors which link all those motives remain uncertainty and changing expectations.

Having discussed the demand for money, it is time to turn to its supply side. In the *General Theory*, 'whilst it is found that money enters into the economic scheme in an essential and peculiar manner, technical monetary detail falls into the background' (Keynes 1936: vii). In particular, in that work, money supply is considered to be completely exogenous. More important for our analysis, though, is that Keynes's insights into the financial dimension of what he later called a monetary production economy are almost all found in the *Treatise on Money*. This remits us to the question of finance, which we discuss below.

FINANCE IN A MONETARY PRODUCTION ECONOMY

Thus far, the financial system (and the banks) has been left aside in the analysis of the monetary production economy. Banks are, nevertheless, important agents in Keynes's theory of employment and output and entrepreneurs. This is because, as will be fully discussed in this section, in an entrepreneur economy, saving does not finance all investment (especially in a growing economy) and finance precedes investment.

The starting point of Keynes's analysis is obviously the 'institution' of bank money. The establishment of private money-creating institutions was a long process in most of the now developed countries (see, for example, Cameron *et al.* 1967). Keynes summarised this process as follows:

> the introduction of money of account gives rise to two derived categories – offers of contracts, contracts and acknowledgements of debt, which are in terms of it, and money proper, answering to it, delivery of which will discharge the contract or the debt. The first of these prepares the way for the next development, namely the discovery that for many purposes the acknowledgements of debts are themselves a serviceable substitute for money proper in the settlement of transactions. When acknowledgements of debt are used in this way, we may call them bank money – not forgetting, however,

> that they are not money proper. Bank money is simply the acknowledgement of a private debt, expressed in the money of account, which is used by passing from one hand to another, alternatively with money proper, to settle a transaction. We thus have side by side State money or money proper and bank money or acknowledgements of debt.
>
> (1930a: 5)

Second, the wider acceptance of bank notes as a means of payment provided banks with credit-creating capacity:

> There has been, indeed, during the past hundred years a steady evolution away from the use of notes to the use of cheques; and the proportion of bank deposits, which in any country we may expect to represent savings deposits, business deposits and income deposits respectively, depends on the stage in this evolution which that country has reached. In the first stage bank deposits are mainly in the nature of investments, most payments being made by notes. In the second stage bank deposits are partly used as a means of holding cash but are generally turned into notes when it comes to making a payment. In the third stage, business transactions are mainly done by cheque, the use of notes being limited to wage-payments and petty cash. In the fourth stage wage payments also are made by cheque, and notes are employed for little except petty cash and out-of-pocket expenditure. Most continental countries are between the second and third stage.
>
> (1930a: 35)

The evolution of privately issued money is critical in understanding the relevance of Keynes's assumption of the independence of finance from saving. For as Chick (1983; 1986) has shown in her theory of the development of the banking system, only in a very early stage of this development do banks depend on previous deposits to create credit. Only in this first stage (Chick's stage 1)are banks' notes restrictively accepted for settling transactions and loans totally backed by previous deposits. Hence, only in this stage do deposits necessarily precede loans and hence saving precede investment.

In Chick's stage 2, however, notes and/or claims on deposits are widely accepted as a means of payment, and thus deposits are made for transactions as well as for saving reasons. In this second stage, banks manage their balance-sheet positions on the basis of the idle balances maintained by depositors, so that daily accruing assets in the shape of cash and claims are as near as possible equal to their daily accruing liabilities (Keynes 1930a).

Bank money creation becomes either a passive or an active book-entry operation: it is passive if 'a member of the public comes along with cash in his pocket or with a cheque drawn on a bank, which he hands in on the understanding that he is entitled in return to a claim to cash (i.e. a deposit) which he can either exercise or transfer to someone'; it is active if the bank creates a claim against itself in favour of a borrower, in return for his promise of reimbursement (Keynes 1930a: 20–1). Accordingly, in an economy with a stage 2 or higher banking system, money can be created by two basic means: through open market operations and by banks' creating deposits. Thus the supply side of Keynes's liquidity preference theory can be told in two complementary 'versions'. In the first version, money is created by an open market operation. Assuming that the liquidity preference is unchanged, an increase in the money supply caused by such an operation will have a direct effect on bond prices and, therefore, on the money interest rates.

In the second version, money is created by banks. In this case, an increase in the money supply has no direct effect on prices of financial assets. Even if banks' reserves are unchanged, banks can create additional deposits, which are exchanged for the IOUs of borrowers and then transferred once the money is spent. Hence, the effect of this operation will depend on how the recipient of such a deposit uses it. If the additional deposit is used for the acquisition of a good or service, it will enter what Keynes called in the *Treatise* the industrial circulation, i.e. the turnover of goods and services of the economy. This will generate the multiplier process which may cause an increase in output, in prices or in both – depending on the level of the use of productive capacity. If it is used to buy, say, bonds, then the effect on the interest rate will be similar to an open market expansionary operation. Finally, if the deposit is hoarded, there will be no immediate effect on the rate of interest.

In stage 1, passive deposit creating dominates, whilst active deposit creation is the norm in stage 2. In the active deposit creation, if cash reserves are depleted below a certain minimum 'margin of safety' (determined by banks' expectations and the institutional structure), banks can borrow surplus reserves from each other, sell other assets or even borrow directly from the money market against certificates of deposits. Given banks' credit-creating capacity, in stage 2 it is banks, and not savers, who provide finance.

The existence of stage 2 credit-creating banks provides the monetary production economy with a flexibility and capacity for accumulation inconceivable in a barter economy.[14] It also increases the complexity of the process of investment finance: the funds available for investment represent only a segment of the pool of funds created by the banking system to finance several activities – from the production of consumption goods to stock exchanges (Keynes 1939: 283).

Therefore, it is important to emphasise that, first, in Keynes's theory finance is determined by the banks' willingness to actively create deposits and credit, and *not* by savers' preferences; and second, the interest rate is neither determined by the forces of productivity and thrift, nor is it the variable that guides the allocation of capital. Rather, the rate of interest is a monetary phenomenon, conjointly determined by monetary policy, banks' credit strategies and the liquidity preference of asset-holders.

In Keynes's economics, thus, the hierarchy of agents in a monetary production economy is such that entrepreneurial and banks' decisions predominate consumers/savers' decisions. In contrast to the view that saving precedes finance, some post-Keynesians assume that the supply of money is always horizontal (e.g. Moore 1988; 1989). In a way, this horizontalist view contradicts Keynes's view that 'banks hold a key position in the transition from a lower to a higher scale of activity' (Keynes 1979: 222): if finance is always forthcoming, what is so important about the role of banks in the dynamics of the monetary production economy? In order to clarify the matter, a simple model of the banking firm under uncertainty will now be given.

A SIMPLE MODEL OF THE BANKING FIRM UNDER UNCERTAINTY

In the perspective of the traditional banking multiplier, banks appear as mere intermediaries between depositors and borrowers. In turn, the supply of deposits will depend on the level of reserves (R) made available by the central bank. Given the public's preference for holding bank deposits instead of cash, the banking firm appears as a *quasi-technical* money creator.

The story told is more or less the following: assuming insignificant operational costs and a perfectly competitive environment, the banking system would expand its loans (L), and hence its deposits (D), to the limit set by the reserves ratio ($r = R/D$). Because the loan of an individual bank will result in an increase of reserves of another bank, the additional supply of reserves by the central bank will go through a bank money multiplier process. Therefore, the supply of deposits (D) is mainly determined by the quantity of base money (B), the bank's minimum reserve ratio (r) and the reserve ratio of the public (c):

$$D = \frac{1-c}{c + r(1-c)} B. \tag{3.5}$$

From a macroeconomic perspective, this implies that the money supply (M), defined as the sum of the public's cash holdings (C) and the deposits with banks, is determined exogenously by the central bank:

$$M = \frac{1}{c + r(1-c)} B. \tag{3.6}$$

This view of banks as mere intermediaries is found in different and even disputing views on the banking firm. As Heise (1992: 285) rightly points out, positions held in this discussion range from the view that banks are 'quasi-technical' money creators, as described above, to the view that banks are risk-neutral portfolio-managers. In the latter version, associated with Tobin's theory of portfolio selection (see, for example, Tobin 1982), banks are risk-neutral agents which choose to hold liquid reserves according to the optimum condition

$$r_A = ef(x)\mathrm{d}x \tag{3.7}$$

where r_A is the yield of an earning asset, which represents the opportunity cost of holding money in liquid form; x is the net withdrawal of reserves; $f(x)$ is the density function of x; and e is the cost of obtaining additional funds. In other words, given the level of deposits available to the banking firm, the optimisation problem that it faces is the following: money, as opposed to loans and other applications, will be held when marginal opportunity costs equal the (expected) costs of restoring liquidity.

In contemporary financial theory, the portfolio theory of the banking firm has become dominant – as much as the portfolio-theoretic approach has become the dominant approach to demand for money. However, as Heise points out, and equation (3.7) implies, the following assumptions underline this type of multiplier: (1) agents must have information about possible yields of other assets, r_A – as opportunity costs of holding money; so far, so good. But also: (2) agents must have information about the density function of net withdrawal of reserves, $f(x)$; *and* (3) agents must have information about future costs of restoring liquidity, e (Heise 1992: 292n). In other words, uncertainty must be assumed away, which, from a post-Keynesian perspective, is not a suitable method to analyse the behaviour of any economic agent in a monetary production economy.

From a post-Keynesian perspective, the conventional banking multiplier as much as the portfolio-theoretic approach are fallacious descriptions of the behaviour of the banking firm. Under uncertainty, competition implies that the individual bank's credit-creating capacity must be sufficiently elastic that it can face an eventual change in its clients' demand for credit.[15] Similarly to other economic agents, banks maintain voluntary reserves and other liquid assets (such as marketable securities) in their portfolio for precautionary reasons.[16]

Banks, like any other agent facing the uncertainty inherent of a monetary production economy, have liquidity preference. This preference is expressed in a similar manner to wealth-holders: as uncertainty rises they will prefer to shorten the maturities of their assets and stretch the maturities of their liabilities. The *prima differentia* of banks in this regard lies in the fact that a significant part of their assets are non-marketable assets (loans).[17] In response to an increase of uncertainty, banks will then express their liquidity preference either by reducing their willingness to lend or by increasing their loan rates, or both.

Let us consider a simple version of a bank's balance sheet: on the assets side we have reserves (R), liquid assets (A) and loans (L). These must equal deposits (D) on the liabilities side:

$$R + A + L \equiv D. \tag{3.8}$$

Even though the compulsory reserves ratio is determined by the monetary authorities, the 'liquid assets ratio' ($\tau = A/D$) will be determined by the strategies of competition of banks and their liquidity preferences. Therefore, loans can be defined as

$$L \equiv (1 - \tau - r)D \tag{3.9}$$

where τ is the ratio of compulsory reserves over deposits. Equation (3.9) may seem similar to the traditional multiplier; however, it is different in fundamental ways. This equation expresses the view that, until our bank has liquid assets ($\tau > 0$), an increase in its loans can be achieved without depletion of reserves. In other words, in case of a fast expansion of loans, r can remain constant while τ declines.

The decline of τ after a certain point (when voluntary reserves equal compulsory reserves) occurs more rapidly than the increase in the deposits created, so that the point where $\tau \approx 0$ can be rapidly reached. However, until this situation (i.e. $\tau \approx 0$) is reached, the supply of loans may be significantly elastic (Figure 3.2). For each level of expectations (E) of the banking system, the supply of loans schedule (L^s) can be seen as almost horizontal until τ approaches 0, when it rapidly becomes vertical.

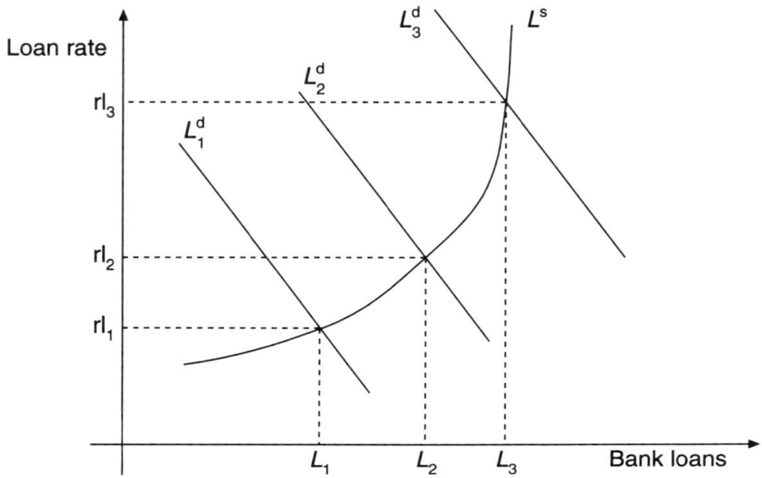

Figure 3.2

As mentioned earlier, some post-Keynesians view this credit-creating capacity as the loss of the discretionary power of the banks in determining their overall levels of lending. For instance, Moore (1988; 1989) maintains that: (1) bank loans are essentially demand determined due to pre-arranged credit facilities (such as overdraft facilities); (2) there is an asymmetry in the capacity of the monetary authorities to influence the level of growth of money stock (central banks can increase it but do not have the ability to reduce it); and (3) monetary authorities, having to fulfil their basic role of lender of last resort and thus their obligation to maintain the liquidity of the system, do not have discretionary control over their own liabilities.

Moore's argument is correct in most circumstances in developed economies. However, the horizontalist view seems to lack the generality to encompass the active role played by banks in inherently uncertain environments. This is where Keynes's (1936) 'state of confidence of banks' (expectations) enters the scheme. As Goodhart (1989) points out in his reply to Moore:

> [Moore] is correct . . . with respect to individual borrowers and in the short-run 'tactical' context. But banks' medium term and longer term 'strategic' decisions to enter and contest this or that credit market (e.g. mortgage lending to persons, syndicated loans to LDCs, etc.) are

of major importance in determining the form and shape of the banking system and its influence on the economy. Of course such decisions are largely shaped by the regulatory and structural context, available technology, etc., but they remain bankers' decisions.[18]

As regards the determination of the lending interest rate, the behaviour of the banking firm will also be affected by uncertainty. In an uncertain environment, where firms do not know the shape and location of their cost and demand curves, the most common pricing procedure is mark-up pricing.[19] This is exactly how the banking firm is seen to proceed in Figure 3.2. That is, in our model, the banking firm will ascertain some percentage mark-up (m) on its normal average cost – which here we assume to be proportional to the basic rate determined in the money market. This mark-up is a sign of the bank's disquietude: for instance, it is stable if it holds sufficient liquid assets which can be used to face change in the demand for loans. If its liquidity shrinks rapidly, our bank will certainly review its pricing policy and raise m.[20]

As regards our bank's cost, bank deposits compete with other liquid assets, such as bonds, hence in equilibrium the deposit rate would equal the rate paid on bonds. The average cost of deposits (r_{d}) depends on the relation between interest-bearing and non-interest-bearing deposits held by the bank. The lending rate of interest (r_{l}) will then be

$$r_{\mathrm{l}} = (1 + m)\,\frac{D}{L}\,r_{\mathrm{d}} \qquad m_{\mathrm{L}} > 0$$

or, what is the same,

$$r_{\mathrm{l}} = (1 + m)\,\frac{r_{\mathrm{d}}}{1 - \tau - \alpha} \tag{3.10}$$

As mentioned earlier, an increase in loans can be achieved without depletion of reserves through the selling of liquid assets. However, if the voluntary reserves fall by too much (i.e. $\tau \approx 0$), banks will have to bid for additional reserves. If the public's average liquidity preference remains unchanged, this will result in an increase in the basic rate of interest (r_{d}).

To sum up, our analysis thus far proposes that banks' capacity to expand loans before deposits is very elastic. However, we can consistently assume that, as banks approach their 'full capacity' ($\tau = 0$), the supply of loans will become vertical. Banks will only be stimulated to increase their loans if they can increase their lending rate at the margin in order to cover the costs of bidding for additional reserves.

FINANCE IN THE CONTEXT OF AN OPEN ECONOMY

In the previous chapter, it was established that the prior-saving argument is as much rooted in closed-economy macroeconomics as it is in open-economy macroeconomics. It was pointed out, for example, that it is common to identify all net capital inflow as the use of 'external saving'. From a post-Keynesian perspective, the distinction between finance and saving must also be applied to the analysis of the role of external debt in financing development – especially in these times, when multinational credit-creating institutions are a part of the world scenario.

A good and relevant example to illustrate the need for this distinction is that of an economy with underdeveloped or non-existent internal mechanisms to finance long-term projects.[21] If investors can find better credit conditions abroad, they will borrow in foreign currency, irrespective of their need to import additional resources (or of 'external saving').

Assume that this hypothetical country is going through an investment boom, departing from an equilibrated current account. If part of the investment finance is obtained through borrowing in foreign currency, the stock of external debt will increase concomitantly. The country's capacity to repay will not rise immediately – even if such external debt is used to finance expansion of export sectors, which will allow the country to repay its debt in the future. Once the stock of external debt has increased, the financial charges also rise and this will produce a deficit in the current transactions account. Can this be accounted for as use of 'external saving'?

Our example shows just how misleading the identification of finance with external saving can be if applied for analytical purposes. But, if such an identification is used for policy recommendation, it can be truly dangerous. For instance, if the increase of external debt is interpreted as a proof of scarcity of internal saving, then the solution is to increase internal saving. Finally, if the prior-saving argument is carried through consistently, interest rates must be raised and internal absorption must be reduced in order to re-establish the external sector equilibrium. This adjustment is almost necessarily recessive; and, as if recession were not enough, the structural problem (the lack of indigenous mechanisms to finance investment) which caused the rise in external debt will remain, and long-term growth may be still threatened.

One way of overcoming this analytical difficulty is to redefine the balance of payments so as to distinguish between what represents real resources transfer from other factors affecting the international capital inflows. This will be discussed in Chapter 6, which deals with the method of analysis of the case study.

SUMMING UP

In this chapter the foundations of Keynes's assumption (that finance and investment precede saving) have been discussed. In addition the consequences of such an assumption in the analysis of finance in market economies have been addressed.

It has been established that the foundations of the post-Keynesian view on finance is the financial dimension of Keynes's paradigm of the monetary production (entrepreneur) economy. In an entrepreneur economy, the means of production are privately owned, so that production is organised by a profit-seeking class through hiring labour. Assuming that the costs of production are known, output decisions will depend on the expectations of demand. Since time is irreversible and production must precede demand, production decisions have to be taken in an inherently uncertain environment. Uncertainty is common to any decision regarding production; however, the return on long-lived assets is more uncertain than the return on current production. This makes the volatility of investment greater than the production of other goods. Furthermore, marginal investment is not financed by current income. Therefore, investment is deemed to be the *causa causans* in the determination of output and employment.

In an entrepreneur economy, finance and investment precede saving. This brings us to the financial dimension of the monetary production economy. It has been shown that in an economy with a developed (stage 2 or higher) banking system, banks can create credit independently from previous deposits. This makes the banking system second in the causal hierarchy in the determination of the level of investment. Saving can only play a role in this hierarchy as part of the determinants of asset prices and thus the interest rate. However, given that financial markets are dominated by stocks rather than flows, the role of saving is limited. More important in the determination of interest rates are the wealth-owners' liquidity preferences and monetary policy.

To sum up, Keynes's and the post-Keynesians' assumption of the precedence of finance and investment over saving completely changes the hierarchy in the process of accumulation in market-oriented economies. Finance and investment decisions are the main determinants and consumption decisions are relatively secondary – though they have an important role in determining the level of aggregate demand.

What is apparently played down by the post-Keynesian analysis is the role of saving, whereas the financial markets are seen with a hint of disguise. The next chapter will show that saving and consequently the financial markets have a fundamental place in the dynamics of the monetary production economy. Therefore this role must be addressed by post-Keynesian theory – especially in models concerned with finance and the processes of growth and development.

Chapter 4

Saving and financial markets in economic growth

INTRODUCTION

In the previous chapter the implications of the following three propositions, which are common assumptions in most post-Keynesian analyses, have been analysed in the context of growth: (1) investment is the causal determinant of output, employment and income; (2) from a macroeconomic standpoint, banks, and not savers, play the most fundamental role in the process of finance; and (3) the rate of interest may affect the investment decision and, especially, the allocation of financial wealth between different existing financial assets. The discussion of the theoretical reasoning behind, and institutional background of, these assumptions has permitted us to unveil the role of banks in a monetary production economy.

We have showed that it is bank credit, and not saving, which plays the crucial role in the financing of investment. This would appear to leave no role for saving, but such is far from being the case. The present chapter develops the supporting role played by saving, and by financial markets in economic growth – a role which has been overlooked even by most post-Keynesian models. For this task, two hypotheses are examined: first, that economic growth is followed by increasing systemic financial fragility; second, that this financial fragility can be mitigated by funding, i.e. the issue of long-term securities by the investing firms to consolidate their short-term liabilities.

The chapter is organised as follows. First, it presents a stock-flow model of finance, investment and saving from a Keynesian perspective. Then Minsky's financial fragility hypothesis is reviewed in the light of the above-cited model; this review establishes that growth, in monetary production economies, increases financial fragility. Further the role of funding, saving and financial markets in achieving a financially stable growth is discussed. Finally, it applies the distinction between finance and funding to the context of an open economy.

THE STARTING POINT: THE FINANCE–INVESTMENT–SAVING CIRCUIT

Keynes's assumption that finance precedes saving has led to much controversy and misunderstanding. This view had already been challenged in a debate which involved Keynes, Ohlin and Robertson.[1] In that debate, Ohlin and Robertson insisted on reinterpreting Keynes's liquidity preference theory within a neoclassical loanable funds framework. Ohlin (1937a, b) claimed that Keynes's *ex post* equality between saving and investment was merely a truism that said nothing about the mechanism by which investment was financed. In contrast, Ohlin maintained that deposits precede loans, and hence saving precedes investment. Robertson (e.g. 1937a) shared Ohlin's view, and claimed furthermore that in the case of a rise in investment, the existing volume of saving would not suffice to finance the latter: an increase in the money supply would have to fill the gap, and that would imply forced saving. If inflation is to be avoided, concluded Robertson, the deposit rates would have to rise in order to stimulate saving.

The controversy was never properly settled; modern post-Keynesians re-opened it, in a now well-known debate started by Asimakopulos (1983) and followed by replies from, among others, Kregel (1984–5), Davidson (1986), Richardson (1986) and Terzi (1986). To clarify the matter, Keynes's view can be approached through a stock-flow model, similar to the one used by Godley and Cripps (1985) for other purposes. This model – the finance–investment–saving (FIS) circuit – is offered as a substitute for the neoclassical, static view of the process of investment finance. In contrast to this view, the FIS circuit integrates finance into the multiplier to show how saving is created as a by-product of the process of income creation. For this reason it has been used by many post-Keynesians to demonstrate the precedence of investment over saving (Chick 1983; Richardson 1986; Terzi 1986; Amadeo and Franco 1989; Carvalho 1992). But the FIS circuit has more to offer as an analytical tool: based on this circuit it is possible to develop a systemic view of the role of banks, saving and financial markets in the process of growth. This is the heart of the approach proposed in this chapter.

A model of investment finance based on the finance–investment–saving circuit

Table 4.1 consolidates the balance sheets of the principal agents – namely the banking system, the entrepreneurs and households – in a Keynesian fashion. Each column corresponds to a period (n) of the multiplier process, and is divided into two other columns, displaying the assets and liabilities of those agents; $n = 0$ is the initial position, followed by three rounds of the sequential process; $n = N$ gives the end-of-process values. All values in these balance sheets are nominal, but prices are assumed to be unchanging. Finally, firms' inventories and households' stocks of durable consumption goods are not considered here. Financial assets are cash, deposits in commercial banks and securities.

For simplicity, the following assumptions are made: (1) only households save; (2) uncertainty has no effect on anyone's current asset-holding behaviour, balances are either held for transactions or for (long-term) saving purposes,[2] (this is similar to assuming that the marginal propensity to buy placements out of household savings (m) is equal to 1 (see Davidson 1978: 272)); (3) the propensity to consume is 0.7 and intended savings are held completely in the form of long-term securities, which are issued by indebted firms in order to repay outstanding debts; and (4) there is a lag between the accumulation of active balances (for consumption purposes) and their expenditures, and between the issue of securities and the repayment of debt.

The model considers a simple income multiplier where investment generates a flow of income, consumption and saving. Suppose that an investment of £50 is entirely financed by bank loans, created as a book-keeping operation. This additional supply of bank money will generate a sequential process of payments – wages and consumption – and, consequently, of transfers of deposits among agents. If we call intended saving the additional holding of securities generated alongside the multiplier process, then in each period 0.3 of the previous additional income will be used to buy securities and, hence, to repay outstanding debt.

As Table 4.1 shows, if the reserves available to the banking system are unchanged, banks must reduce their liquidity in order to finance investment.[3] It must be stressed though, that, since deposits remain within the banking system, investment finance need not represent a drain of cash from the banks as a whole.

In the process of financing investment, the corporate sector must also increase its financial vulnerability – here defined by the ratio between its

Table 4.1 The financial side of the multiplier process: a numerical example

		Period (n)										
		0		*1*		*2*		*3*		...	*N*	
		A	*L*	*A*	*L*	*A*	*L*	*A*	*L*	...	*A*	*L*
Banks												
Reserves	(1)	100		100		100		100		...	100	
Loans	(2)	50		100		85		74		...	50	
Deposits	(3)		150		200		185		174	...		150
Firms												
Deposits	(4)	100		115		110		107		...	100	
Capital	(5)	50		100		100		100		...	100	
Loans	(6)		50		100		85		74	...		50
Securities	(7)		0		15		25		33	...		50
Net worth	(8)		100		100		100		100	...		100
Households												
Deposits	(9)	50		85		74		67		...	50	
Securities	(10)	0		15		25		33		...	50	
Wealth	(11)		50		100		100		100	...		100
Total	(12)	350	350	515	515	495	495	482	482	...	450	450
$Y^{(*)}$	(13)			50		85		110		...	167	
$S^{d(*)}$	(14)			15		25		33		...	50	
R/D = (1)/(3)%	(15)	67		50		54		57		...	67	
L/NW = (6)/(8)%	(16)	200		100		100		100		...	50	

Notes: *A*, assetsl *L*, liabilities; *Y*, income; s^d, intended saving; *, accumulated values; *R/D*, bank reserves over deposits; *L*/NW, loans over net worth.

loans and its net worth (*L*/NW). The macroeconomic reason for this result is that until the multiplier is complete part of the additional savings are not intended, but result from acceptance of deposits in the course of transactions.

Because at each period the whole of the additional intended saving is used to buy long-term securities, at the end of the process aggregate intended saving will be asymptotically equal to investment ($S^{d} \approx I =$ £50).[4] And since firms use those funds to repay their short-term debts, when the multiplier process following a one-shot investment is completed, bank loans will be reduced to their initial position (£50).

Banks hold a key position[5]

The above model assumes that bank loans are a causal variable in determining the level of investment. An applied economist may rightly challenge this assumption, since corporate finance statistics show a higher proportion of self-finance (retained profits) as a source of investment financing in most developed economies (e.g. Mayer 1988). So why not assume that finance comes totally from retained profits or other sorts of previous saving?

The logic which underlies Keynes's claim that finance comes from banks rather than saving rests upon a view of finance as a sequential process similar to the one employed in the above model. If this view is taken to its logical limits, then only in a stationary state, and then only under strict assumptions concerning the portfolio choice of savers, can previous saving finance investment. This can be demonstrated by using Robertson's (1937a: 171–5) suggestion about the role of saving in financing investment when investment is steady throughout time.

Robertson pointed out that, where investment is made at an equal and steady pace for a certain period of time, the sum of the additional intended saving equals the demand for investment finance at any point. In Robertson's words:

> If the act [of investment] is repeated a sufficient number of times, we can regard the sum of the increments of saving being done in any one period of time as balancing the investment done in that period; and if, with Mr. Kahn, we are prepared to forget about the period of transition, we can declare that the problem of the finance of the process of investment to be self-solving.
>
> (1937a: 172)

This view is illustrated by Table 4.2, where *c* stands for the propensity

Table 4.2 A Robertsonian view of overlapping multiplier processes

	Period							
Period	*1*	*2*	*3*	*4*	...	*N*	*N + 1*	S^d
1	$1-c$	$c(1-c)$	$c^2(1-c)$	$c^3(1-c)$	...	$c^N(1-c)$		≈ 1
2		$1-c$	$c(1-c)$	$c^2(1-c)$	...	$c^{N-1}(1-c)$	$c^N(1-c)$	≈ 1
3			$1-c$	$c(1-c)$	...	$c^{N-2}(1-c)$	$c^{N-1}(1-c)$	< 1
4				$1-c$	...	$c^{N-3}(1-c)$	$c^{N-2}(1-c)$	< 1
⋮						⋮	⋮	...
N						$1-c$	$c(1-c)$	< 1
$N+1$							$1-c$	< 1
S^d	< 1	< 1	< 1	< 1	...	≈ 1	≈ 1	

to consume; the rows represent the multiplier processes initiated by an investment I equal to £1, undertaken in each period; and the columns represent the intended saving (S^d) created as a product of the multiplier process.

Notice that from $n = N$ the aggregate demand for securities (S^d) equals the demand for investment finance (I). Thus, in a stationary state (from $n = N$ onwards in Table 4.2), no additional creation of liquidity is necessary in order to finance accumulation: the investing firms may always finance their investment projects through the issue of securities. This result was accepted in Keynes's response to Robertson, i.e. his view of finance as a '*revolving* fund which looks after a flow of investment [and] does not absorb or exhaust any resources' (1937b: 209; 1937c: 219–20). However, as Keynes rightly pointed out elsewhere (1939: 284–5), the existence of a *revolving fund* of credit does not reduce, but consubstantiates, the causal importance of bank credit for the process of growth. To demonstrate this is simple if one assumes that the economy is growing and that this growth (g) is investment-led:

$$I_t = (1 + g)\, I_{t-1}.$$

Since the increase of investment only affects the additional income created immediately after it, then

$$I_t - mS^d_t = gI_{t-1} > 0$$

where m is the marginal propensity to buy placements out of household savings.

Therefore, only in the stationary state ($g = 0$) can investment be totally financed by prior saving, and then only if savers agree to hold all their intended saving in the form of long-term securities ($m = 1$). Yet any increase of investment above previous investment levels will generate a demand for money for finance motive that is not automatically provided (Keynes 1937b: 209–10).

Assume that banks do not accommodate an increase of the demand for finance. If the public's liquidity preference is unchanged, then either the rise of investment will be halted by the lack of funds, or investors will bid for funds in the money market,[6] which may cause an increase in the rate of interest.[7] Since the interest rate is a main determinant of the level of investment, this rise may abort the process of growth.

To sum up, it is banks, and not savers, who hold a key position in the process of growth. Only if they share the optimism of entrepreneurs in periods of growth or are led, for any other reason, to accommodate the demand for investment finance can the monetary production economy grow. This conclusion would appear to leave no role for saving, but such is far from being the case, as the following two sections will demonstrate.

GROWTH AND FINANCIAL FRAGILITY

Minsky's financial fragility hypothesis (e.g. 1982) describes the inherent tendency of investors and speculators to rapidly increase their level of indebtedness in moments of optimism. If such optimism is shared by lending institutions, they will accommodate the demand for loans by reducing their margins of safety. The net result is an increase in the vulnerability of the network of financial commitments of the monetary economy. In turn, the viability of such a network depends upon the ability of the borrowing units to honour their debts (see Minsky 1982: 204).

The FIS model presented above illustrates another facet of Minsky's hypothesis: a growing market economy is inherently more fragile. First, borrowing from banks to finance investment increases short-term indebtedness. Firms' capacities to repay with their own cash flows have to wait until their investment projects mature and their productive capacities expand. Therefore, a bank-financed expansion leaves the corporate sector in a more vulnerable financial position. Second, in increasing the supply of investment finance banks are reducing further their margin of safety. In other words, both firms and banks are augmenting the vulnerability of their businesses and, potentially, their dependence on alternative sources of liquidity.

Below, Minsky's hypothesis of financial fragility is briefly reviewed. This will permit us to establish the risks that a process of increasing fragility can impose on growth. Once this has been done, the microeconomic and macroeconomic roles of saving and financial markets in supporting growth can be fully unveiled.

Minsky's hypothesis of financial fragility briefly revisited

There are many formal interpretations of Minsky's financial fragility hypothesis. See, for example, Taylor and O'Connell (1985) and Lavoie (1986–7). Here a simple model, based on Minsky (1986: 335–41) and Gatti and Gallegatti (1990), is used.

Assume that a firm borrows the sum D from a bank which generates cash commitments of CC each period i. These commitments will be met either from quasi-rents Q or from additional debt or from both. Businessmen, and their bankers, expect the borrowing firm to yield quasi-rents Q_i and allow a variance of $\sigma^2_{Q_i}$ in their expectations. For the *hedge financing* of a position, the expected quasi-rents will always exceed the contractual cash payment commitments on debts, i.e.

$$\mathrm{CC}_i < Q_i - \lambda\sigma^2_{Q_i} \qquad \text{for all } i \tag{4.1}$$

where λ denotes the degree of subjectivity attached to the probability distribution of Q_i and is sufficiently great to guarantee that the subjective probability of CC_i being smaller than Q_i is acceptably small. A *hedge financing* implies that the debtor maintains a great margin of safety in their cash flow. If such a margin is defined as θ, then equation (4.1) can be rewritten as follows:

$$\mathrm{CC}_\mathrm{i} = \theta(Q_i - \lambda\sigma^2_{Q_i}) \qquad \text{for all } i,\ \tau < 1. \tag{4.2}$$

A *hedge financing* position also implies that the capitalised value of the expected quasi-rents ($P_k = V(Q_i - \lambda\sigma^2_{Q_i})$) exceed the capitalised value of the debt service (i.e. interest charge plus amortisation, $V(\mathrm{CC}_i)$) by a significant margin. If this margin is defined as μ, then

$$P_k = \mu V(\mathrm{CC}_i) \qquad \mu > 1 \tag{4.3}$$

where V represents the capitalisation function, which is assumed to be equal for the debt service and for the quasi-rents.

Finally, because of the uncertainties related to the future quasi-rents and to future credit conditions, the hedge borrower will normally hold balances, in the form of money and marketable financial assets, beyond what is needed for transactions. This precaution is especially important, since any extraordinary expense may affect the firm's capacity to honour its financial commitment or to finance its productive operations or both. Therefore, assuming that these balances are a function of the total debt, the borrower's balance sheet can be described as follows:

Assets	*Liabilities*
$\eta V(\mathrm{CC})$	$V(\mathrm{CC})$
$P_k K$	Eq

where $P_k K$ is the market value of the firm (liquid and fixed) capital; η is what Minsky names the *liquid asset kicker*, the ratio between the firm's precautionary provisions of liquid assets and the total debt; and Eq is the equity of the firm. The characterisation of a hedge financing can be summarised as the position where $\theta < 1$, $\mu > 1$ and $\eta > 0$ for all periods. Further, if the expectations of the *hedge unit* are fulfilled and therefore the realised Q_i always exceeds the CC_i, the firm may, if it wishes, increase its liquid asset kicker η by acquiring more liquid marketable financial assets; this will in turn increase μ and its equity.

The characterisation of *hedge financing* makes it possible to identify two further financial postures in the context of this model: speculative and Ponzi financing. Speculative financing is the case when the firm pays only the interest charges in the periods until near the maturity of the debt, leaving the amortisation of the principal to be paid in subsequent periods. In other words, in equation (4.2), if $i = 1, \ldots, m$ for a considerable part of the periods, say from $i = 1$ to $i = m - n$, $\theta > 1$; and $\theta \leqslant 1$ from $i = m - n + 1$ to $i = m$.

Applying the same example above, one can see that, for the *hedge unit*, the capitalised value of expected quasi-rents will still be superior to the capitalised value of the debt service ($\mu > 1$) for the whole period. But for the dates of speculative debts ($i = 1, \ldots, m - n$), $\mu < 1$. Therefore, the speculative firm expects to meet the difference between CC_i and Q_i in these earlier dates by *refinancing*.

The need to refinance its debt makes the speculative firm highly dependent on the future conditions of credit. Rising interest rates will force the speculative firm either to sell its precautionary balances or to increase its debt only to refinance its outstanding debt. In this context, the firm will see its margins of safety decreasing and, in the limit, 'if interest rates fluctuates widely, technical, and hopefully, transitory insolvency is likely to occur for organisations that engage in speculative finance' (Minsky 1986: 337). As Minsky himself emphasises, this characteristic of speculative finance has important, and '*obvious policy implications: the larger the weight of speculative finance, the greater the importance of preventing the emergence of very high interest rates*' (op. cit.: 339, Minsky's emphasis).

The speculative unit is likely to maintain precautionary balances of money and liquid marketable assets, i.e. $\eta > 1$. These balances will be held in order to protect the firm against transitory quasi-rent or money-market difficulties (Minsky 1986: 338). It is important to notice, though, that this increases rather than decreases the dependence of the financial position of speculative firms on shifts in interest rates. For if interest rates are rising, this is normally attached to a fall of financial asset prices. Thus, not only are the firm's financial commitments rising, but its liquid asset kicker η is decreasing proportionally.

Having characterised the speculative firm, we can now proceed to define the Ponzi case. In the Ponzi case, the firm's expected quasi-rents are not enough to pay even the interest component of the debt. *Ponzi finance* is thus defined as 'the payment of cash to debt holders with funds raised by either additional debt or decreasing cash kickers' (Minsky

1986: 340). Ponzi schemes are highly dependent upon the continued sale of additional debt, and therefore firms engaging in such a financing scheme should carry large liquid asset kickers (hence $\eta \gg 0$). But if the firm finds difficulties in selling liabilities during the period in which it is refinancing debt, the firm's liquid assets are rapidly depleted and therefore its equity is being continuously eroded.

Even though the Ponzi finance is evocative of fraud, this is a finance posture which is a normal situation of growing firms, for instance in heavy industry. In such industries, if the firm wishes to expand there may be the need to finance long-lived assets which will only produce income in the long run.[8] The three financial postures are summarised in Table 4.3.

Notice that so far, the financial postures have been defined in terms of entrepreneurial and banks' expectations. However, a financial position can change because of an unanticipated decline in the quasi-rents or of a rise in the rate of interest. A change in Q may affect hedge, speculative and Ponzi firms alike: hedge units may be forced into a speculative posture, speculative financing may become Ponzi, whereas Ponzi businesses may simply go bankrupt for lack of refinancing of their debts. As regards a change in the rate of interest, this will only affect those firms with speculative and Ponzi financial postures, because only those have to renegotiate the terms of their debts at each repayment period.

A change in the financial positions may also affect the general conditions of credit and the prices in organised financial markets. As regards the lending conditions, if this change is perceived by banks as a sign of an increase of lender's risk, then credit rationing may occur. In terms of the model of the banking firm presented in the previous chapter, this will result in an increase of the desired liquid asset ratio because banks now have to make more provisions for bad debts. In other words, the liquidity preference of the banking firm will rise.[9]

Table 4.3 Typical financial positions of hedge, speculative and Ponzi units

	θ	μ	η
Hedge	< 1	> 1	≥ 1
Speculative	> 1	> 1	$0 < n < 1$
Ponzi	> 1	> 1?	≈ 0

Financial instability can deter growth

In what concerns financial markets, a deterioration of the financial postures will have two effects. On the one hand, wealth-owners will revise the capitalised values of the listed firms. On the other hand, those firms under speculative and Ponzi financial postures will be willing to deplete their stocks of marketable assets to honour their financial commitments. This increase of liquidity preferences by both wealth-owners and firms is likely to bring down securities prices, which causes the financial situation of the speculative and Ponzi players to further deteriorate. From a macroeconomic perspective, this means an increasingly fragile economic system.

Financial fragility in itself is not a constraint to growth, but it may disrupt the process of expansion. This is especially true if an increase of fragility causes a debt-deflation, an expression of the exhaustion of financial arrangements which may lead to depression (Minsky 1982; Fisher 1933). Debt-deflation can be triggered by units attempting to sell their liquid assets in order to raise cash (indebted firms), to re-establish their liquidity positions (banking and other financial institutions) or to satisfy some bearish change of expectations (speculators). This run to regain liquidity affects real expenditures through its effects on interest rates, on the availability of funds to finance and fund investment and on long-term entrepreneurial expectations.

To sum up, the fact that banks can finance investment through book-keeping creation of money does not warrant a financially stable process of growth. Growth increases financial fragility, and financial instability can halt growth. Having said this, we are now in position to assess the role of saving and financial markets in the process of growth.

FUNDING, FINANCIAL MARKETS AND SAVING

Even if, in post-Keynesian theory, individual savings and financial intermediation are secondary in the determination of the aggregate supply of investment finance, they do matter in a different context – the question of funding.

From the microeconomic perspective, entrepreneurs and bankers desire to fund their long-term commitments on a stable basis because of the uncertainty about the prospective conditions of credit and levels of interest rates. Thus, the reason for funding can be interpreted as a response to a menacing increase in both borrower's and lender's risks (Keynes *C.W.* VII: 144). Hence, investment finance in a world of uncertainty is characteristically a two-fold process of finance and funding:

> The entrepreneur when he decides to invest has to be satisfied on two points: firstly, that he can obtain sufficient short-term finance during the period of producing the investment; and secondly, that he can eventually fund his short-term obligations by a long-term issue on satisfactory conditions. Occasionally he may be in a position to use his own resources or to make his long-term issue at once; but this makes no difference to the amount of 'finance' which has to be found by the market as a whole, but only to the channel through which it reaches the entrepreneur and to the probability that some part of it may be found by the release of cash on the part of himself or the rest of the public. Thus it is convenient to regard the twofold process as the characteristic one.
>
> (Keynes 1937c: 217)

Being the *loci* where funding takes place, financial markets have an important role in supporting growth. From a microeconomic perspective, they may increase the predisposition of firms and banks to engage in the financing of long-lived assets. Another interrelated microeconomic function is the provision of information for firms issuing securities, underwriters and demanders of securities. This informational role can be summarised as follows: (1) secondary markets signal the price of new issues of securities; (2) secondary markets make underwriting by specialised financial institutions a less risky business;[10] and (3) secondary markets enable investors to evaluate the prospective profitability of newly issued securities by enhancing the flow of information (Bain 1981: 61).

From a macroeconomic viewpoint, funding and, therefore, financial markets also bear a role which is seldom spelled out. That is, the role of mitigating the increasing financial fragility inherent in a growing monetary economy. This macroeconomic role will very much depend upon two interrelated characteristics of the financial markets: their size and their stability. A thin financial market is unlikely to be able to increase its levels of operation without significant shifts of asset prices; and a volatile financial market can provoke sudden shifts of the rate of interest and, therefore, be more damaging than supportive of the process of growth.

Finally, it is worth remembering that not only are thin markets highly speculative and volatile, but also speculation a short-term phenomenon which tends to disappear in the long run. Much to the contrary, the very existence of the secondary markets (where old securities are sold and bought) relies on continuous trading, which provides the liquidity that makes it less risky for wealth-owners to hold long-term securities. It is this provision of liquidity which makes long-term bonds and securities attractive to savers – who, as Davidson has rightly put it, are searching for safe liquidity time-machines, and rarely wish to be locked in to holding an asset for a long period of time.

Therefore, financial markets have an important, but yet ambiguous, role in supporting growth. They intermediate between the demanders of securities and those firms wishing to fund their short-term liabilities. But one cannot forget the negative side, i.e. the instability brought by the speculative nature of these markets.

One final remark must be made about the role of financial intermediaries in the process of financing/funding investment. One of the assumptions of the FIS model given earlier was that all 'intended savings' were held in the form of long-term securities. This is not only unrealistic, but also reduces the importance of the financial intermediaries (or 'middlemen') in the process of funding accumulation.

As stressed earlier, what makes the financial markets functional actors in reducing the financial fragility inherent in growth are their ability to transform short-term assets which are demanded by savers as forms of 'liquidity time-machines' into long-term sources of funding. This maturity transformation assumes different forms according to the institutional background behind the financial structure. For instance, as Davidson (1986) illustrates, in the segmented financial markets which existed in the USA before the deregulation of the 1980s, the commercial

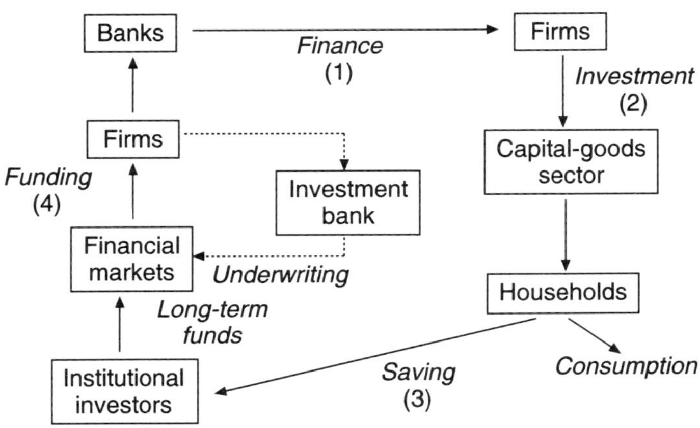

Figure 4.1

banks provided sight and short-term deposits against short-term commercial and industrial loans; investment banks were specialised in converting short-term borrowing into long-term borrowing through underwriting operations; and institutional investors (e.g. insurance companies and pension funds) would invest savings on behalf of the general public. The finance–funding mechanism of this specific institutional structure is illustrated by Figure 4.1.

To sum up, the existence of financial intermediaries broadens the system's ability to transform maturities. Therefore, financial intermediaries also have an important role to play in supporting a financially stable process of growth and development.

FINANCE AND FUNDING IN THE OPEN ECONOMY

It has been indicated in the previous chapter that the distinction between finance and saving must also be applied to the analysis of the role of external debt in financing development – especially in these times when multinational credit-creating institutions are a part of the world scenario. Another important distinction is, of course, that between finance and funding.

This distinction can be straightforwardly used in the analysis of the less developed countries' (LDCs') debt problem. One of the main problems about the recent experience with LDCs' debt was that, even though the international banking system substantially increased their capacity to *finance* firms in developing countries, the institutional mechanisms to *fund* them were not available in the 1970s and 1980s. The reasons for this are many, but one of them is that few companies in LDCs are large enough or well enough known internationally to be able to float stocks and long-term securities in the organised international financial markets.

This lack of mechanisms to fund LDC firms may partly explain why in the 1970s, when there was a significant increase of international bank loans to LDCs, banks preferred to lend with floating interest rates (or at short maturities) and the guarantee of LDCs' national governments was commonly required for such operations. The short-term maturities of the rapidly increasing loans to LDCs almost immediately put LDCs and the international banking system into a more fragile position. For even if such debts had been used to finance expansions of the productive capacity to export (which was not, incidentally, always the case), LDCs could not repay their debt before such capacity was put to use. Indeed it only took a rise of interest rates, caused by the monetary policies of the developed countries at the end of the 1970s, to turn the financial fragility of the LDCs' position into the debt crisis of the 1980s.

SUMMING UP

The fact that finance is independent of previous saving does not guarantee that growth can be sustainable from a financial perspective. Even in economies which have highly developed and competitive financial systems, economic growth is normally accompanied by increasing financial vulnerability of firms, banks and other financial institutions; hence, growth increases the economy's financial fragility. This in itself does not threaten the process of growth, but it can be disruptive if it degenerates into financial instability and debt-deflation.

Financial fragility can be mitigated by funding, i.e. the issue of long-term securities by the investing firms to consolidate their short-term liabilities. Consequently, saving and financial markets may play a fundamental role in a financially stable process of growth/development. This role, however, is ambiguous because of the inherent volatility of those markets.

In the next chapter, we shall build on the framework developed in this chapter to discuss the constraints caused by the underdevelopment of financial markets, which is the case normally identified for LDCs.

Chapter 5

Financial structures, financial development and economic development

INTRODUCTION

It was pointed out earlier in this book that less developed countries (LDCs) commonly have thin or even no organised financial markets (see, for example, Goldsmith 1969; McKinnon 1973; World Bank 1989). According to the mainstream view, this institutional underdevelopment is the result of the 'long history of financial repression in developing countries' (Fry 1989: 233). It is further assumed that financial development can be promoted by financial liberalisation, which is alleged to increase saving and therefore investment.

An alternative view on financial structures, financial development and economic development, which is consistent with the theory presented in the previous chapters, is presented in this chapter. In this view, the role of banks in the process of growth is to supply finance, whereas saving and financial markets provide funding. Therefore, from our perspective, the concept of capital market efficiency – which is only applicable to the neoclassical analysis, where the main role of the financial system is to allocate saving between competing investment projects – must be replaced with the new tool to compare and address different financial structures in their roles as promoters of growth. Instead, the concept of capital market functionality is proposed, which has both microeconomic and macroeconomic foundations. Rather than assuming that there is an 'optimal' financial structure, we shall then be in a position to assess and compare different financial structures according to their potential functionality.

Having defined the concept of functionality, the main features of two different financial systems, the capital-market-based systems and the credit-based systems, are compared in this chapter. This comparison establishes their relative strengths and shortcomings in supporting financially stable growth. Further, we investigate the reasons why rapid developing economies tend to have credit-based systems and examine the compensating structures created in some successful developing countries in order to overcome the imperfections of their financial structures. Finally, we indicate why the establishment of an appropriate financial structure should be a pivotal part of development policies.

THE CONCEPT OF FUNCTIONALITY OF THE FINANCIAL STRUCTURE

The measure of efficiency of the financial system in contemporary financial theory is based upon the competitive capital market paradigm (see Lewis 1992). From a neoclassical perspective, in a competitive capital market saving/capital is allocated optimally; hence inefficiency attaches to anything outside that paradigm: real-life institutional arrangements are implicitly seen as distortions in relation to the optimal outcome of the idealised structure. The role of analysis is thus to point to the imperfections of such structures and, perhaps, to the ways of re-establishing the sovereignty of the market forces (e.g. financial liberalisation).

From a post-Keynesian perspective, financial systems are more than intermediaries between saving and investment: they create saving (through finance) as much as they allocate saving (through funding). Both roles are equally important in an entrepreneur economy: finance creates the means of commanding resources that will permit entrepreneurs to implement their production and investment decisions; funding represents an incentive for both banks and wealth-holders to hold securities and, additionally, reduces the financial fragility inherent to growing monetary economies. Since neither the availability of finance nor the existence of mechanisms for funding can be warranted by the pure forces of free competition, the meaning of efficiency here must forcibly have a different connotation in our analysis. In order to stress this difference, we shall use another term: functionality.

Functionality is defined as follows: a financial system is functional to the process of economic development when it expands the use of existing resources in the process of economic development with the minimum possible increase in financial fragility and other imbalances that may halt the process of growth for purely financial reasons. Functionality has two distinctive dimensions: one concerns the stability of the financial system and another is related to the allocation of real resources. This first is the macroeconomic dimension, the second, the microeconomic.

In the macroeconomic dimension, the functionality of the financial structure should be judged by how well it performs the functions of financing and funding; in other words, how it supports financially stable growth. As regards the microeconomic dimension, functionality relates not to the static allocation of existing resources, but to the *dynamic* allocation of resources, which must encompass economies of scale. Since the under-employment of potential resources is characteristic of developing market economies, investment will not only increase the use of existing (and possibly idle) available productive resources, but will also create them.

Concerning the macroeconomic functions described above, it is important to stress that, from the perspective adopted here, there is no reason why appropriate mechanisms to finance and fund accumulation will spontaneously evolve in the process of economic development, especially when such development is rapid. Financial institutions (and especially banks) will, because of the liability structure, prefer to remain in the shorter end of financing if that is possible. In a fast-growing economy, with constant pressure on finance, the financial institutions can profitably grow simply by providing short-run finance to credit-thirsty enterprises. Neither private banks nor other financial institutions will have the competitive stimulus to finance long-term positions. In this case, in order to grow, firms will have recourse to renewable short-term credit, self-funding or foreign indebtedness in order to implement their investment projects.

As regards funding, it is important to recognise that the development of stable financial markets may require a long-term strategy and not simply short-term incentives to securities buyers. Thin financial markets – which are the rule in LDCs (Goldsmith 1969; McKinnon 1973; World Bank 1989) – tend to be highly speculative and manipulated by a few big insiders, which creates a comprehensive mistrust by most small savers and even some potential institutional investors, such as those using pension funds. Therefore, such development must be carried out with careful regulation by the authorities. This regulation can be loosened according to the development of such markets, but it is unlikely that complete deregulation will ever be compatible with financially stable growth.

Finally, it is important to remember that in countries where financial markets did not develop sufficiently to support financially stable growth, compensating structures are normally found. These compensating structures will be the main topic of the next sections of this chapter.

CAPITAL-MARKET-BASED AND CREDIT-BASED FINANCIAL SYSTEMS

Institutional environments are, by nature, constantly changing and, notwithstanding deterministic faith, nothing can guarantee that development will lead to a unique financial structure. For instance, one of the characteristic developments in the early years of industrialisation in Britain, where the Industrial Revolution began, was the rapid evolution of the banking system, which enhanced investment and speeded up economic growth.[1] The market for long-term securities came later and consolidated at a slower pace than the banking system. For instance, whereas the London stock market originated between 1689 and 1720, only by the early decades of the nineteenth century had it acquired a key position in the British financial system, rivalling in importance that of the Bank of England. Until the mid-nineteenth century it dealt chiefly in government securities. The insurance companies, conversely, did invest a portion of their assets in industrial projects.

But, as the mechanisms to fund investment were poorly developed, the role of banking was crucial in providing an increased supply of means of payment to meet the rapidly increasing demand for money associated with industrialisation, higher incomes and the monetisation of the entire economy (see Pollard 1964: 41).[2]

However, the development of capital markets has not been so uniform in many other nations – a phenomenon confirmed by Zysman's (1983) classification of financial systems as capital-market-based and credit-based systems. The capital-market-based system is one where securities (stocks and bonds) are the main source of long-term funding. There is a wide range of capital and money-market instruments, a large number of specialised financial institutions offer competing services and prices are determined by the interplay of supply and demand. In credit-based financial systems, on the contrary, the capital market is weak and firms depend heavily on credit for raising finance beyond retained earnings.

In a nutshell, what differentiates the two types of financial structure is the existence or not of funding mechanisms. This difference has, in turn, consequences as regard the ways which investment can be supported by the existing financial institutions. From the theoretical perspective adopted thus far, the lack of organised financial markets can have two destabilising consequences for development: first, finance will tend to be very short term and credit rationing may occur in times of growth; second, if finance is forthcoming to sustain growth, the financial position of both firms and banks will become more fragile (how rapidly depends on the rate of growth). Let us investigate these two consequences.

As regards finance, the supply and the average maturity of loans made available for investment will be determined by the banks' liquidity preference. If financial markets remain underdeveloped and funding is not available, banks' liquidity preference will be high and they may refrain from expanding their lending activity. And even if they do lend, banks will almost certainly prefer short-term loans (say towards the financing of consumption, working capital and/or speculation) to longer-term, and hence riskier, investment projects. As Zysman points out, this is directly linked to the risks of long-term lending:

> Any loan is a gamble on the future solvency of the client, but a long-term loan involves a new kind of risk. Obviously, a long-term loan on the business of a client cannot in reality be secured by any physical assets. Moreover, a bank gets the bulk of the money it uses from funds deposited for a short term at the going interest rate. If it lends a firm money for five years, during the period, the depositors may withdraw their funds at which point the bank's reserves drop and it must reduce its loans: in an extreme case it might not be able to pay claims presented to it. Another, potentially more serious, problem may occur should interest rates change in unexpected ways. If the short-term rates go down and the bank has lent long, its margin of profits increases, but if the rates go up, its profit margins are cut or it loses money.
>
> (1983: 63)

In what concerns the financial fragility of the economy, if banks are still prepared to finance expansion despite the lack of appropriate mechanisms to fund investment, the indebtedness of the corporate sector has to increase. Growth will only be sustained if a section of investing firms borrows short, hoping to repay by borrowing until their investment matures and begins to produce additional cash inflows.

Credit-based systems are thus extremely vulnerable to changes in credit conditions in times of growth, because the weight of speculative finance tends to increase with the acceleration of investment. If the financing of long-lived assets is supplied mainly through short-term renewable loans, a change in the rate of interest will represent a significant rise in firms' financial expenditures; if firms try to adjust by cutting other expenditures simultaneously, this may set in motion a vicious circle of financial reactions which could reduce effective demand even further.

As many authors have demonstrated (for instance, Goldsmith 1969),

LDCs tend to have credit-based financial systems. The reason behind and the consequences of this fact are discussed below.

DIFFERENT FINANCIAL STRUCTURES IN A HISTORICAL PERSPECTIVE

In order to illustrate the difficulty of matching financial and economic development in a rapidly growing economy, let us assume an economy with the following characteristics: fast economic growth and structural change and high levels of accumulation in the form of industrial investment – say, a passage from an agrarian to an industrial urban economy.

In a primarily agricultural economy, the needs for financing are relatively small. For instance, in a non-subsistence plantation, the financing of production involves not much more than the payment of labour. If credit is needed, the producer can always use his/her own land as collateral for borrowing. Land is the main physical capital and can be expanded by simple incorporation (especially if the agricultural frontiers are still very wide, such as in the case of many LDCs), which may require little financing.

Changes in the productive structure affect financial requirements within the three great productive sectors: the primary, the industrial and the services sectors. Industrialisation changes the financial requirement of the primary sector in at least two ways. First, urbanisation of the economy is normally attached to the process of industrialisation, which in turn expands the demand for agricultural products. Second, the spacial detachment between producers and consumers increases. This in turn stretches the process of intermediation and creates new financial requirements. In addition, the change in techniques of production may require non-conventional inputs and equipment, which again creates new sources of demand for long-term financing.

As regards the industrial sector, the internalisation of the productive process increases the phases of production and introduces new links between primary production and final goods. This implies an expansion in the financial requirements per unit of production. Industrialisation also changes the composition of investment towards sectors with higher capital intensity, larger scales and longer terms of maturation. Finally, the process of industrialisation affects the services sector due to the inherent process of urbanisation, which extends the needs of the infrastructure, and the expansion of the commercial sector.

To sum up, in addition to the financial requirements inherent in the process of growth, the structural changes intrinsic to economic development generate pressure on the financial system. Even though the demand for short-term and medium-term finance increases, long-term finance is perhaps the most problematic aspect of financial development for two reasons. First, financial institutions (and especially banks) will, because of the liability structure, prefer short-term assets. Second, financing the accumulation of physical capital requires increasing the vulnerability of financial institutions. Therefore banks will only accept the risk of financing long-term projects if competition drives them to and if they can mitigate their risk through funding. However, in a rapidly growing economy, financial institutions can grow profitably simply by providing short-run finance to credit-thirsty enterprises. In this case, in order to grow, firms will need to have recourse to renewable short-term credit, self-finance or foreign indebtedness in order to implement their investment projects.

Finance in the early stages of industrialisation

Given the pattern of financial and economic development during England's Industrial Revolution, which we briefly discussed above, it is not surprising that Anglo-Saxon economic literature has always elected saving as the main source of finance. For, in this phase of British development, reinvestment of profits was the norm among businessmen,[3] even though banks did have an important role in the financing of accumulation.

This view of finance cannot be extended to the analysis of development finance nowadays for three main reasons. First, the pace of growth and change in the early stages of industrialisation was nothing like that which we are used to today; second, the rate of capital accumulation was hardly spectacular either; and third, the structural changes in the economy were not as dramatic as those in modern industrial development. This can be shown by some facts about the British Industrial Revolution.

In England, the annual rates of yearly growth in the first half of the eighteenth century scarcely averaged more than 0.5 per cent; this rose to about 1.5 per cent yearly after 1750 until it fell during the American Revolution; finally, it started rising again by 1785 reaching an average overall yearly rate of some 3 per cent in the 1830s.[4] Further, according to Deane (1961), at no time in eighteenth-century England did the ratio of capital formation to national income rise above 7 or 8 per cent and for most of the century it remained below 5 per cent. In addition, Pollard (1964: 301) notices that the 'amount of fixed capital involved in industry, compared with circulating capital, has often been exaggerated'.[5] Pollard also shows that direct suppliers' credit was the main source of financing of working capital, so that

> It was . . . possible for firms beginning in a small way and with greatly inadequate capital resources of their own to insert themselves into the circulation of credit and, in this way, to acquire working capital by a process of running credit balances of much larger amounts than debtors'. Conversely, firms of merchant origins, or otherwise well provided with capital, could find themselves, even in the factory age, using it to finance other firms' current needs rather than their own productive base.
>
> (1964: 306)

Finally, data compiled by Cameron *et al.* (1967: 33–5) allows us to show that the structural changes in the economy were not as dramatic as one is used to in modern industrial development (Table 5.1).

Comparing these data with recent experiences of development (see Table 5.2), changes in the size and structure of the productive basis in the early stages of industrial development were not very rapid.

Table 5.1 Participation of great productive sectors in national income in England (per cent, selected years)

Sector/year	*1688*	*1801*	*1841*
Agriculture, forestry and fishing	40	32.5	22.1
Mining, manufacturing and building	21	23.6	34.4
Trade and transport	12	17.5	18.4

Source: Cameron *et al.* 1967: 33–5

Table 5.2 Some indicators of recent experiences of economic development

	GNP growth (1)		*Investment/GNP* (2)		*Industry/GNP* (3)	
	1965–73	*1973–80*	*1965*	*1980*	*1965*	*1980*
Low-income economies	6.5	4.7	19.0	25.5	28.0	37
Middle-income economies	7.0	4.7	21.8	27.8	34.0	39
High-income economies	4.8	3.1	16.7	22.1	42.0	37

Source: World Bank 1991: 184–6

Therefore, in the early stages of industrialisation the pace of growth and accumulation allowed the volume and maturity of loans to evolve slowly without causing major disruption to the process of development. Hence it is not surprising that the evolution of the financial structure, besides the banking system, could be very slow too.

To sum up, in the early stages of industrialisation it is evident that the slow pace of change in the financial structure matched well enough the changes in the financial requirements of the time, for

> insofar as the newer forms of industry had a greater need for capital, both fixed and circulating, than the old, the transition was gradual, not sudden. The size of the average firm increased somewhat over time, and new firms entering most industries in the 1830s were probably larger than new firms entering the same industries in the 1780s; but for the most part growth was internal – within the firm – by means of reinvested profits. The proportion of working capital varied from industry to industry and may have increased slightly over time. Rarely, however, did the 'representative firm' in any industry invest as much as 50 per cent of its total assets in fixed capital. Of greater importance collectively were the liquid funds or access to credit needed for the purchase of raw materials, the payment of wages (and in some cases of rents and royalties), and the extension of credit to buyers. In this respect the difference between the new industrialism and the old was one of degree only, not one of kind.
>
> (Cameron *et al.* 1967: 36)

In the English case, therefore, the financial markets developed *spontaneously* and partly as a response to the needs created by industrialisation. In contrast, in late developing countries, the process of industrialisation was much more an intensive, and frequently State-oriented, process. The development of financial institutions was often a policy to facilitate rapid growth and high levels of accumulation – especially with regard to the financing of long-term, highly capital-intensive investment projects – where *finance* mechanisms were previleged to the detriment of *funding* mechanisms.[6] This is what we shall discuss next.

Investment finance in rapidly growing economies with underdeveloped funding mechanisms

The supply of long-term finance by private banks is inherently dependent upon the existence of mechanisms to provide funding. This may partly explain why in countries where funding channels did not develop, compensating structures are normally found, such as a strong commitment on the part of private banks or close government intervention – for example, the creation of development banks and the use of a regulated selective credit mechanism.

The German universal banks provide an example of a compensating structure: it was basically the great banks which geared and sustained the fast pace of industrialisation in the last half of the eighteenth century. Schumpeter (1939: 349) describes that role undertaken by the German great banks as follows:

> [the banks] took care of the necessary issues of stocks and bonds, thus helping the enterprises to redeem its short debt and providing it with additional means. In order to effect this they were ready to take these stocks or bonds for their own accounts, not only if they were unable to place them, but in the ordinary course of their business routine . . . When they placed the securities acquired, they again financed the private investors so that, temporarily at least, the transaction often meant no more than a shift in assets.

This was especially true after the 1870s, but was already clear before then (see Tilly in Cameron *et al.* 1967). Another interesting characteristic of the German case was the entrepreneurial element of the association between business and the banking system:

> In some instances the bankers initially perceived new opportunities for investment and suggested methods of exploiting them. More important, however, were entrepreneurial tasks that were allied with financial ends. Frequently, interested bankers obtained government approval and support for the projects of others. Then they had to create a market for the new securities. Finally, it was essential for them to ensure that the policies, financial and otherwise, of enterprises newly created or enlarged would continue to favor, or at least not interfere with, their own banking interests.
>
> (Op. cit.: 178–9)

But Germany was not the only case where a credit-based financial structure had a wide role in the process of accumulation. For example, between 1868 and the Second World War, Japan industrialised vigorously and developed a sophisticated, modern banking system, well structured to meet the needs of economic development. This was not coincidental but a planned policy of the government, which clearly favoured the evolution of the system as a tool for promoting economic growth.

In Japan, although the initial capital for industrial investment came primarily from stock subscriptions by industrialists (especially members of the wealthy merchant–landowner–financier group and in some instances, notably railways, by the aristocracy), it appears that commercial banks financed most individual subscriptions to both new and existing enterprises (Cameron *et al.* 1967: 235). Further, banks also appear to have directed funds to specific enterprises. And not only did new enterprises benefit from this sort of financial arrangement:

> Industrial enterprises relied on two main sources of funds: new capital stock issues, sold mainly to existing stockholders; and short-term and long-term loans from banks. It was not clear which was more important in the early years [of the industrialisation process], but by the turn of the century bank loans were clearly the major source.
>
> (Op. cit.: 283–4)

In fact, many big conglomerates (*zaibatsu*) owned their own banking institutions or at least maintained a very close relation with them. This made it relatively easy to transfer funds among affiliated enterprises and to collect private individual savings to finance *zaibatsu* investment. Generally speaking then, large banks were increasingly important in financing both the initial and the continued development of large-scale enterprise, based on high indebtedness and stable interest rates.[7]

More recently, modern Japan and some of its neighbours, notably Taiwan and the Republic of Korea, appear to have inherited this kind of institutional arrangement, where government, banks and enterprise have strong links (see Foley and Lazonick 1986; and Wade 1989). According to Zysman's classification, all these three East Asian countries have credit-based financial systems, with government-administered prices. The tight control of the banking system on credit supply is evident from the fact that, for instance, in Taiwan virtually the entire banking system is government owned; and in the Republic of Korea, even after the denationalisation of banks in 1980–3, the government exerts an important influence through the direct appointment of senior managers and personnel.

Hence, the institutional mechanisms created to finance investment exemplified above seem to be institutional alternatives to the difficult problem of financing development in circumstances when the rate of growth and changes in the productive structure are speeded up and the development of private financial markets is slowed down. The problem of financing is as important a factor for the process of economic development now as it was in the early stages of the development of Western European countries (Wade 1989: 137). The only difference seems to be in the circumstances of late development, with the 'demonstration effect' and the availability of high technology, raising both attempted growth rates and capital costs. These exacerbate the need for further institutional arrangements – to promote development by overcoming the relatively slower evolution of long-term financing mechanisms and by supplying the volume of capital required to set up modern industrial plants.

Functionality in different financial structures

As was discussed earlier, a credit-based financial system requires further compensating structures in order to be functional in the process of development, especially with regard to the financing of long-term projects. In a credit-based financial structure dominated by institutions, if growth is to take place at all then one of two possibilities must occur. First, banks must maintain a long-term relationship with their clients, consistent with the financing of the latter's long-term positions. Credit-granting is based on the firms' long-term prospects, but financial institutions are pressed into a close monitoring of management and their decisions.

Second, where this spontaneous institutional arrangement does not evolve, it is common to find that the State has had to intervene in order to secure long-term funds. This situation seems to be the origin of Zysman's credit-based financial systems with administered prices: government either creates institutional arrangements to reduce the risk private institutions undertake (e.g. rediscount windows for long-term loans) or they set up their own development agencies. In both cases, the government can exercise a more direct influence on firms' decision making and the direction of development.

The functionality of any financial system functionality cannot be assessed, nor a policy proposed, without a close examination of the existing institutions and their role in the financing of accumulation. It is thus naive to assume that institutional arrangements outside the capital-market-based paradigm are less efficient; or to expect that financial liberalisation, including positive real rates of interest, in itself will suffice to solve the problem of the lack of long-term finance.[8]

To sum up, different financial structures may be viewed as the institutional means of overcoming the problem of financing growth. It seems, however, that the faster the pace of growth and structural change in the productive sector, the more unlikely it will be that investment finance and funding will develop spontaneously. History shows, for instance, that the German universal banks and strong government intervention in the mechanism of finance were used by late-comers to the now developed countries to establish their own finance-funding mechanisms. But for many other countries (like Brazil), the recourse to profit-inflation and to foreign indebtedness to finance internal accumulation has played an important role, with great costs in terms of financial and macroeconomic stability.

Policy towards enhancing the functionality of the financial system for economic development should focus as much on an appropriate financial policy as on institutional development. As regards financial policy, it must be remembered that in a fast-growing economy, with constant pressure on finance, private financial institutions can profitably grow simply by providing short-run finance to credit-thirsty enterprises. If neither private banks nor other financial institutions have the competitive stimulus to finance long-term positions, firms will have to resort to short-term credit, self-finance or foreign indebtedness in order to implement their investment projects.

With regard to institutional development, this must be a long-term policy. Thin financial markets, which are the rule in LDCs, tend to be highly speculative and manipulated by a few big 'insiders'. This creates a comprehensive mistrust amongst most small savers and even some potential institutional investors (e.g. pension funds). Therefore, such development must be carried out with careful regulation by the authorities – regulation which can be loosened according to the development of such markets. It is unlikely though that complete deregulation will ever be compatible with financially stable growth.

Finally, it is important to remember that in countries where financial markets did not develop sufficiently to support financially stable growth, compensating structures were created – such as, for example, a strong commitment on the part of private banks (e.g. the German universal banks), the development of financial/corporate conglomerates (e.g. the Japanese financial/corporate conglomerates) or close government intervention such as the creation of development banks and the use of regulated selective credit mechanism (e.g. the South Korean case). It seems that LDCs, and perhaps multilateral development agencies, have more to learn from these experiences than from the capital-market-based paradigm of an efficient financial structure.

SUMMING UP

In order to be functional in the process of growth, a financial system must have credit-creating power and funding mechanisms and must maintain robustness throughout the process of growth. As indicated in previous chapters, all of these roles depend upon the current stage of development of the financial structure. This institutional evolution is not always spontaneous, especially with regard to mechanisms for *funding*. In fact history gives us plenty of examples of successful developing economies where the evolution of credit-based financial structure was part of a wider development strategy.

A fast developing economy will tend to develop a credit-based financial system for three reasons. First, growth depends on additional credit, whatever the existing type of financial structure. Second, if growth is high, only if the marginal propensity to buy placements out of households' savings is equal to one, long-term funds will not be available to fund all existing outstanding debt. Third, if development creates constant excess demand for financing short-term operations (working capital, for instance), financial institutions (especially banks) may have no competitive stimuli to finance long term or to promote funding.

Credit-based financial systems cannot support high levels of growth unless other financial arrangements are created. These arrangements exist in order to overcome shortcomings created by the lack of mechanisms to fund investment and the increasing financial fragility inherent in growing economies. In many LDCs the process of growth and structural change is faster than one can expect the financial structure to develop, especially as regards the capacity to fund ongoing investments. This means that, unless other arrangements exist to overcome the gap between financial and economic development, growth will be constantly constrained by the lack of sources for financing or surges of financial instability. Such seems to have been the case of Brazil in its recent experience of rapid industrialisation. This is the topic of our next four chapters.

Chapter 6

From theory to evidence

INTRODUCTION

This chapter marks the transition between the theoretical and applied parts of the book. It summarises the story of Brazil's development from 1947 to 1983, concentrating on the relation between real and financial development, with three aims: (1) to justify concentrating on this period, in particular to justify stopping in 1983; (2) to indicate the questions raised by applying the approach of the first four chapters to this period of Brazilian economic experience; (3) to indicate the method of application.

The chapter is organised as follows. First we provide an overview of the problems dealt with in the case study and explain the choice of the overall period. The importance of the financial reforms of 1964–6 is highlighted in order to explain the demarcation into two sub-periods, before and after the reform, which is followed in subsequent chapters. Then, we show how the post-Keynesian framework developed earlier will be used to structure the questions to be addressed in subsequent chapters.

A SUMMARY OF THE PERIOD AND ITS SUB-PERIODS

In our case study we compare the functionality of Brazil's financial structure before and after the financial reforms of 1964–6. The study deals with the period from 1947 to 1983, which is divided into the periods of 1947–66 and 1967–83. These sub-periods were chosen for reasons concerning both the economic and the financial developments of the period.

The year 1947 is a watershed in Brazil's economic development after the Second World War, because it was then that the first steps to the rapid process of import-substitution were taken by Brazil's government. This process had already started spontaneously in the 1930s and 1940s, with the subsequent import constraints caused by the world trade crisis and the Second World War. However, with the raising of import tariffs to counter the increasing balance-of-payments deficit, 1947 marks the beginning of an increasing involvement of the State in the process of industrialisation which culminated with the *Plano de Metas* (Target Plan) from 1956 to 1960. The Plan promoted an unprecedented industrial development, which increased the pace of accumulation and boosted output and employment. This boom finished in 1961, and from 1962 to 1966 the country saw its first industrial recession.

The period between 1967 and 1979 marks another phase of Brazil's import-substituting development. First, growth was resumed by a boom in the consumption of durables and in the housing sector. The exhaustion of the inherited productive capacity at the beginning of the 1970s signalled to the fact that the continuance of Brazil's development required a renewed rise in investment. This time again the government led the process of import-substitution with its Second National Development Plan (1974 Plan), which rapidly raised the accumulation. The growth-*cum*-debt strategy of the 1974 Plan ended in 1979, with the highest levels of external and internal debts ever in Brazil, soaring inflation and menacing financial fragility. The 1980s, therefore, are characterised by subsequent stabilisation plans, resilient inflation, several accords with the International Monetary Fund (IMF), but no true continuance to the process of economic development. To use a well-established *cliché*, the 1980s were in many aspects a lost decade.

The second reason for choosing the period between 1947 and 1983 is the fact that the 1964–6 financial reform substantially changed the way accumulation was financed and the relation between the financial system and productive sectors in general. Until the 1960s the Brazilian financial system was dominated by the banking system, which was in turn dominated by the government's bank, the Banco do Brasil. This institution shared the responsibility of financing investment with the Treasury and the National Development Bank (BNDE).[1] In contrast, the private banks concentrated their operations on the short term and maintained high levels of mark-up. Finally the financial markets were underdeveloped (see Table 6.1) and dominated by operations not related to the financing of productive investment.

As discussed earlier, despite the underdevelopment of the financial system, a fast process of import-substituting industrialisation took place in the period 1947–61, which was followed by a contraction which lasted until 1966 (Table 6.2). The contraction had to do with the decline of

Table 6.1 Brazil: some indicators of the development of the financial system (1947–83) (selected years)

		1947	*1961*	*1964*	*1967*	*1973*	*1978*	*1983*
Number and types of institutions								
Commercial banks	(1)	444	332	328	261	115	107	111
Bank branches	(2)	1,783	4,949	6,389	7,357	7,931	10,222	14,336
Savings banks	(3)	–	1	1	1	6	6	5
Branches	(4)	–	561	595	517	608	736	2,490
Investment banks	(5)	–	–	–	–	45	39	39
Finance/investment companies	(6)	–	–	–	–	152	119	114
Development banks	(7)	–	1	1	1	14	16	16
Federal	(8)	–	1	1	1	1	1	1
State	(9)	–	–	–	–	13	15	15
Savings/loans associations	(10)	–	–	–	–	36	36	22
Real estate credit societies	(11)	–	–	–	–	44	40	76
Brokerage firms	(12)	–	–	–	–	569	477	426
Brokerage houses	(13)	–	–	–	–	414	280	249
Stock exchange	(14)	–	–	–	–	16	12	12
Insurance companies	(15)	–	–	–	–	110	96	95
Credit co-operatives	(16)	–	–	–	–	324	367	530
Other	(17)	–	–	–	–	–	–	74
Other quantitative indicators (%)								
Financial assets/GNP	(18)	41	27	21	26	51	43	53
Loans/GNP	(19)	30[a]	17	13	32	85	108	75
Monetary assets/total assets	(20)	59	84	92	73	38	31	14
Public debt/total assets	(21)	13	6	1	12	29	26	45
Banco do Brasil's loans/total	(22)	26	29	30	20	15	15	10
Financial system product/GNP	(23)	3	3	3	4	5	8	11
Bank branches per 10^6 inhabitants	(24)	37	70	81	86	79	90	112

Sources: rows 1–17, 1947–78, *Brazil, a Handbook of Historical Statistics*, 1978, Cambridge, Mass.: Hall; 1983, Goldsmith 1986: 529; rows 18–22, 1945–78, Central Bank Bulletin 1965: table 1.11; 1980 and 1983, Central Bank Bulletin 39 (3), March 1985: 150; row 23, IBGE 1987: 118–20; row 24, number of branches from row 7, population from IBGE 1987: 33 (1940) and 111 (1947 onwards)

Note: [a] 1951 data.

Table 6.2 Brazil: macroeconomic indicators from 1947 to 1983

		1947–61	*1962–6*	*1967–73*	*1974–80*	*1981–3*
GNP	(1)	7.0	5.0	11.2	6.8	−0.8
Per capita GNP	(2)	4.2	1.0	8.5	−3.1	5.4
Industry	(3)	8.7	4.9	13.5	7.0	−3.4
Agriculture	(4)	4.1	4.4	4.9	5.4	−0.1
Inflation (WPI)[a]	(5)	15.8	81.9	19.4	49.2	123.0
External sector[b]						
Imports/GNP	(6)	6.5	4.5	6.0	8.5	7.2
Exports/GNP	(7)	7.5	5.4	6.1	6.9	8.4
Debt/GNP	(8)	7.9	15.7	12.8	18.7	27.5
Debt/exports	(9)	123.6	291.8	208.3	274.2	327.6
Investment indicators						
Total (percentage of GNP)[c]	(10)	15.4	17.4	20.4	23.6	19.5
Total (growth rate per cent)[d]	(11)	9.5	6.6	14.5	6.4	11.9
Private (percentage of total)	(12)	73.4	65.6	57.5	60.7	63.2
Private (growth rate per cent)[d]	(13)	6.7	15.0	21.2	6.2	−8.5
Government (percentage of total)[e]	(14)	26.6	34.5	42.5	39.3	36.8
Government (growth rate per cent)[d]	(15)	12.0	12.6	14.3	3.5	−16.2

Sources: rows 1–2, IBGE 1987: 111; rows 3–4, 1947–70; Instituto Brasileiro de Economia–Fundação Getúlio Vargas/IBGE (as published in *Anuarios APEC*, 1987: table I–2); 1971–83, IBGE 1987: 122; row 5, IBGE 1987: 111; rows 6–7, ibid.: 536–7; rows 8–9: ibid.: 543; rows 10–11, 1934–45, Goldsmith 1986: 152; from 1947 onwards: IBGE, 1987: 114–116 and 126 (see observation below); rows 12–13: 1947–66, Werneck 1969; 1967–79, Trebat 1983: 130; 1980–1; Dismoor 1990: 62; rows 14–15, nominal private investment obtained by subtracting government investment from total investment

Notes: [a] Rates of change of average general price index (IGP–DI).

[b] Dollar values transformed into cruzeiro using the implicit exchange rate as in IBGE 1987: 524–5.

[c] Total investment includes changes in inventories.

[d] From 1947 to 1969 real total investment was obtained by deflating nominal values by GNP implicit deflator; data for 1970–83 obtained from IBGE 1987: 126.

[e] Includes investment of government-owned enterprises.

investment after a period of intensive accumulation. But the financial structure did represent an important constraint to the resumption of growth: the unsophisticated financial system was inadequate even to finance consumption of durables and medium-term working capital, expenditures which were fundamental to permit the use of the newly installed industry.

In 1964–5 a financial reform was undertaken in order to increase the diversification of the assets and the institutions of the financial system. The view behind the reform was that financial repression had deterred the development of the financial structure in the 1950s and 1960s. This was associated with the usury law and the gold clause, which restricted interest rates to a maximum of 12 per cent a year, when the average inflation was superior to this. It was alleged that low (even negative) real interest rates had reduced the supply of voluntary savings into the financial system and, therefore, the supply of loanable funds available to investing firms was lower than the potential. The national private firms were, according to the same view, the ones to lose the most from this financial repression – as the public firms had access to public funds (such as funds from BNDE) and the international corporations could always count on loans in foreign currency and direct investment from abroad.

The reform was indeed successful in increasing the diversification of assets and boosting the consumption of durables and the housing market, which led the period of high growth from 1967 to 1973. But far more important than the achievements of the financial reforms seem to be the long-run effects of such reform to the process of economic development in Brazil. First, in order to raise interest rates, the government introduced indexation – basically of those assets issued and loans granted by the monetary authorities and the public financial institutions. The failure of government attempts to impose the same practice on private institutions created a severely fragmented financial system – where indexed and non-indexed assets co-existed. This increased the scope for speculation and the fragility of the system.

Second, the highly speculative financial markets and the persistence of inflation increased, rather than reduced, the risk-aversion of financial institutions and savers. So the private financial system continued to be dominated by the shorter end of the financial operations. The longer-term credit, such as the financing of industrial investment and civil constructions, was left to the State.

Third, the reform further opened up opportunities for firms to borrow abroad, allegedly in order to capture foreign savings. Given that the reforms had failed to increase the channels of finance for national firms, the result of such openness, associated with the exceptional conditions in the international financial markets in the 1970s, was a boost of foreign borrowing far above the finance requirements of the economy, especially in the period 1967–73. After 1974, the government continued with the growth-*cum*-debt strategy, this time also explicitly stimulating public enterprises to borrow in order to finance the investment projects associated with the Second National Development Plan.

The inadequacy of the financial system that emerged after the 1964–6 reforms and their consequences for the developments in the 1970s are overlooked by the existing literature, in view of the intensity of the disequilibria caused by the subsequent oil shocks and the interest shock. The importance of those shocks is not reduced in our analysis. But emphasis will be placed on the constraints, imposed by the financial structure, in overcoming the challenges of the 1970s.

To sum up, what is claimed here, and what will be demonstrated in the subsequent chapters, is that the financial structure represented (and still does represent) one of the main obstacles to a stable process of development in Brazil. However, the reforms in 1964–6, rather than solving the main structural weakness of the financial system, worsened it. The choice of periods of analysis is thus justified by our understanding that the causes of the problems behind Brazil's lost decade are completely characterised by the events up to 1983. In other words, to proceed from then on would extend significantly the scope and size of this book, without contributing to our conclusions.

THE METHOD OF ANALYSIS

The choice of a method cannot be dissociated from the paradigm which underlies the theoretical analysis. For instance, within the mainstream approach, it is only natural that the method should involve a precise specification of the hypothesis and test it. Or alternatively, that two competing hypotheses are specified in such a way that data can discriminate conclusively between them. But as Dow points out:

> Leaving aside the methodological problem with this procedure when applied to short-period analysis, it has severe shortcomings when applied to long-period analysis. Over the long period, the very changes in economic structure, institutions and behaviour which are the object of a study of economic development evade capture by formal mathematics or observation by consistent data series.
>
> (1990: 2)

Our analysis concerns the relation between financial structure and economic development, where, by definition, the institutions and therefore the behaviour of the main protagonists are evolving through time. In this case, more than ever,

> The scope for universal laws in economics is restricted by the capacity of the economic system to evolve over time; the majority of the general statements must be conditional on the environment in which they are formulated. In particular, as Hicks . . . points out, the time element in statements of cause and effect becomes important if structural change can occur during that time period. In order to retain the causal statement, therefore, it must incorporate a statement about behaviour reacting to the structural change, as well as the initial cause. This requirement to account for historical development further impedes the ability of an economist to conform to the traditional rules of scientific enquiries.
>
> (Dow 1985: 35)

Therefore, in our case, where the 1964–6 financial reform fundamentally changed the conventions of economic agents, a political economy approach seems more suitable to the analysis of development processes. This approach 'forgoes precision in the narrow sense of amenability to mathematical expression, in the interests of depth and breadth of understanding of complex causal process' (Dow 1990: 3). The causal process that will be analysed in the next chapter is the relation between financial and economic development in Brazil from 1947 to 1983. This analysis will be centred on the concept of functionality defined in the previous chapter.

The main questions that are addressed by the empirical analysis of this book are (1) how the 1964–6 financial reforms changed the functionality of the mechanisms to finance and fund accumulation; and (2) to what extent the reformed financial structure can be blamed for the severe macroeconomic/financial imbalances of Brazil's development in the 1970s and 1980s.

Testing the functionality of the financial system is to analyse the behaviour of separate, and yet integrated, financial institutions and markets, and their role in financing and funding accumulation. The structure that seems to fit this type of analysis is the following.

First, a summary of the main macroeconomic indicators will be presented for each period, in order to establish the pace of growth and accumulation as well as to indicate the economic agents leading the process of accumulation.

Second, the interrelation between financial structure and economic development will be analysed through the following topics: (i) the main institutional features of the financial system; (ii) banks and other suppliers of finance; (iii) the stage of development, the size and the volatility of financial markets and their role as suppliers of funding; (iv) the role of foreign capital inflows in financing internal accumulation; and (v) the system's financial robustness and the mechanisms of contagion of instability.

Finally, we analyse the compensating structures – i.e. the institutional arrangements are created to compensate for the lack or deficiencies of the traditional mechanisms to finance and fund investment – and their shortcomings to the process of development. The theoretical reasons behind this structure are now briefly reviewed.

The importance of the institutional setting

Financial systems are institutional environments whereby the command of a significant part of the real resources is determined. In monetary-production economies, the existence of a Stage 2 banking system allows the economy to accumulate at a faster pace than previous saving would permit. Since saving is not causally important in the financing of investment, the institutional setting determines a hierarchy in the system, where banks' credit policies and firms' decisions, both based on their expectations, define the levels of investment, output and employment, and thus income. As regards saving decisions, they will delimit the availability and direction of the supply of funding. However, it is again the institutional setting and the preferences of wealth-holders which determine whether these funds will be functional or not to economic growth. In other words, the existence of both a developed financial market and a favourable state of liquidity preference will facilitate the redirection of additional savings to funding.

The post-Keynesian theory of finance normally assumes an institutional environment that includes a banking system that has at least reached Stage 2, and organised financial markets. However, it also provides the analyst with a theoretical framework to understand the consequences of most LDCs not having their financial markets developed: on the one hand, credit-based systems provide the economy with a great capacity to accumulate; on the other, they also tend to enlarge financial fragility. Hence, fast-developing countries may need compensating mechanisms to finance accumulation and to avoid financial instability.

Therefore, in order to assess the functionality of the financial structure, the institutional analyses must evaluate the inherited institutional setting as regards the mechanisms and structures to finance and fund accumulation and the possible structures created to compensate for the lack of developed capital markets. In the specific case of Brazil, the financial reforms of 1964–6 represent the main watershed as regards such mechanisms and structures. Accordingly, most of the analysis will be concerned with the comparison of the financial structures and their functionality before and after the above-mentioned reform.

Once the institutional setting has been investigated, then the analysis can proceed to describe the behaviour of the most relevant financial agents in the process of financing accumulation.

The analysis of main suppliers of finance

In post-Keynesian theory, growth and investment are determined by entrepreneurial long-term expectations and the availability and cost of finance. Finance should be sharply distinguished from saving which derives from, rather then being a precondition for, growth. The supply of finance, in economies with a developed financial structure, is determined by the banks and their expectations.

In Brazil's case in 1947–61, the credit-creating capacity of the banking system was significant because of the dual role played by Banco do Brasil as monetary authority and commercial bank. As monetary authority, the Bank had direct access to the Treasury funds which could, accordingly, accommodate any demand for additional reserves required. Any increase in Banco do Brasil's loans represented a direct increase in the reserve base of other commercial banks.

However, in this period, the mechanisms to fund investment were very underdeveloped. Consequently private investment finance relied greatly on a tripod consisting of government finance (directly through government investment, and indirectly through funds released by public agencies, such as BNDE and Banco do Brasil), foreign capital inflows and inflationary self-finance.

In this environment, the pace of growth of the level of activity produced a constant demand for credit on the finance account. Because non-inflationary mechanisms to fund accumulation were lacking, firms usually resorted to inflation as a means to repay these debts. From the supply side, inflation affects lending decisions, creating a bias towards the short term and high levels of liquidity preference. From the demand side, inflation plays a role in the growth of demand for finance by creating increasing *illusory profits* and making the firms more inclined to *Ponzi* financing.

If the official ceiling of the rate of interest cannot be blamed for the underdevelopment of the financial markets, the usury law did make bond-issuing by the government impossible, especially when inflation rose. This did not affect fiscal policy, for the government has an unconstrained capacity to finance its deficit with money issues. But it greatly limited the availability of alternative assets for inactive holders of money. This is why the basic rate of interest for small savings (set by bank deposit rates) remained almost steady at 4 per cent, much below the 12 per cent ceiling on interest rates. Despite the negative real loan rates, banks could maintain high mark-ups in their loan operations, because the system lived in a constant situation of excess demand for loans.

In a nutshell, the institutional arrangement to finance investment described above permitted growth, but there were side-effects: inflation, constant government deficits and rising external debt. Furthermore, the functionality of such a mechanism depended on the maintenance of investment growth, low rates of inflation and the continuing refinancing of external debt. Indeed, as inflation rose significantly in the beginning of the 1960s, both the government's financing capacity and the firms' capacity for self-financing collapsed into the crisis which began in 1961.

With the 1964–6 financial reforms, indexation was introduced in government bonds and other liabilities of public institutions. Indexation of savings accounts also had the full backing of the monetary authorities. Given their new liquidity, government bonds became the standard in the determination of other assets' own rates. The existence of other liquid indexed assets with non-indexed assets in an environment of persistent inflation made the newly born financial market very speculative from the outset. This speculative demand and the monetary policy became the main determinants of the interest rate in the money market.

The behaviour of the banking system also changed substantially with the financial reform. Until 1964 the bank-dominated financial structure was involved in financing business. The financial reform permitted the development of financial institutions specialising in the financing of consumer durables and housing. But it also permitted the system to profit from the speculative uses of its funds, especially with government bonds. Further, the deliberate policy of government to let banks hold reserves (even their voluntary reserves) in the form of public bonds, not only restricted the scope of monetary policy but also made speculation an alternative means of expansion of the banking system. Indeed, when inflation (and along with it uncertainty) started to rise, the financial institutions' performance became closely linked to the gains related to the refinancing of the rapidly expanding public debt.

The examination of the mechanisms of funding

Saving funds, but does not finance capital accumulation. Funding means the transformation of the short-term debts incurred by investing firms into long-term securities issued through the financial markets. As such, the allocation of savings may have an important role in maintaining the financial stability of the growing economy, especially in periods of acceleration of accumulation.

We have seen earlier that the conventional financial-repression literature sees any process of financial deepening as a sign of improvement of the efficiency of the financial system. From our perspective, the innovations and diversification which characterise most processes of financial deepening are only functional to the process of growth if they create conditions for the development of stable mechanisms to finance and fund accumulation. If such innovations only swell up what Keynes called the 'financial circulation', then they have little, if not a negative functionality to economic development.[2]

A functional system of long-term financing and funding of modern capitalism requires a certain type of institutional evolution, including the development stock markets, specialised financial institutions and institutional investors. Thin financial markets – which are the rule in LDCs (Goldsmith 1969; McKinnon 1973; World Bank 1989) – tend to be highly speculative and manipulated by a few big insiders, which create a comprehensive mistrust by most small savers and even some potential institutional investors, such as pension funds. The development of growth-supporting, financially stable securities markets can also be imperilled by the pace of growth. For, if financial institutions can comfortably expand by profiting from short-term financial operations, they will have no stimulus to enter into long-term contracts. Finally, inflation, another characteristic of many LDCs, increases the risk of capital loss in long-term operations; hence persistent inflation creates a *culture of the short term*, which cannot be easily changed, at least in the short run. Therefore it is important to recognise that the development of stable financial markets may require a long-term strategy and not simply short-term incentives to securities buyers.

The financial reforms of 1964–6 correctly perceived the need to develop a private long-term capital market. But the implicit assumption that the creation of institutions such as investment banks and the rise of real interest rates would suffice to stimulate such development was misleading. The introduction of indexed government bonds raised the floor of the nominal asset rates offered to asset-holders and the financial costs to firms. However, this did not lengthen the maturity of loans to the productive sector. Furthermore, the possibility of capital gains that the coexistence of indexed and non-indexed short-term securities provided, stimulated speculation in which both wealth-holders and financial institutions engaged. Finally, the rise of real deposit rates caused an expected rise in real loan rates.

In addition, government's attempts in 1964–6 to develop a private long-term financial market, based on investment banks and fiscal incentives to acquire shares, was a significant failure. Investment banks never fully acted as suppliers of long-term funds or represented an important stimulus to the development of long-term securities markets. In effect, in 1971 the feeble stock market suffered a crash from which it never fully recovered until the 1980s.

To sum up, the failure to develop a private capital market and the rise of speculation created a financial system which was *more* short term and speculative than the underdeveloped system of 1947–61: in other words, the reformed system was less functional to development. As a result, when accumulation was resumed in 1974–8, *ad hoc* measures had to be taken to finance accumulation. These measures included the rapid increase of subsidised loans from public financial institutions. Another effect of the financial reform was the increased use of foreign indebtedness. We turn to this next.

The role of foreign capital inflows

The first problem that one has to face when analysing the role of foreign capital in economic growth is to measure the contribution of such funds to the financing of economic development in the period under analysis. Certainly the definition of 'external saving' is not helpful, as it fails to distinguish what represents effective net finance from purely accumulation of international reserves and from the use of additional reserves to cover financial costs of previously obtained debt.

One way of overcoming the analytical difficulty is to redefine the balance of payments so as to distinguish what represents real resources transfer (RRT) from other factors affecting international capital inflows. The RRT comprises approximately the trade ($X - M$) and non-factor (NF) payments. RRT is financed by capital inflows (CI) minus what we call costs of capital (CC) – i.e. interest payments i, amortisation a and profit remittances π – and changes of international reserves (Res). Finally, capital inflows encompass transfers (T), foreign direct investment (FDI) and loans (L). So we have:

$$\text{RRT} = (X - M) + \text{NF} = \text{CI} - \text{CC} - \text{Res} \tag{6.1}$$

$$CI = T + \text{FDI} + L \tag{6.2}$$

$$\text{CC} = i + a + \pi \tag{6.3}$$

This classification permits the analyst to distinguish, in a time series of the balance of payments, the purely financial causes of an increase of external debt from a gap between internal supply and demand. Given this reclassification, here we can advance the method that we shall adopt in analysing the Brazilian case.

Without ignoring the 'supply side' of the debt crisis (i.e. the increase in liquidity of the international banking system in the 1970s and the interest rate shocks which occurred from 1978), the analysis will focus on the 'demand side' of the problem. The position adopted in the analysis is summarised below.

If firms do not have access to long-term financing and funding internally, they will resort to foreign borrowing even if they do not require to import capital goods for their investment projects. From a macroeconomic perspective, this will result in increases in the level of investment being pegged by an increase in the external debt, above that required to finance trade of services and goods. This is the starting point of our analysis.

In the period from 1947 to 1961, there was indeed a constant excess demand for foreign currency to finance an increasing positive real resources transfer generated by the rapid internal accumulation. Since most private national enterprises (including the public firms) did not have access to credit from the international financial system, the financing of the mentioned gap involved three main mechanisms: (1) direct foreign investment; (2) the transfer of purchasing power in foreign currency from the surplus export sector to the investing national (public and private) firms; and (3) borrowing with the government's help.

The financial reforms of 1964–6 opened access to the international financial system for both public and private enterprises. It dismantled the previous controls on loan capital inflows and left a significant part of their allocation to private banks. Furthermore, by reducing the flow of investment funds to public enterprises, it stimulated those firms to borrow directly from abroad. The result of this opening to the international financial system was an unprecedented increase in the demand for foreign loans in 1967–73, much above the requirements to finance RRT.

From 1974 the access to international financial markets was only useful in a very short period (until 1977), when the oil shock created a severe increase in the trade deficit. But from 1977 the structural tendency to borrow above what was required to finance the trade deficit, imposed by the need to refinance the outstanding stock of debt, was repeated. The cost of such a strategy was to augment the financial vulnerability of the country to the credit conditions in the international market. Finally, with the change of monetary policy in the United States in 1979 and the sharp rise in interest rates, the rolling-over of the external debt became infeasible and the debt crisis dragged the country into the stagflation of the 1980s, the so-called lost decade.

It is important to stress that the development strategy undertaken by the government in the 1970s – the so-called growth-*cum*-debt strategy – was not caused merely by a misleading policy during the 1980s. It was also forced by the failure of the 1964–6 reform to develop appropriate mechanisms for financing accumulation domestically, and the lack of alternatives in 1974 for the financing of the Second Development Plan.

The assessment of the system's financial robustness

Financial fragility should be measured by indicators of the firms' levels of indebtedness and their capacity to repay the services of their outstanding deficit. This, as Taylor and O'Connell (1985) pointed out, is in itself a difficult task, as it implies the availability of precise firms' balance-sheet data and some subjective forecasting of firms' capacity to generate cash flows in the future in order to repay their debts. In our case, the lack of firms' balance-sheet data of Brazilian firms in the 1950s and 1960s makes the analysis of systemic financial fragility very limited. Nevertheless here we can put forward few theoretical considerations of the relation between the inherent financial fragility of economic development and the evolution of the financial system in Brazil in the period.

In credit-based financial markets, an increase in long-term commitments will be followed by rising indebtedness of firms. This leads to a higher degree of general financial fragility, expressed by elevated leverage ratios of banks and non-financial enterprises.

In Brazil this fragility was mitigated in the 1940s and 1950s by the fact that firms used profit inflation as a means of funding their investment. However, as inflation rose and aggregate demand decelerated at the end of the 1950s, this mechanism became increasingly dysfunctional. Intervention by the monetary authorities increased, but was not sufficient to avoid the increase of bankruptcies in the productive sector and the collapse of financial institutions and the 'curb' market for bills of exchange.

The financial reforms did not reduce this tendency to fragility; in fact it increased. First, the introduction of indexation raised the nominal interest rates. Second, because of the commitment to stimulate internal saving and attract external saving, the monetary policy targeted the real interest rate during almost the whole of the 1970s. On the one hand, this increased the external and internal debts disproportionately, as we have already pointed out. On the other hand, the speculation by both private financial institutions and firms in financial assets (especially government bonds) created an intricate network of financial commitments, the stability of which increasingly depended on the government's expanding the internal public debt.

Finally, in the 1970s the debt of the corporate sector also expanded significantly, because of both the rapid accumulation and the high interest rates in the period. This meant that, once aggregate demand started decreasing in the 1980s, the financial assistance of the central bank to financial institutions had to rise. Nevertheless, this was not enough: bankruptcies increased again. The surviving firms had to go through an intensive process of financial restructuring. This was made possible by significant transfers of government funds to the financial system and, indirectly, by the private sector's capital gains from dealing in government bonds.

SUMMING UP

This chapter has established the method and the structure of the analysis that will be used in the case study. This compares the functionality of Brazil's financial system before and after the reforms of 1964–6. The structure of the analysis of each period will be analysed according to the criterion of functionality as defined in the previous chapter. The structure that seems to fit this type of analysis is the following. First, a summary of the main macroeconomic indicators will be presented for each period, in order to establish the pace of growth and accumulation as well as to indicate the economic agents leading the process of accumulation. Second, the interrelation between financial structure and economic development will be analysed through the study of (i) the main institutional features of the financial system; (ii) the behaviour of banks and other suppliers of finance; (iii) the stage of development, the size, the volatility of financial markets and their role as suppliers of funding; (iv) the role played by foreign capital inflows in financing internal accumulation; (v) the system's financial robustness and the mechanisms of contagion of instability; and finally, (vi) the compensating structures – i.e. the institutional arrangements which are created to compensate for the lack or deficiencies of the traditional mechanisms to finance and fund investment – and their shortcomings to the process of development.

Having defined the method and structure of the analysis, given the theoretical framework we are using here, a detailed empirical analysis will follow.

Chapter 7

Financial system and industrialisation in Brazil, 1947–66

INTRODUCTION

During the period 1947–66, Brazil lacked developed mechanisms to finance and fund accumulation. Long-term finance was limited to two government banks, whereas private lending institutions confined their operations to short-term loans for working capital. Financial markets were poorly developed and dealt in few securities. Finally, access to foreign loans was limited to official loans from governments and multilateral agencies. Despite the shortcomings of the financial structure, the Brazilian economy grew 7 per cent per year on average and investment over gross national product (GNP) was 15 per cent between 1947 and 1961. This extraordinary growth changed the economy from a primary exporter with a nascent non-durables industrial sector into a relatively mature economy with a small import coefficient, diversified consumer non-durables and durables sectors and a budding capital goods sector.

In the light of the approach set out in the previous chapter, here we investigate how this rapid industrialisation was possible despite financial underdevelopment, without causing financial instability. We then discuss the institutional arrangements – or compensating structures – created to overcome the limits of the financial structure. Further we indicate how the economic downturn in 1962–6 is associated with the mismatch between the financial and the economic development in the period.

THE POLITICAL ECONOMY OF GROWTH

Since its first stages, Brazilian industrialisation has been led by the process of import-substitution. This process began as a spontaneous response to the import constraints, caused by the decline of international trade during the World recession of the 1930s and then the Second World War (see Malan *et al.* 1980). Industrialisation in itself had caused several changes in the structure of the economy, which in turn had political effects. These were, for instance, expressed by the political demands of the urban working class and the industrialists.[1] The economic and political stage was thus set for the populist governments of the 1950s, and industrial policy increasingly became a part of the political agenda.[2]

Perhaps the first indication of the strength of the new political forces was the government's choice of restrictive measures to deal with balance-of-payments problems in 1947.[3] These measures clearly protected the indigenous industrial sector and guaranteed the continuation of the import-substitutive industrialisation. Already in 1948, the choice for industrialisation became transparent as President Dutra's government requested planning aid from the US government to evaluate and propose solutions for the problems of the Brazilian economy. Although the report of that joint Brazil–United States Commission did not constitute a plan in itself, and the promised credit of US$500 million was never actually granted, many of its recommendations were carried out.

In 1951, under President Vargas, another joint Brazil–United States Economic Development Commission was created with the specific purpose of providing technical assistance to speed up the preparation of applications for loans for the development projects which would be submitted to the United States and international lending agencies.[4] The commission's report resulted in the Plan for Retooling and Stimulating the National Economy and the creation in June 1952 of the National Bank for Economic Development (BNDE), which was to be responsible for executing the plan. The founding of the BNDE in 1952 was the first step towards raising and allocating funds to finance the high levels of accumulation anticipated.

A second important step was taken in October 1953, when the monetary authority (SUMOC) instituted Instruction 70, a five-compartment exchange system in which the government ranked imports according to their essentiality. More than just being a simple solution to the balance-of-payments problem, Instruction 70 represented a stimulus for industrialisation for at least three reasons: first, by raising the internal prices of specific imports it consolidated protection for producers of industrial goods which were in process of substitution; second, it provided the concession of exchange subsidies for capital goods and basic inputs required for the process of industrial development; and third, with the additional revenues obtained by the auctioning of foreign currency to importers of 'non-priority' goods, it raised public funding for government investments in infrastructure. Furthermore, in terms of investment finance, Instruction 70 represented a purposeful transfer of purchasing power in foreign currency from the import sector to the developing industrial sector. This was a feature which was to characterise the process of industrialisation from then until the 1960s (see Leff 1968: 16–17).

Political commitment to industrialisation was also an essential feature of the 1955 election campaign. The newly elected Kubistchek administration, which during the campaign had promised to make Brazil 'grow fifty years in five', created the Council for Development at the beginning of 1956. This was directly linked to the presidency and was responsible for the planning and execution of a development plan. Based almost entirely on the recommendations of the Joint United States/Brazil Technical Commission, and those of the United Nations Economic Commission for Latin America/BNDE Joint Commission, the Council for Development put forth in 1956 an audacious five-year development plan – the *Plano de Metas* (Target Plan).

The Plan aimed to intensify the process of import-substitution of industrial goods. Industrialisation was to be through the integrated development of a domestic consumer durables sector, an intermediary industry and an adequate energy and transport sector. In particular, the government allocated 92 per cent of the forecasted budget of public investment to investments in transport, basic industry and energy. The consequence of such a plan was the extraordinary process of growth and accumulation during the period.

Even though the pace of growth changed substantially, from 1947 to 1961 Brazil's economy grew on average by 7 per cent, and GNP per capita rose 4.2 per cent yearly.[5] The industrial sector led this growth with an average annual rate of expansion of 8.7 per cent. Not only was the pace of growth significant, but the rate of accumulation was high and increasing: from 1947 to 1955 the investment/GNP ratio ranged from 12.3 per cent (1948) to 16.7 per cent (1954). With the government committed to industrialisation, the heavy investment in infrastructure and physical capital took the ratio of investment to GNP from 16 per cent in 1955 to 21 per cent in 1959.

This fast pace of growth and accumulation changed the productive structure of the economy significantly. In addition to the construction of the new capital, Brasília, in the short period from 1956 to 1960, the automotive, shipbuilding and heavy electrical materials industries were set up and, furthermore, basic industries such as steel, non-ferrous metals, heavy chemistry, oil and cellulose were considerably expanded.[6]

Table 7.1 Sectoral distribution of GNP

	Agriculture	*Industry*	*Commerce*
1947	27.6	19.9	19.4
1955	25.1	24.4	16.3
1964	21.5	25.7	13.8

Source: Goldsmith 1986: 225

In a nutshell, the industrial sector consolidated its leading position in the sectoral distribution of GNP (Table 7.1) and for the first time in Brazil's history the internal market became the main determinant of growth.

Another important consequence of the development of the 1950s was the increase of the average size of the industrial firms. Now large companies, both national and multinational, predominated the family owned businesses. Furthermore, these firms were installed to produce mainly for the internal market, using internal resources. As a consequence, as Table A.1.1 in the Appendix indicates, the ratio of imports and exports over GNP fell from 23 per cent in 1947 to 11 per cent in 1961 and to 10 per cent in 1966, whereas the proportion of imports in the total internal consumption of industrial goods decreased from 15.6 per cent in 1949 to 11.3 per cent in 1958 and 9.7 per cent in 1961 (Tavares 1972: 92). In turn, the share of durable consumer goods in the composition of imports fell from 10.3 per cent in 1935–9 to 2.4 per cent in 1964 (Fishlow 1972: 44).

The effects of these structural changes on the financial requirements of Brazil's economy cannot be exaggerated. On the one hand, the newly established industrial structure was highly dependent on medium-term credit to finance its operations (see Tavares 1972: 127–52).[7] On the other hand, the durables sector had been the fastest growing sector in the 1955–61 period, its productive capacity having increased far ahead of existing demand. Given poor income distribution, the existence of term sales to finance the consumption of durables had become essential for the full use of this sector's capacity.

Given the gap between financial and economic development, it is not surprising that once the investments of the Target Plan matured, the economy entered a recession.[8] The decline of private investment and, consequently, of the rate of growth brought further destabilising consequences, as inflation accelerated (from around 10 per cent in 1958 to the unprecedented level of 90 per cent in 1964) and the government budget deficit rose (from 1 per cent of GNP in 1959 to 2.2 per cent and 2.9 per cent respectively in 1961 and 1962). In addition, there was a significant deterioration of the balance of payments because of the increasing financial costs associated with the outstanding external debt.

The deterioration of the economic environment increased the pressure on the government for stabilisation.[9] Two adjustment programmes were attempted between 1962 and 1966: one from the end of 1962 to 1963 (the three-year plan) and another from 1964 to 1966 (the government's action plan). The short-lived 1962 plan was a mixture of gradualist but orthodox monetary and fiscal policies, which anticipated a reduction in the government budget and restrictions on loans from Banco do Brasil. As regards the balance of payments, the plan proposed an exchange rate policy which would stimulate exports and discourage imports.

Despite very strict monetary policy from 1962 onwards (shown by Table 7.2), the reduction of government subsidies plus an increase of 56.2 per cent in the minimum wage in January 1963 accelerated, rather than reduced, inflation. The credit squeeze resulted in an intensification of the political pressure on the government to ease its monetary policy (see Resende 1982: 770). With the money supply and inflation increasing beyond projections, the three-year plan lost political support and failed soon after its implementation.

A second stabilisation plan was to be tried in 1964 by the military government, which had overthrown the elected government of President Goulart in March of that year. The military *junta*'s plan for economic action (PAEG) had an approach very similar to the three-year plan: (1) rigorous control over money and credit expansion; (2) rigid control over public expenditures and an emergency fiscal reform in 1965; and (3) strict wage policy and control of commercial and residential rents and prices of goods and services produced by public enterprises.

The emergency fiscal reform involved rises in federal government's revenues through changing some of the mechanisms of taxation and the centralisation of receipts from the States to the federal union.[10] The reform did allow a significant reduction of the public deficit from 2.8 per cent of GNP in 1964 to 0.9 per cent in 1966 (Table 7.3). However, despite the rhetoric, government's capacity to control the money supply was limited just as it had been under the 1962 plan: even though the monetary base decreased in the fourth quarter of 1964 and the first quarter of 1965 (respectively –8.0 per cent and –4.6 per cent per annum), in the last period M1 and M2 rose above inflation. Therefore, the key to the success of the plan in reducing inflation from 1965 onwards is to be found neither in fiscal nor in monetary policy, but in the wage policy that

Table 7.2 Money: real yearly growth rate of the monetary base M1 and M2 (deflated by the general price index IGP–DI) (per cent)

Year	*Quarter*	*Monetary base*	*M1*	M2
1961	1	9.5	11.0	12.0
	2	0.6	1.6	2.3
	3	1.9	1.3	0.8
	4	−3.1	−0.4	−2.1
1962	1	−11.0	−7.6	−9.4
	2	0.3	0.5	−1.8
	3	7.4	7.8	5.8
	4	15.7	12.7	10.3
1963	1	1.1	−6.2	−7.9
	2	−3.0	−10.7	−11.9
	3	−4.9	−14.5	−15.4
	4	−3.7	−10.1	−10.3
1964	1	5.3	−0.1	−0.8
	2	8.6	7.6	6.9
	3	2.2	6.3	5.6
	4	−8.0	−1.4	−1.6
1965	1	−4.6	7.3	7.0
	2	3.0	14.8	14.4
	3	12.4	27.1	26.6
	4	28.4	36.6	36.3
1966	1	17.9	17.8	16.4
	2	3.4	−0.3	−1.0
	3	−8.4	−15.5	−15.7
	4	−11.2	−19.6	−19.4

Source: IBGE 1987: 503–4

was implemented. This involved the re-adjustment of the minimum wage, wages of public servants and of workers in the private sector, according to an official index which was repeatedly below inflation. This procedure significantly compressed the real wage in a short period of time.[11]

Despite the reduction in the rate of inflation from 84 per cent in the last quarter of 1964 to 31 per cent in the last quarter of 1966, the social costs of the 1964 stabilisation programme outstripped the benefits. For instance, in a country where income distribution in the 1960s was already one of the worst in the World (see Serra 1982: 64 for data), the compression of wages and the stagnation of output caused a sharp decline in the urban population's standard of living (Resende 1982). The political costs were also significant, as the *junta* launched a wave of

Table 7.3 Some indicators of government deficit and its financing (1959–66)

				Financing			
				Monetary authorities			
Year	*Revenues (million cruzeiros, 1959)* (1)	*Expenditures (million cruzeiros, 1959)* (2)	*Surplus/deficit (%)* (3)	*Banco do Basil (%)* (4)	*Other (%)* (5)	*Public debt (%)* (6)	*Column (3) as percentage of GNP* (7)
1950	108.6	125.3	−16.7	84.4		15.6	1.1
1951	136.3	125.1	11.2	108.3		−8.3	−0.7
1952	134.2	124.0	10.2	84.0		16.0	−0.6
1953	131.1	165.4	−34.3	−91.6		191.6	2.2
1954	138.6	149.6	−11.0	−162.5		262.5	0.6
1955	136.0	149.1	−13.1	10.0		0.0	0.7
1956	149.9	198.0	−48.1	99.2		0.8	2.3
1957	172.5	245.9	−73.3	100.0		0.0	3.3
1958	169.9	209.6	−39.6	69.4		30.6	2.0
1959	180.9	221.4	−40.5	78.0		22.0	1.7
1960	180.3	236.1	−55.8	90.6		9.4	2.4
1961	178.1	244.1	−66.0	98.9		1.1	3.0
1962	156.2	233.8	−77.6	87.9		12.1	3.8
1963	152.2	225.3	−73.1	84.5		15.5	3.8
1964	196.3	263.4	−67.1	101.1		−1.1	2.8
1965	260.1	299.6	−39.5	−52.2	−3.5	155.7	1.4
1966	306.0	336.4	−30.4	5.9	−38.4	132.5	0.9
1947–55				13.6		53.0	1.5
1956–61				89.3		10.7	1.1
1962–6				45.4	−8.4	62.9	0.5

Source: Brazil's Central Bank, August 1971: 51–2

repressive interventions in unions and popular movements. This repression inaugurated a dark period of political persecution, especially after 1968, which would last until the mid-1970s. As if these social and political costs were not sufficient, the draconian stabilisation programme could not in itself tackle the causes which had triggered the recession. One of these causes, as mentioned earlier, was the mismatch between financial and economic development – to which the next section draws attention.

THE UNDERDEVELOPMENT OF THE FINANCIAL STRUCTURE AND ITS CONSEQUENCES

The financial system of the 1930s was essentially a carry-over from the late nineteenth century. Given the fact that Brazil was mainly a primary exporter, this system concentrated on financing export production and trade, and contributed to infrastructural development only to that extent. Most of the undertakings which required long-term financing were owned by entrepreneurs with a direct link to the developed financial markets abroad. For instance, the railways were almost exclusively owned by British companies and linked coffee producing areas to ports; most of them received direct financing from British banks (Sochaczewski 1980: 17–18).[12]

The financial requirements changed after the 1930s because of the process of industrialisation. First, the emerging industrial sector demanded short to medium-term financing for working capital, which could not normally be based on collateral. Second, investment in industrial plants required longer-term financing to which the banking system was not normally used. And finally, the increasing level of internal activity generated a growing demand for infrastructural services, especially transportation and energy – services whose provision normally requires great volumes of financing with long maturities.

In the 1940s and 1950s, the financial structure developed largely in response to the government's pragmatic attempts to deal with the problem of financing accumulation. An assessment of this development is best begun by analysing the formal structure of the financial system. In 1947, the monetary authority in Brazil comprised the Superintendency of Money and Credit (SUMOC) and the Exchange Department and the Mobilisation Department of the Banco do Brasil. These divided (chaotically) the regulation of the financial system: the Treasury had a monopoly over currency issue; the SUMOC regulated monetary and credit policies but had no executive powers; and finally, Banco do

Brasil was simultaneously the government's bank, a commercial bank and a development agency.

The banking system dominated the financial structure. In the period 1950–61 monetary assets were more than 60 per cent of total assets, and the banking system was responsible for over 80 per cent of the total loans to the private sector. In turn, the Banco do Brasil accounted for no less than 26 per cent of the loans (see Tables A.3.4 and A.4.3 in the Appendix). The Bank acted as a central bank, receiving deposits from other member banks as legal reserves, and, because of its role as financial agent of the government, the Treasury maintained an account directly with Banco do Brasil. Given its privileged position as a monetary authority and a commercial bank, the creation of deposits by the Bank to finance government deficit represented an almost straightforward increase in reserves for the whole banking system. Therefore, it was the Bank's lending policies and the government's fiscal and credit policies which determined the amount of reserves on which banks could expand their own loans.

Regarding the financial markets, there were stock markets in all state capitals and in Santos (in the state of São Paulo). However, only in Rio and São Paulo were there dealings in shares and public bonds. In the remaining capitals, the main activity of stock markets was not to deal in securities, but to auction foreign currencies held monopolistically by the monetary authorities and negotiated through publicly appointed brokers. Even in Rio de Janeiro and São Paulo, the lack of interest of most brokers in stock transactions and the thinness of the markets were such that most issues were made outside these institutions.[13] Therefore, even though the proportion of share subscriptions in cash to the total issues of shares ranged from 6 per cent (1950) to 15 per cent (1956) (see Table A.6 in the Appendix), only one quarter of this amount is estimated to have been issued directly in stock markets.[14] Considering that total share buys never represented more than 14 per cent aggregate investment, this means that issues of shares through stock markets provided less than 4 per cent of the funds available to investment.

There are at least four reasons for the underdevelopment of the financial markets. As mentioned earlier, up until the 1950s most of the firms in Brazil were family owned. Second, the poor income distribution made even the prospects of the development of institutional investors very limited. Third, inflation and the relative illiquidity of most shares (as indicated by the very low turnover ratio of shares in Table A.6 in the Appendix) made the holding of a share a very risky business. Finally, the prices of shares in the period were very volatile and actually declined in the 1950s (see column 9 of Table A.6).

Given the poor development of financial markets, when studying the mechanisms to finance investment in the 1950s the analyst must turn to the role played by banks and other lending institutions. This is our next topic.

BANKS AND OTHER SUPPLIERS OF FINANCE

Not only was the financial structure poorly diversified, but it was also largely restricted to providing short and medium-term credit. Except for the official banks, the banking system specialised in the provision of short-term credit (30, 60 and 90 days) which was eventually renewed, often for as long as four or five years, at floating interest rates (*Conjuntura Econômica* 1972: 54). Medium-term finance was mainly provided by Banco do Brasil, other official banks and, after 1959, finance companies. The main sources of long-term financing were: (1) Banco do Brasil (especially for agriculture); (2) the National Bank of Economic Development (BNDE), after 1952; and (3) the federal savings bank (Caixa Econômica Federal).

Given the pace of growth and accumulation and the underdevelopment of mechanisms to finance working capital and accumulation, one may assume that this was a period of constant excess of demand for credit. Many analysts, e.g. Simonsen (1969) and Cysne *et al.* (1990: 15), have blamed the interest ceilings then existing and inflation for such a state of credit rationing.[15] In our view, there is a great misunderstanding about both the actual performance of the lending institutions in the 1950s and the causes behind it. Because this is an important issue in understanding the shortcomings of the financial reforms of 1964–5, a brief analysis is in order.

As Table A.3.2 in the Appendix indicates, it is a fact that time deposits in the banking system decreased on average by 7 per cent yearly in the period 1947–61. It is also true that this was partly related to the negative interest rates caused by the association of the usury law and creeping inflation. However, this did not stop Banco do Brasil and the other commercial banks from increasing their loans, in real terms, at an average of 2.4 per cent a year in the period (Table A.4.1 in the Appendix). Besides, given that in an inflationary context the maturities of loans tend to be reduced, and these data are based on end-of-period balances (and not on flows), this rate actually underestimates the growth of the volume of loans supplied by the banking system.[16]

Furthermore, even though the usury law might have represented a threat to the normal operations of the system, in practice the private lending institutions did find ways to by-pass this legal imposition. On the one hand, it was a normal procedure for banks (especially private ones) to charge commissions and request an average deposit balance from their borrowers. Such a hidden charge allowed the banking system to maintain a substantial differential between loan and deposit rates, and thus to obtain substantial profits (despite increasing costs). This is what Figure 7.1 indicates.

On the other hand, finance companies (*financeiras*) operated a market in exchange letter discounts and also charged higher loan rates. This may explain why this limited segmentation in the financial market could hold even when inflation, especially in the mid-1950s and 1960s, went far beyond 12 per cent, the legal nominal interest rate ceiling.

This behaviour by the banks and finance companies is compatible with the view expressed in Chapter 3 that a high level of real growth will lead to a continuously growing demand for finance. This leaves commercial banks in the comfortable position of assured demand and rising profits (see Figure 7.2), by restricting their operation to the very short term, especially when creeping inflation is constantly expanding the risk of longer-term operations.

Hence, it is legitimate to ask whether the non-existence of long-term private finance in the period was due to financial repression or to the lack of interest of the financial institutions in operating in the long term. Given the good performance of banks operating in the short term and the non-existence of funding mechanisms, it is likely that the banks would

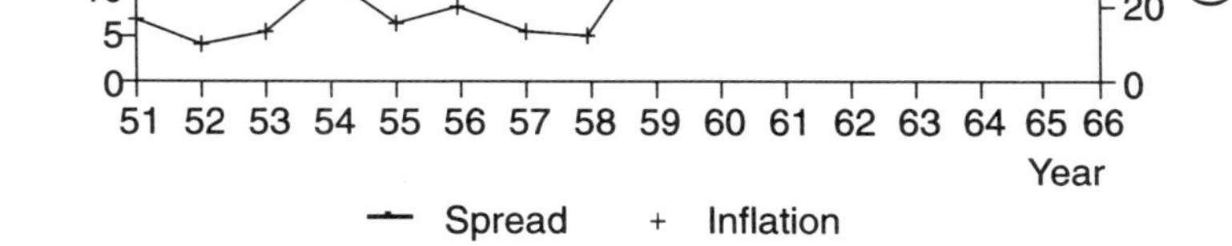

Figure 7.1
Source: Table A.5.1

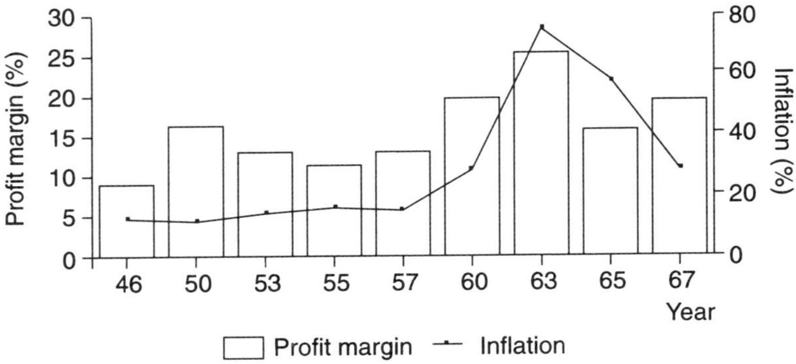

Figure 7.2
Source: Portocarrero de Castro 1981: 101

not have had much incentive to risk long-term positions even if they were allowed to offer and charge real positive rates of interest.[17]

We have thus far seen that the mechanisms to finance and fund investment were both very limited in this period, and that this was not solely caused by *financial repression*. Given the political commitment of the government to speed up industrialisation and growth, it remains to indicate what were the compensating structures created to overcome the shortcomings of the financial structure and the limitations of these structures from the point of view of their functionality to development.

THE COMPENSATING STRUCTURES: FUNCTIONALITY AND SHORTCOMINGS

From a financial point of view, fast growth was only possible in the 1950s because the main investing agents (the public firms, international enterprises and national firms) found ways of by-passing the lack of long-term financing with specific institutional arrangements. Like in many other developing countries, the State played an important role in shaping these compensating structures.

After the war, and after a very brief period of liberalism (from 1945 to 1947), interventionism returned to Brazil's politics. Government intervention in the period 1947–61 can be divided into two sub-periods: before and after the beginning of the Target Plan (1956–61). Under the Target Plan, the government's share in total fixed capital investment increased from 22 per cent in 1956 to 39 per cent in 1960,[18] representing an almost steady average annual rate of growth (around 20 per cent) of total government expenditure on capital formation (see Table A.1.2 in the Appendix). This rising investment effort contrasts with the relatively small taxation base of the country and the thinness of the market for government debt. As regards the former, most of the taxes were *ad valorem*, and tax revenues were small relative to the GNP. In contrast, government expenditure as a proportion of GNP increased at a much faster pace, so that the public deficit tended to increase in the periods of intensive accumulation – as indicated by Figure 7.3 which shows the ratio of government deficit over GNP in the period from 1950 to 1966.

The possibility of financing the deficit – leaving aside public investment – by issuing bonds was even more difficult than increasing ordinary taxation. As the usury law limited the government to issuing bonds with a return of 12 per cent, a ceiling which private institutions and the curb market could find ways to by-pass. This meant that the government's capacity to get the public to hold bonds voluntarily was inversely related to the rate of inflation. Indeed, the proportion of government bonds in the total financial assets decreased from 9.1 per cent in 1947–55 to 2.6 per cent in 1955–61.

After 1952, the government could also count on the newly created BNDE to finance public investment. However, the BNDE was not, strictly speaking, a bank (since it could not accept or create deposits); its main source of funds until the mid-1960s was the additional income tax for the re-tooling of the economy.[19] Therefore, BNDE's capacity to finance investment was very limited in quantitative terms.[20] Over the

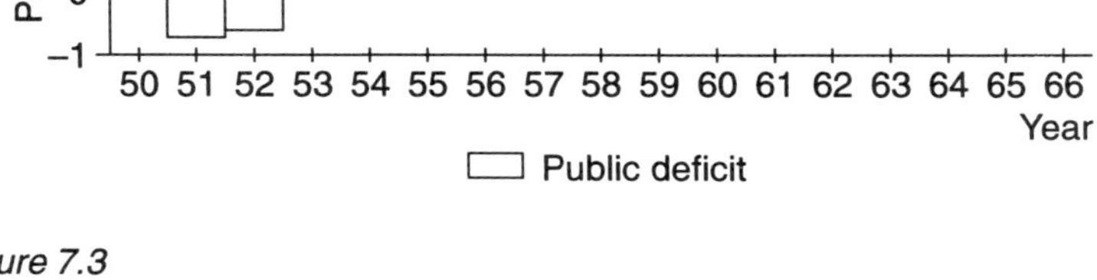

Figure 7.3
Source: Table 7.3

whole period, the BNDE's contribution never represented more than 20 per cent of the government's total investment – or 4 per cent of total capital formation in the country – despite the extraordinary average increase of these funds in real terms (10.9 per cent per annum), especially during the period of the Target Plan (11.8 per cent per annum).

The two sources of financing left to the government were the extraordinary taxes and credits drawn against the national central bank (money issue). As regards the extraordinary taxes, two are worth mentioning: the extra-budgetary export tax and exchange confiscation. For instance, Instruction 70 (discussed earlier) allowed the government to yield revenues with the exchange rate premium between selling and buying prices. According to Leff, the extra-budgetary revenue provided by these means represented 16 per cent of the federal government's tax revenues on average in this period (1968: 15–16). Table 7.4 further indicates the funds created in the 1950s and their significance in the financing of public investment.

The government's direct access to the finance provided by the Banco do Brasil also represented a very functional arrangement in facilitating the financing government expenditure. For, since the Banco do Brasil was also the government's tax collector, the deposits created to finance government expenditure would generate inflows in the form of tax receipts through the tax multiplier.

Figure 7.4, which shows the participation of the credit drawn by Banco do Brasil in the financing of the public deficit, indicates that the *conta movimento* was the main source of government's finance until 1964. It was the possibility of counting on credits from Banco do Brasil and on extra-budgetary taxation that allowed the government to proceed with its investment projects without any financial planning (on this see Lessa 1982).[21]

The underdevelopment of the financial structure was not much of a problem for foreign investing firms either. Most of their investments were made under Resolution 113 of 1955, which modified the exchange rate system so that foreign private investors in high-priority sectors could import capital goods at a lower exchange rate. Resolution 113 also allowed foreign firms to register their capital at free-market rates and to remit up to 10 per cent of capital yields at privileged rates. Finally, because profit remittances corresponded with registered capital, foreign firms not only had privileged rates when registering their investment, but also had the security of being able to remit substantial volumes of foreign currency if circumstances required. Furthermore, foreign

Table 7.4 Funds created by the Federal Government to finance its own investment projects (in billion cruzeiros and per cent)

	1959	*1960*	*1961*	*1962*
Treasury funds	12.88	16.86	23.33	28.53
Fundo Aeronautico	0.07	0.07	0.05	0.47
de Reaparalhamento Economico	7.16	9.92	14.24	20.14
Especial de Valorizacao da Amazonia	3.06	4.21	5.91	–
Federal de Eletrificacao	0.59	0.68	0.77	2.51
de Valorizacao da Fronteira do Sudoeste	0.50	0.55	0.55	–
da Marinha Mercante	1.50	1.43	1.81	5.40
Special funds	50.44	65.29	106.33	157.93
Rodoviario Nacional	19.20	23.10	44.90	59.10
da Marinha Mercante	3.40	4.00	5.60	9.40
Portuario Nacional[a]	27.84	38.19	55.83	89.43
Other special funds	10.00	13.56	23.87	15.77
Funds administered by BNDE	10.00	13.56	23.87	15.77
Total	73.32	95.70	153.54	202.23
Percentage of the total public investments[b]	61.04	53.27	56.24	44.38

Source: MiniPlan 1965: 47–57
Notes: [a] Estimated according to the information provided by the above-cited document, p. 52.
[b] Public investment from Werneck 1969: 99.

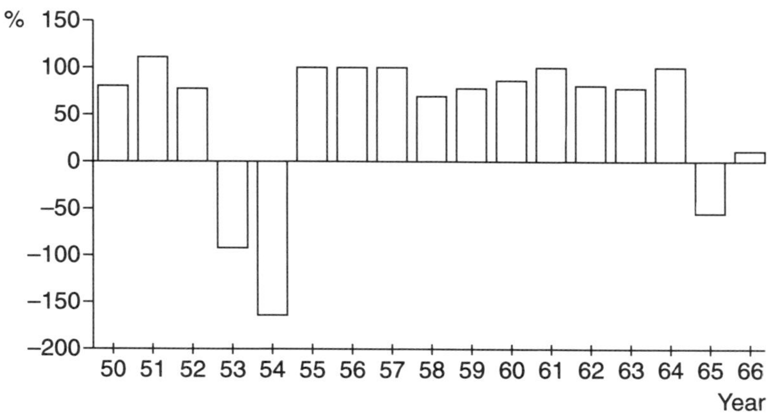

Figure 7.4
Source: Table 7.3
Note: Negative values indicate surpluses

Table 7.5 Banco do Brasil's loans to the public sector (as percentage of its total loans)

1951	*1952*	*1953*	*1954*	*1955*	*1956*	*1957*	*1958*	*1959*	*1960*	*1961*
52.9	47.2	48.9	47.6	49.1	54.0	58.0	55.8	58.7	61.5	65.6

Source: *Conjuntura Econômica*, February 1969: 82

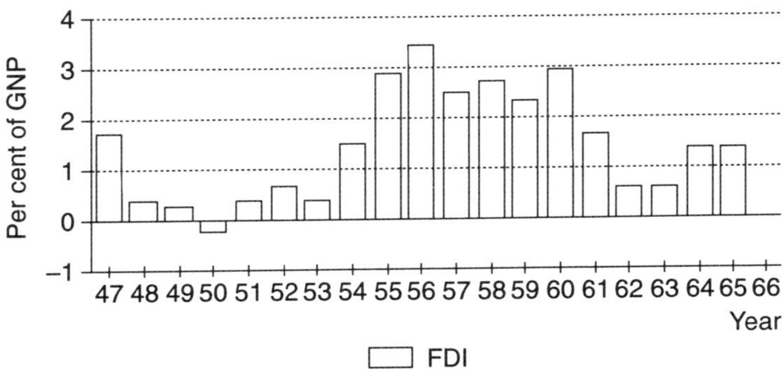

Figure 7.5
Source: As in Table A.7.1

borrowing in the form of interest remittances and the amortisation of loans could take advantage of favoured exchange rates (of up to 8 per cent of the outstanding debt), provided that the credit had maturities of five years and above. These incentives, and the favourable climate for foreign investment deliberately created by the Kubistchek administration, did succeed in attracting increasing amounts of foreign investment from other countries. However, this amount should not be overestimated: the participation of such investment in total fixed capital formation during this period never exceeded 4 per cent – as Figure 7.5, which presents the ratio between net foreign investment (FDI) and GNP, shows.

It must be stressed, though, that, if FDI did not contribute significantly to the total allocation of resources during this period, it had, nevertheless, a strategic place in Brazil's development process. For, it created a dynamic sector of consumer durables which stimulated domestic or indigenous entrepreneurs to invest in complementary activities.

Finally, in what regards the national firms, they certainly had little access to investment funds in the quantities required by the proposed industrial projects. Finance was mainly provided by the banking system at short-term maturities (30, 60 and 90 days) and, to a much smaller extent, by finance companies at medium-term maturities. Therefore, firms who had no access to the long-term funds provided by Banco do Brasil had to self-finance their accumulation. At the macroeconomic level, this means that the firms had to borrow short in the hope of being able to repay their debt with the cash flows of subsequent production periods. This mechanism of self-finance requires that the firms maintain high levels of mark-up and be capable of increasing them at periods of expansion.

Indeed this is what Table 7.6 indicates. This shows that firms simultaneously experienced an increasing demand for external funds and a high level of retained profits, which suggests the following mechanism: (1) firms took recourse to banks' short-term lending for their investment finance; (2) because the exchange reform of 1957 provided complete protection against foreign competition for national firms in priority sectors, expanding firms had privileged access to an increasing internal market, therefore a strong mark-up position; (3) due to their high

Table 7.6 Flow of funds of commerce and industry: external (A) and internal funds (B) as percentage of total funds and retained profits (C) as percentage of total profit (1952–66)

	Industry			*Commerce*		
Year	*A*	*B*	*C*	*A*	*B*	*C*
1952			65.0			77.4
1953	56.3	43.7	69.0	51.5	48.5	61.7
1954	69.4	30.6	69.5	83.6	16.4	67.9
1955	43.9	56.1	71.8	28.1	71.9	67.8
1956	88.5	11.5	70.3	96.0	4.0	64.7
1957	75.7	24.3	69.7	100.3	−0.3	69.2
1958	70.0	30.0	76.5	67.1	32.9	76.7
1959	63.6	36.4	75.6	76.7	23.3	70.7
1960	63.4	36.6	75.2	74.7	25.3	68.5
1961	65.9	34.1	74.4	73.5	26.5	72.7
1962	64.1	35.9	82.5	77.1	22.9	76.3
1963	60.8	39.2	85.7	74.1	25.9	83.8
1964	47.3	52.7	90.1	64.9	35.1	87.8
1965	47.4	52.6	84.4	61.5	38.5	86.2
1966	48.8	51.2	81.1	64.5	35.5	74.6

Source: Sochaczewski 1980: 65

mark-up and the continuous increase of government investment financed by drawing credit on Banco do Brasil, firms could maintain high levels of profits which allowed them to repay their short-term debts.

THE ROLE OF FOREIGN CAPITAL INFLOWS

Until the 1970s the banking system of the developed economies was very much inward-looking. This means that the sources of foreign finance to less developed countries were mainly limited to suppliers' credit, aid and FDI. For Brazil, which strove to industrialise, this lack of international finance meant that the foreign currency produced by its exports had to be carefully allocated to priority sectors. This explains Instruction 70 and other measures taken by the government during the period.

The method of analysis of the contribution of external finance to the financing of Brazil's economic development has already been described in Chapter 5, and now it remains to present a summary of the most important variables for the period 1947 to 1966, which is done in Table A.7.1 in the Appendix. This indicates that the period was indeed characterised by the need to finance a real resources transfer and that this was closely associated with the pace of accumulation. Further, it can be seen that with the Target Plan (1956–61) accumulation did increase the need for external finance. However, even in this period, the ratio RRT/GNP never exceeded 3 per cent. Comparing the latter figure with the rate of accumulation (investment/GNP) of over 18 per cent, one sees that rapid industrialisation required relatively little use of external resources.

Furthermore, in the period 1956–61, the financing of the real resources transfer represented on average 20 per cent of the total capital inflows whereas the costs of capital absorbed 80 per cent of these inflows (CC/CI). This indicates that whenever part of internal accumulation was financed by short-term external funds, the external debt rapidly became dysfunctional to economic development. Furthermore, one of the causes of the recession of the 1960s was the pressure exercised by the IMF in order that Brazil increased its exports to repay its debt. The development strategy of the 1950s was an inward-looking rather than outward-looking type. Therefore, when the need to expand exports emerged, the government had little room for manoeuvre except to cut imports which were essential to Brazil's growth.

THE INHERENT FINANCIAL FRAGILITY OF THE INDUSTRIALISATION

Financial fragility should be measured by indicators of the firms' levels of indebtedness and their capacity to repay the services of their outstanding deficit. As mentioned earlier (Chapter 5), this is in itself a difficult task, as it implies the availability of precise firms' balance-sheet data and some subjective forecasting of firms' capacity to generate cash flows in the future in order to repay their debts.

In the period under analysis, the lack of firms' balance-sheet data of Brazilian firms makes the analysis of systemic financial fragility very limited. However, a measure of this fragility can be obtained by using a ratio (DEF) of the total value of notes on which the borrowers defaulted over the total value of the loans provided by the banking system to the private sector. This measure has at least two more shortcomings: first, the data on notes defaulted are limited to Rio de Janeiro and São Paulo; second, part of the loans corresponds to consumer credit. These shortcomings are mitigated by the facts that (a) those two states produced more than 75 per cent of the total GNP; and (b) only a small fraction of the above-mentioned loans was given by finance companies to consumers.

Notwithstanding the shortcomings of the measure DEF, Figure 7.6 indicates that rapid accumulation in the period did not increase financial fragility. In fact, it is exactly when the economy shows signs of slowdown (in the beginning of the 1960s) that DEF declines and it is only after 1964 that it rises very rapidly. The reason for this behaviour is related to the financing mechanisms of the period: first, as firms saw a reduction of their cash flows, they increased their mark-ups in order to pay their debts and to enlarge their liquidity; second, the rise of inflation caused the real financial services to decline in real terms because of the ceiling on the rate of interest. This partly explains the negative correlation between inflation and DEF from 1960 to 1964. Finally, only in 1964, when the government deepened the recession by simultaneously tightening credit control and squeezing the purchasing power of the urban population, did financial fragility rise significantly.

To sum up, the compensating structures which permitted Brazil's economy to grow rapidly in the 1950s also significantly reduced the risks of financial instability. What they could not avoid was the increasing gap between financial and economic development, which accounts for much of the constraints on further economic development in the 1960s. This is the topic of the next section.

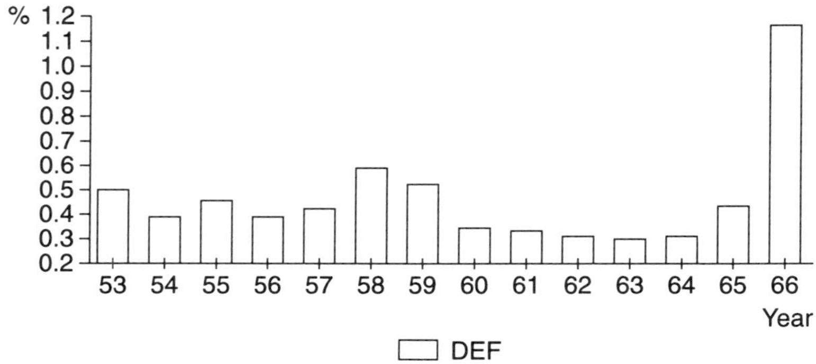

Figure 7.6
Source: *Conjuntura Economica*, December 1972: 63

LIMITS ON THE FUNCTIONALITY OF THE FINANCIAL SYSTEM

The financial arrangement that allowed the extraordinary growth in the period 1947–61 is illustrated in Figure 7.7. The numbers in parentheses indicate the causal chain in the process of investment finance. This process logically begins with investment being financed by transfers of public funds, FDI or (especially) short-term bank loans. This investment would produce a multiplier effect which provided the government with additional tax revenues and firms with additional profits. Because mechanisms to fund short-term debt did not exist in the period, the only way private firms could repay the short-term debt to finance long-term projects was by increasing their mark-ups; this is the role inflation played in the process of financing accumulation.

In the light of Figure 7.7, the functionality of this financial arrangement can be shown to depend on at least three conditions: (1) continuous growth of effective demand, in order to guarantee that firms could increase their mark-ups and repay their past debts; if effective demand was not expanding, then part of the outstanding short-term debt of the corporate sector could not be repaid and the economy would rapidly become more financially fragile; the expansion of effective demand could come from either a rise of investment or a boost in the demand for consumer durables; (2) relatively low levels of cost inflation, so that firms could keep their mark-ups and thus self-finance their investments; and (3) the continuous refinancing of the external debt.[22]

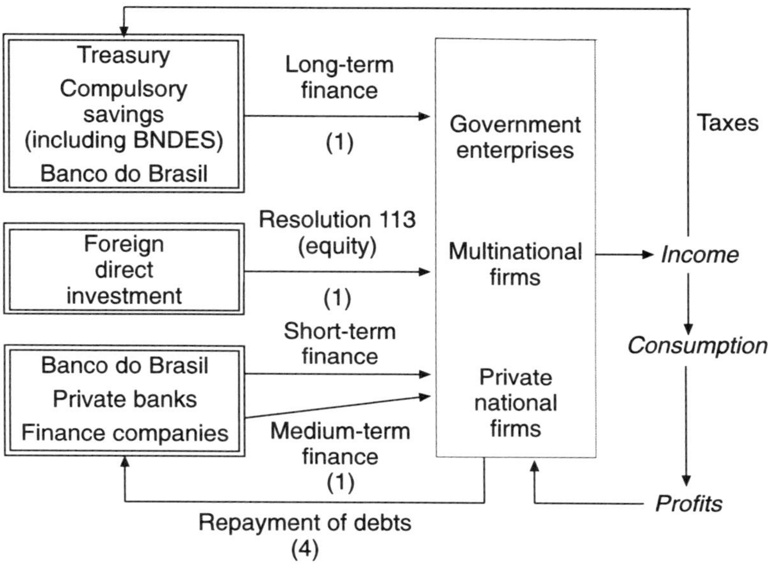

Figure 7.7

Those conditions did not exist any more by the end of the 1950s. First, concerning investment, because Brazil's industrialisation took place in blocks of industrial investment, productive capacity expanded far ahead of contemporary demand.[23] Therefore, it was unlikely that the private sector would venture to expand even further its productive capacity. In addition, although there was an increasing need for investment in basic infrastructure, public investment was running into problems due to the diminishing financing capacity of the public sector. As inflation rose, not only did it become more difficult to finance real expansions of public expenditure without a tax reform (because of the so-called Oliveira–Tanzi effect), but the political pressure on the government to reduce its deficit increased as well. With consumption of durables, the problem was located, as noted earlier, in the highly uneven income distribution and the lack of mechanisms for the provision of consumer credit.

The government's stabilisation plans in 1962 and 1964 actually contributed to the deepening of inflation and the financial difficulties of the corporate sector, for, as mentioned earlier, they did not attack the central problems behind the recession begun in 1962 – among which was the mismatch between the economic and the financial development.

SUMMING UP

The financial mechanisms that supported the extraordinary capital accumulation in Brazil during the period 1947–61 can now be summarised. The underdevelopment of funding mechanisms and the uncertainty of the inflationary environment meant that private financial institutions could not and did not provide long-term finance to private enterprises. Foreign borrowing, which did play a role in the financing of investment of foreign enterprises, was also not very significant in quantitative terms.

The bulk of the finance was provided by macroeconomic mechanisms which articulated the financing of public investment with the self-financing of private firms. This process causally began with the financing of government's investment, through an association of extra-budgetary taxation and monetary expansion. Private firms could count on short-term loans provided by the commercial banking system, finance corporations and even the incipient curb market for acceptances. However, such loans could only be repaid given the continued increase of nominal demand generated by the financing of government deficits and the high level of mark-up in the Brazilian industrial sector.

This mechanism could only be sustained if the government continued to finance its increasing expenditure and deficits by additional money creation, and if firms could keep their prices growing at a faster pace than their costs. With escalating inflation, however, it becomes difficult for firms to keep increasing their mark-ups and for the government to augment their expenditure without increasing taxation or taking recourse to bond-issuing. Without the stimulus of government expenditure and money creation, the scheme breaks down and firms are forced to try to increase their mark-up. This creates an inflationary pressure and enlarges the overall fragility of the financial system. This is one of the main features of the slow-down during the 1960s.

To sum up, the compensating structures created in the 1950s, in order to overcome the shortcomings of Brazil's financial structure, were significantly functional in providing the financial basis for industrialisation. However these had two weaknesses which proved unsurmountable: first, they were not capable of resisting declines in effective demand without enforcing macroeconomic imbalances, especially inflation. Second, they did not provide the mechanisms to continue accumulation once this stage of industrialisation (of the import-substitution of durables sectors) was concluded. For this, the financial system would have to possess mechanisms to finance middle-term operations (such as industrial working capital and consumption of durables) and long-term operations (such as mortgages and, especially, investment of larger scales and maturities).

The gap between financial and economic development and the need for financial reform was widely perceived by economists in the 1960s; however, when the time came for the military government to opt for a financial reform it took the 'prior-saving argument' as its theoretical background. This, as will be demonstrated in the next chapters, had important and disastrous consequences for future financial and economic development in Brazil.

Chapter 8

The financial reforms and the 'economic miracle'

INTRODUCTION

In the previous chapter it was shown that, before 1964, financial development in Brazil lagged behind the rapid progress made by the productive sectors. This created constraints on the country's development, which required appropriate medium- and long-term financing mechanisms. In other words, a new articulation between the financial and the productive spheres was needed.

In 1964 a military coup brought to power a group of neoclassical economists who believed that this partnership between the financial and productive spheres had to be based on the stimulus of individual saving. From 1964 to 1966, this group implemented a series of reforms of the financial system. One of the basic guidelines of these reforms, according to an official government document, was to guarantee higher interest rates for savers and lower rates for borrowers and all investors (MiniPlan 1965: 21). The reformers blamed the usury law and inflation for the negative rates of interest paid to savers; and the lack of competition and inefficiency of the financial structure for the increasing gap between deposit and loan rates. The solution for the problem was threefold. First, in order to reduce inflation the government introduced a severe stabilisation programme, which has already been described in Chapter 7. Second, the government indexed its bonds and loans and determined that private financial institutions did the same with theirs. Finally, to increase the competition and efficiency of the financial system, the reforms promoted a segmentation of its structure according to the maturity of assets and loans; and facilitated the access of firms to foreign indebtedness.

This chapter analyses the logic behind the financial reforms. Further, it shows how the reformed system deviated from what was expected by the reformers and how such structure contributed to the economic boom from 1967 to 1973. Finally, it explains how the reforms failed to create a financial structure functional for development and indicates the reason for and the consequences of such failure for the future economic and financial developments of the country.

THE RATIONALE OF THE REFORMS OF 1964–6

After the *coup* of 1964, the new administration, as often happens with new administrations, was very much willing to present itself as the saviour of the country, which, as they perceived it, was on the verge of an economic and political collapse. For them, the former governments' inefficiency and the inflation caused by their populist policies were to be blamed for most of the evils of the previous period of development in Brazil. These evils, they claimed, included the subversion of order and social hierarchy, the disorganisation of the credit and capital markets, the distortions in the exchange market, the allocative distortions caused by 'illusory profits', the lack of stimulus to invest in basic sectors and residential construction, and speculation (see MiniPlan 1965: 30–4). The predominant opinion within the government, expressed in several interviews and official documents of the time, was that the 'discipline of the market' should be imposed so as to correct these shortcomings in Brazil's development.[1]

The stabilisation programme of 1964–6 – comprising fiscal, monetary and wage policies[2] – was already a step towards the 'discipline of the market'. Concerning fiscal policy, the budget would have to be balanced and the traditional inflationary financing of public deficits had to be suppressed by introducing mechanisms to finance it through public debt. This was the main goal of the 1965 emergency fiscal reform, which raised the tariffs of the public sector and introduced an indexed bond, the Readjustable National Treasury Bond (ORTN). Further, in 1966, a definitive fiscal reform was introduced.

The banking reform had the objective of providing the government with tighter control over the money supply. The Superintendency of Money and Credit was abolished and the National Monetary Council (CMN) created and given the task of setting monetary, credit and exchange policies. The reform also created a central bank which was supposed to execute the policies determined by the CMN and to incorporate the function of bankers' bank and lender of last resort – until then assumed by Banco do Brasil. Finally, Banco do Brasil was expected to give up its function as the monetary authority but to remain the government's financial agent and a commercial bank.

The strategy also involved the reforms of the housing and of the capital markets. With regard to the housing market, the reformers alleged that the two main factors which constrained its development were negative real interest rates and the ceiling on rents. The negative rates were seen as a discouragement to long-term saving. In turn, the ceilings on rents dissuaded wealth-owners from investing in the construction of new residences. The consequence of this double repression, the argument continued, was a broad excess demand for housing – or the 'housing deficit' as official documents used to call it. Accordingly the market-oriented solution to the problem was threefold: to introduce a new tenancy law which allowed the inclusion of a indexation clause in tenancy agreements; to stimulate long-term saving by indexing housing bills and to promote their transfer to finance construction; and to create institutions specialising in mortgage financing.

The new capital market law was the star of the reforms proposed by the government. Again, it was alleged that the market for long-term securities did not develop in Brazil due to the lack of stimulus to save and that this was caused by three interrelated factors, two of which have already been noted: creeping inflation, interest rate ceilings and the inefficiency of the existing financial institutions and markets. According to many official documents, there was no scarcity of long-term savings, but these were not channelled into investment because of the factors mentioned above.[3]

Finally, the reformers blamed the excessive regulation of profits remittance and the discriminatory exchange policy for the limited use of foreign saving. This was then to be stimulated by a consistent exchange policy pegging the cruzeiro to the dollar, by a more liberal policy towards foreign capital and by introducing new institutional mechanisms for indigenous firms to borrow abroad.[4] There already existed a mechanism which permitted the contracting of loans in foreign currency with a minimum maturity of six months.[5] In addition, the reform permitted the contracting of loans in foreign currency directly between firms abroad and in the country; and of loans in foreign currency by commercial banks, investment banks and the national development bank, the BNDE.[6] The latter type of loans could be split into cruzeiro loans of shorter maturity, to finance investment and working capital for national industrial and commercial firms.

The financial structure envisaged by the reform is summarised in Table 8.1, where the segmentation is ordered according to an ascending scale of the maturities of the financial operations from both savers' and borrowers' sides.

Table 8.1 The financial structure proposed by the reforms of 1964–6

Type of savings	*The institution*	*The use of funds*
Sight deposits	Banco do Brasil (BB) Private commercial banks	Rural credit (only BB) Consumer credit Short-term credit to firms
Bills of exchange	Finance companies	Working capital
Savings accounts Housing bills	Housing finance system	Mortgages
Certificates of deposits	Investment banks	Long-term investment
Shares and debentures	Stock markets	Equity
Government bonds	Bonds market	Eventual government deficits

As the table indicates, the banking system was expected to continue to issue sight deposits in order to provide firms and individuals with short-term credit. The only difference proposed by the reform was the reduction in the competitive advantage of the Banco do Brasil by abolishing its function as the monetary authority, and by eliminating its link with the Treasury represented by the *conta movimento*.[7] Banco do Brasil, however, was to remain the government's financial agent, and, as such, to implement government programmes to finance agriculture.

Finance companies were expected to continue to finance medium-term working capital, but also to change their method of funding their operations. The government publicly declared a war against the *ágio* – i.e. the spread obtained by the finance companies in their previous method of discounting bills of exchange – which was alleged to have a strong inflationary bias. The reformers assumed that the large *ágios* between borrowing and lending rates were caused by finance companies having to cope with the higher actuarial risks of inflation. But, in turn, these spreads also contributed to inflation as they imposed high financial costs on firms. Therefore, the curbing of inflation required an immediate reduction of these spreads, and the indexation of both ends in the market for bills of exchange was seen as the means to achieve this.[8] Once inflation had fallen, the argument continued, the actuarial lending risk would fall, and finance companies would be able to fund their indexed loans by borrowing with indexed rates (see MiniPlan 1965: 69–71).

Furthermore, savers holding indexed bills of exchange would receive positive rates, so it was expected that the supply of medium-term credit would increase rapidly and firms would have access to non-inflationary sources to finance their operations.

One of the two main institutional innovations of the 1964–5 reforms was the creation of the National Housing Finance System (SFH).[9] The SFH had the National Housing Bank (BNH) as central bank and lender of last resort to a system of various private saving and loans associations. These associations were allowed to hold indexed savings accounts and to index their loans; up to a high amount, the individual savings deposits were fully guaranteed by the BNH.

Investment banks were to be the stars of the reformed financial structure. They were designed in the image of the American investment bank, and were expected to assume a leading role in the capital market. In addition to capturing funds through foreign exchange loans, it was anticipated that these banks would issue long-term certificates of deposit in order to finance long-term investment projects, and that they would engage in underwriting operations (see Almeida 1984: 26; and Sochaczewski 1980: 381–7). It was also hoped that the active role of investment banks and the introduction of indexation would stimulate the development of organised markets for shares and long-term debentures.

Interestingly, the reformers saw no need for any major change in the operation of the stock market. Despite the importance placed on that market in the reform, the policy-makers seemed convinced that all the market required in order to boost its operations was a modern regulation and fiscal incentives. Accordingly, Law 4728 introduced new regulations for the market – which were subsequently reviewed by Central Bank Resolution no. 39 of October 1966 – and reduced the taxes on dividend receipts. Furthermore in February 1967, the Decree-Law 157 allowed corporate and non-corporate taxpayers to invest, respectively, 10 and 5 per cent of their tax expenses in special funds (*Fundos 157*) administered by investment banks.

To sum up, the financial reform was guided by the view which earlier we called the prior-saving argument. That is, the ultimate source of finance is saving, which has to be stimulated by the provision of positive interest rates to savers and channelled to productive investment through specialised financial intermediaries. The main obstacles to achieving this goal, it was believed, were inflation, financial repression and inefficient (non-competitive) financial institutions, all of which were associated with some form of misguided intervention of former governments. The solution was then to stabilise price through tighter fiscal and monetary policies, to dismantle the mechanisms of financial repression (through indexation) and to stimulate competition between private financial intermediaries. Further, competition was to be enhanced by privatising the credit market (or by reducing the competitive advantage of Banco do Brasil) and opening access for national firms to foreign saving.

The four main financial innovations regarding the capital market introduced by the financial reform of 1964–5 were: (1) the introduction of the indexation of financial assets (*monetary correction*); (2) the establishment of financial institutions and instruments specialised in long-term financing, namely the investment banks and the housing financial system; (3) the creation of fiscal incentives to stimulate purchases of shares and debentures; and (4) Resolution 63, which opened access for national firms to foreign loans. In a nutshell, the idea was to replace the State and inflation as sources of investment finance with savings from the private sector; and to replace the public agencies with private institutions as intermediaries of such savings to the private sector. With the creation of investment banks, indexation, incentives for the stock market and the reduction of the lending capacity of Banco do Brasil, the government thought it had corrected the main distortions in the capital market. It was expected that the freer, more competitive market would be able to increase private savings and loanable funds to finance development thereafter.

This is not quite what happened. The financial structure which emerged from the implementation of the 1964–5 reforms is significantly different from that envisaged by the reforms. First, the government never succeeded in extending the indexation to the private sector, which continued to operate with nominal rates and with wide *ágios* between lending and borrowing rates. Second, the maturities of operations within the private financial system never lengthened, as was expected by the reform; in fact, such operations remained very short term and became highly speculative. Third, the initial segmentation soon gave away to a rapid process of financial conglomeration, led by the private commercial banks. Fourth, long-term finance continued to rely on government agencies. Finally, the external debt very soon became more a source of instability than a complement to the loanable funds available to finance internal accumulation. These 'deviations' are closely interrelated, and will be discussed in detail below.

INDEXATION AND THE MATURITY OF FINANCIAL OPERATIONS

The government expected that indexation would, at the same time, stimulate long-term savings flowing into the financial system and neutralise the effects of inflation on rates of interest – reducing the *ágio* obtained by lending institutions such as the finance companies. In turn, given the expected enhancement of competition in the reformed system, these two effects would increase the maturities of the loans and improve the efficiency of the allocation of savings. Indexation was to be imposed on all public and private medium- to long-term assets and loans, which included the operations of finance companies and investment banks.

Contrary to what was anticipated by the reforms, indexation proved to be an unsurmountable problem of liability management for private investment banks. These were expected to fund part of their operations by issuing long-term indexed certificates of deposits. However, from the start they found it very difficult to place their long-term certificates of deposit, because of the similarity of these financial instruments to the 180-days bills of exchange issued by the finance companies. The government was nevertheless convinced that the success of the certificates of deposit (CDs) was a matter of time and, as a compromise move, allowed the investment banks to discount bills of exchange (Resolution 18 of 1966). The measure was meant to be provisional, as such operations were only allowed until 1972. Nevertheless, already by 1967 the government had permitted investment banks to issue *discounted* CDs.

In other words, investment banks began their operations in a way which clearly contradicted the functional segmentation proposed by the reforms: instead of issuing long-term indexed CDs to finance long-term investment, they were issuing *discounted* CDs with (high) nominal interest rates and acted as mere privileged intermediaries by transferring the funds obtained through their access to foreign loans (Resolution 63). Consistent with their liability structure, they reduced the maturities of their loans and specialised in the financing of short- and medium-term working capital. Indeed, by 1971 loans for working capital represented more than 80 per cent of their freely allocated loans.[10]

The government also attempted to force finance companies to adopt indexation through fiscal means, as Law 4728 of 1965 imposed a heavy tax (15 per cent) on revenues obtained from discounting bills of exchange – the *ágios*. Despite this measure, the market for discounted bills of exchange expanded rapidly, at an average yearly rate of 46 per cent in the period from 1966 to 1970. Already in June 1966, the government introduced an emergency measure by delimiting the *ágio* charged by the finance companies to a maximum ceiling. This in practice institutionalised the *ágio* under the awkward title of 'pre-fixed monetary correction' (correção monetária *a priori*). One month later, the government finally accepted the *ágio* (Central Bank Resolution 32) and, furthermore, permitted finance companies to reduce the minimum maturity of acceptance contracts to six months.

Therefore, in a short period of time, the government's grand dream to create a private market for long-term loanable funds was over, and the private financial sector went back to (short-term) business as usual. Furthermore, the reduction of maturities of assets issued by investment banks and finance companies set in motion another deviation from the reform which had long-lasting consequences for Brazil's development. That is, the overall reduction of the maturities of loans from specialised private lending institutions. This began with the government allowing investment banks to discount bills of exchange in 1966 in order to compete with those issued by finance companies. Because of the short maturity of these assets, investment banks rapidly shifted their operations towards the more secure financing of working capital for its clients, a market which traditionally belonged to finance companies.

In the competition between finance companies and investment banks for loans to finance working capital, the former were at a clear disadvantage. This was because the latter were also allowed to obtain foreign funds through Resolution 63, at a time when the liquidity in the international banking system was high and international interest rates were falling rapidly.[11] Therefore, the shortening of the maturities of loans offered by investment banks precipitated the move of finance companies to the financing of consumer credit, which occurred rapidly from 1966 onwards. In that year, the government institutionalised the 'direct consumer credit' (CDC),[12] which was fundamentally based on a system of collateral (the so-called *alienação fiduciária*) by which the consumer good remained in the property of the finance company until the total repayment of the loan.

Finally, the banks also started pressurising the government to allow them to issue deposit certificates. Not only did the government concede, but it also reduced the minimum maturity of that instrument to 180 days. Therefore, the private institutions were concentrating on the short end of financial operations. In turn, the fact that the maturities of loans from the

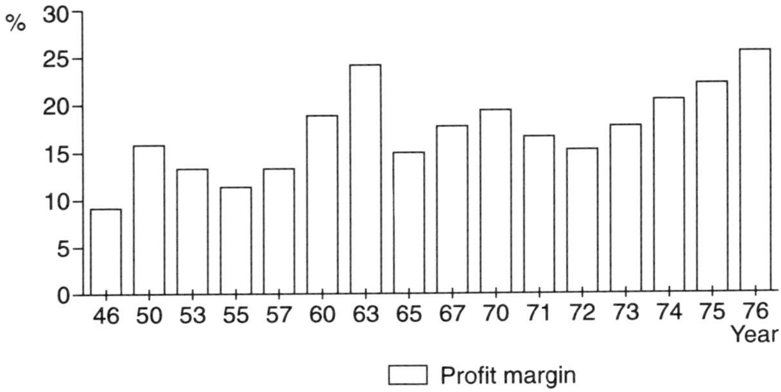

Figure 8.1
Source: Portocarrero de Castro 1981: 101

private financial sectors continued to be very short, opened another important chapter in the financial development of Brazil after the reforms of 1964–6: the process of financial conglomeration. This conglomeration should be seen as a direct result of two factors: first, the reduction of the competitive strength of Banco do Brasil in the mid-1960s, exactly when deregulation of the interest rates allowed banks to obtain significantly high profits (see Figure 8.1); second, the process of shortening of the maturities of financial operations dealt with by private institutions.

Regarding the second factor, as the maturities of financial assets and loans in these markets shortened, segmentation rapidly lost any practical meaning. In turn, the fact that banks were financial powers and had a wide branch infrastructure, even before the financial reform, made them the strongest competitors. Hence they managed to absorb rapidly within their departments operations typical of investment banks, finance companies and insurance companies. In aggregate terms, this meant that, whereas in 1966 the five largest banks held 32 per cent of total deposits of the public in the private banking system, 3 per cent of total loans and 24 per cent of total net worth of the system, in 1975 these same numbers were, respectively, 45, 43 and 38 per cent (see Table 8.2 for detailed data).

To sum up, the fact that the government did not manage to impose indexation on the private financial sector triggered a complex interplay

Table 8.2 Indicators of concentration of the banking system

Year	*1966*		*1970*		*1975*	
	Private	*Total including Banco do Brasil*	*Private*	*Total including Banco do Brasil*	*Private*	*Total including Banco do Brasil*
Participation in total deposits (%)						
The largest	8.2	55.5	11.1	43.4	15.7	34.6
Five largest	32.1	66.6	39.7	61.2	44.8	55.2
Ten largest	49.7	75.0	60.5	73.1	64.5	68.1
Participation in total loans (%)						
The largest	1.1	57.2	7.8	44.0	14.9	43.5
Five largest	3.3	61.6	28.8	58.7	42.7	60.3
Ten largest	4.7	62.8	47.3	67.6	62.9	69.7
Participation in total net worth (%)						
The largest	7.0	57.2	9.8	44.0	13.9	43.5
Five largest	24.5	61.6	27.9	58.7	38.0	60.3
Ten largest	40.1	62.8	43.7	67.6	56.9	69.7

Source: Moura da Silva 1979: 48

of market responses and political pressures which ended up with the full acceptance by the government of the *ágio* under the pompous name of '*pre-fixed* monetary correction'. In turn, this was closely followed by the reduction of the maturities of the financial operations. In other words, the government permitted the private financial sector to continue to operate in the very short term, issuing assets which paid nominal rates, and to maintain the old regime of discounting firms' bonds. Once the maturities of all financial assets issued and loans offered by the private financial sector were significantly reduced, the segmentation proposed by the financial reform lost any practical meaning. Now the market forces led the private financial sector towards a completely different direction from that anticipated by the reformers: instead of more competition, financial concentration and conglomeration; instead of more supply of long-term funds to finance development, a rapid expansion of financial circulation on speculative accounts. But not only in the implementation of the reform of the credit system was this the case, as we shall now demonstrate.

THE SPECULATIVE BIAS OF THE REFORMED CAPITAL MARKET

As part of the liberal direction of financial reform, the government attempted to stimulate the 'democratisation' of the stock market by giving new fiscal incentives to share-holders and firms. These were: zero taxation on share bonus payments; reduction of taxation on revenues accrued from transactions with shares;[13] and *monetary correction* of firms' long-term and fixed assets (which meant that share values would be automatically revalued according to the official price index). Finally, the government allowed corporate and non-corporate taxpayers to invest, respectively, 5 and 10 per cent of their tax expenses on funds administered by investment banks (the so-called *Fundos 157*). This was perhaps the most important fiscal incentive. Even though part of these *Fundos 157* had to be remitted to the government after some period of time, in effect this allowance meant that the government was giving up tax receipts in order to stimulate the development of stock markets and investment banks.

These additional incentives generated an unprecedented boom in Brazil's thin stock markets, as Figure 8.2 illustrates. However, the market showed clear signs of fragility due to its thinness: already by August 1969 it had suffered a violent downturn which led to a decline in transactions until 1970. The government was nonetheless determined

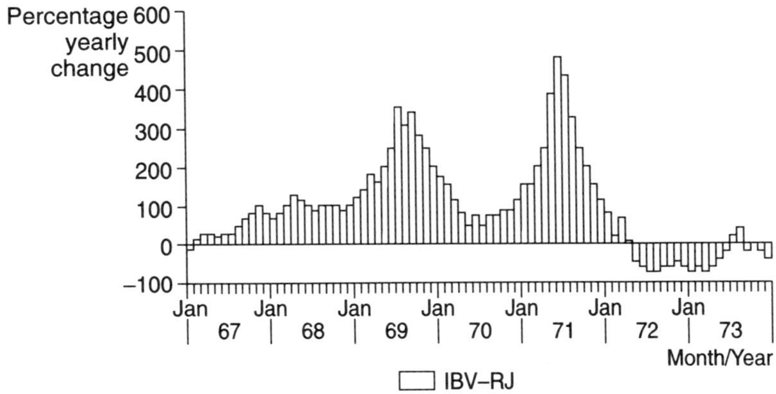

Figure 8.2
Source: Banco Central do Brasil, *Boletim Mensal*, 1977, 13 (3): 96–8

to foster the market and extended the fiscal incentives by allowing for the stretching of the redemption maturity date of the fiscal funds and by exempting taxes on the retained profits of open companies. The result was again a boom, where price–profit earnings ratios of 50 to 100 were commonly observed.

Even though the stock market boom stimulated share issues, the trend was not sustained. The boom was followed by another crash in 1971, which led not only to a shrinkage of share dealings but also of new issues (Table 8.3). Indeed, the violence of the crash created an overall mistrust of stock markets as a provider of firms' financing.

Another important trend of the reformed financial structure is revealed by the rapid financial 'deepening', which was observed after 1964 and is normally indicated by both the rise of financial assets (FA) as percentage of GNP and of non-monetary assets as a percentage of total financial assets (Figure 8.3). As noted earlier, this process is interpreted by many authors as representing a genuine improvement in the efficiency of the financial system (see, for example, Cysne *et al.* 1990: 241–2). What is often overlooked is that this financial *widening* took place in an increasing speculative atmosphere, and contributed little to the increase of the supply of loanable funds.

Two interrelated factors led to such a speculative atmosphere: first, the co-existence of indexed and non-indexed assets in an environment of persistent inflation; second, the shortening of the maturities of assets

Table 8.3 Some indicators of the stock market (1967–73)

	Volume of stocks traded on the Rio and São Paulo stock exchanges		*Primary issues of shares*			
Year	*Cr$ billion* (1)	*Real growth of column (1)*[a] (2)	*Cr$ million* (3)	*Real growth of column (3)*[a] (4)	*Column (3) as percentage of aggregate investment* (5)	*Column (3) as percentage of column (1)* (6)
1967	0.3	38.3	86.0	257.2	0.5	28.7
1968	0.4	21.0	527.0	393.8	2.0	131.7
1969	2.5	391.6	468.0	−26.1	1.3	18.7
1970	4.6	56.7	531.0	−5.0	1.1	11.5
1971	25.6	377.9	119.0	82.9	1.8	0.5
1972	18.0	−40.0	1357.0	−1.0	1.6	7.5
1973	17.9	17.7	913.0	−41.5	0.7	5.1

Source: Banco Central do Brasil, *Boletim Mensal*, October 1978: 178–9
Note: [a] Deflated by the general price index (IGP–DI).

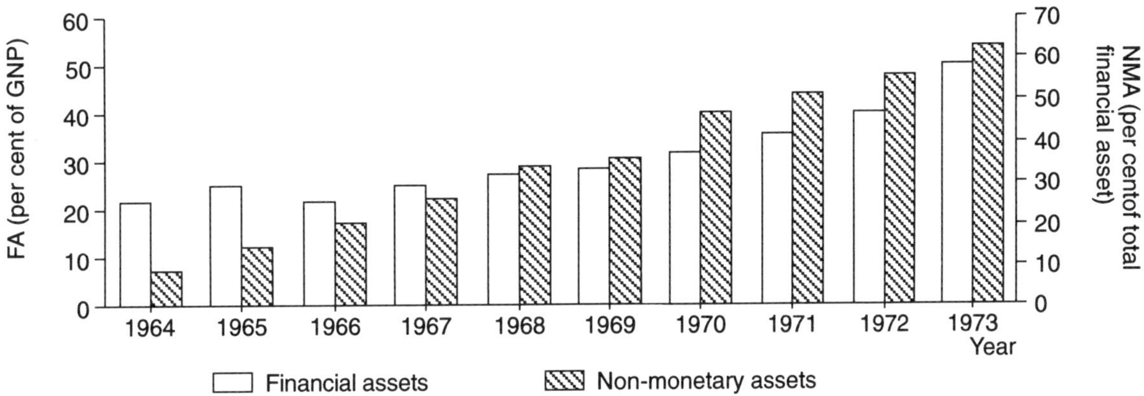

Figure 8.3
Source: Table A.3.4

issued by both private and public institutions. The process of the shortening of maturities and its relation to indexation has already been discussed above, so now it only remains to explain the speculative bias of the segmentation of interest rates.

The introduction of monetary correction generated a dichotomic structure, where some assets were indexed and others bore nominal interest rates. This permitted investors between different assets whenever inflationary expectations changed dramatically.[14] Suppose that a private financial institution funds its operations by issuing non-indexed assets of shorter maturity than its loans. If it is assumed that the carrying cost of such an asset is zero, the initial equilibrium position can be represented as follows:

$$q_i + r_i + a_i = q_n + r_n + a_n \tag{8.1}$$

where q is the own-rate, r is the liquidity premium and a is the capital-gain or loss due to inflation; the subscripts i and n stand, respectively, for indexed and non-indexed assets.

Because a for indexed assets will only be determined at the end of the period, any change in expectations of inflation will change this equilibrium, causing a shift of funds to or from indexed assets. If, for instance, there is an upward revision of such expectations, then it is worth selling the non-indexed asset in order to buy the indexed asset; and vice versa.

In the context of Brazil's post-1964 financial structure, non-indexed assets either funded the operations of some private institutions (e.g. finance companies) or corresponded to voluntary reserves of banks. The shift of funds as described above would provoke an immediate reaction of those institutions, which would have to bid for funds to replace those lost in the shift. Hence, an upward revision of inflationary expectations could also cause very abrupt upward changes in the rates of interest of various assets.

The first consequence of this tendency was the convergence of the nominal rates (Figure 8.4) towards the rates paid by the re-adjustable treasury bond (ORTN). This convergence was only possible because the rate of inflation was actually declining during the period 1966 to 1970, but in subsequent periods the non-indexed rates tended to be higher than the indexed ones. Regarding the loan rate, however, lending institutions continued to behave as suggested by the model developed in Chapter 3. That is, they maintained a mark-up pricing system. The mark-up, however, would increase as inflation rose. In contrast to the earlier period, indexation and then the liberalisation of interest rates in 1976 meant that loan rates could reach very high levels.

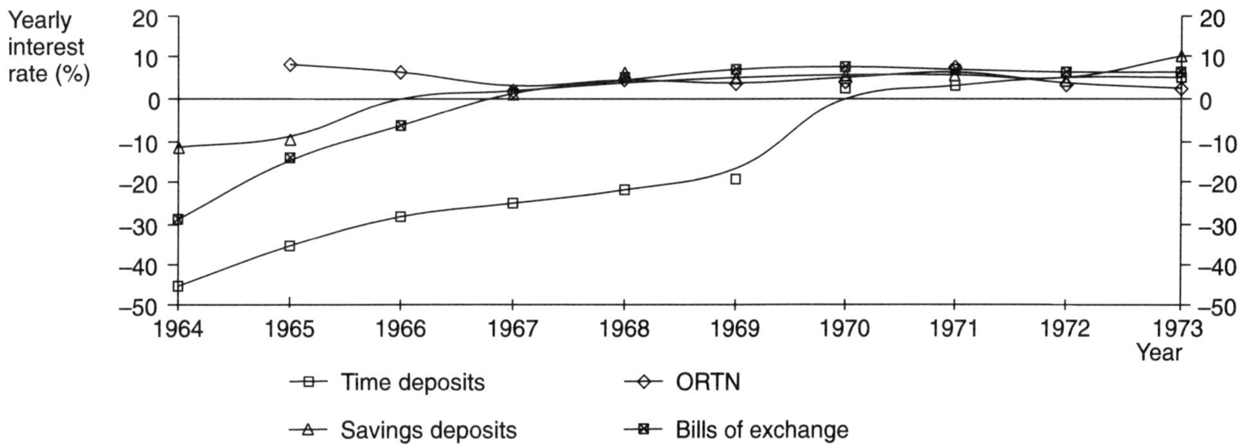

Figure 8.4
Source: Table A.5.2

THE REFORM AND THE FOREIGN DEBT

The financial system that emerged after 1964 was significantly more open to foreign borrowing than the one which existed in the 1950s. Prior to the reform, national private corporations had the least access to sources of long-term financing. Resolution 63 provided national firms with the capacity to borrow foreign currency on conditions (maturities and interest rates) which the internal financial system had not, until then, been able to provide.

These legal changes affected the flows of foreign borrowing almost immediately: foreign borrowing rose from US$373 million in 1965 to US$508 million in 1966, and then increased almost steadily from US$583 million in 1968 to US$4.5 billion in 1973. The financing needs relating to the transfer of real resources also rose in this period; however, the continuous rise of international reserves occurred because loans rose faster than these needs.

This trend of borrowing beyond the needs of the country for purely financial reasons can be better illustrated with the help of the classification of the balance of payments developed in Chapter 5. According to this, real resources transfers (RRT) comprise the results of the trade and the non-factors accounts; the capital costs (CC) encompass interest charges, amortisation of loans and profit remittances; and the capital inflows (CI) consist mainly of net foreign investment and loans. Given that the sum of these three must equal the change in reserves (Res), and that CI is representative of the net increase in debt, the ratios of the three aforementioned variables (RRT, CC and Res) over CI give an indication of the causes behind the increase of the external debt.

Figure 8.5 indicates that during 1967, the use of external borrowing to finance the transfer of real resources was at a minimum if compared with the increase in reserves that such loans caused and the payment of the costs of capital. These consisted mainly of interest charges, which grew proportionally with the increase of the external debt. This tendency for over-borrowing was caused by both internal and external reasons. The internal reason was pointed out above: in contrast to the period 1947–55 it became much easier, especially for national firms, to borrow abroad. From the external (supply) side, the development of the Euromarkets in the 1960s and 1970s greatly extended the credit-creating capacity of the international banking system, which was indeed flooding LDCs with cheap money (on this see, for example, Aglietta 1985). Due to this increase in liquidity in the international banking system, credit was abundant and at costs

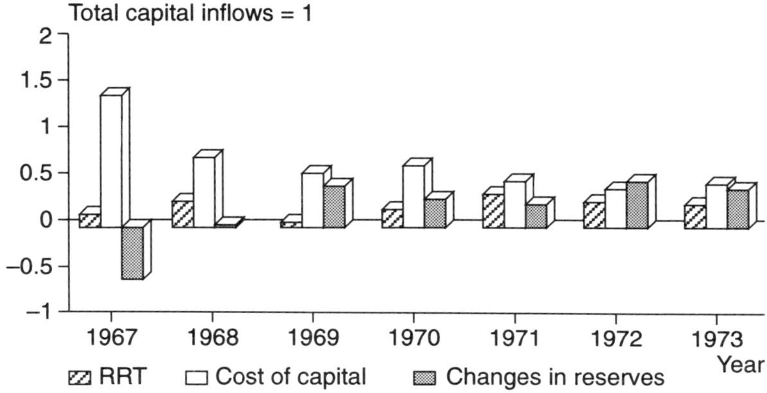

Figure 8.5
Source: Table A.7.2

and terms which were infinitely more favourable than the ones available in Brazil (Davidoff Cruz 1984: 34). And given the structural deficiencies of the national financial system, it was only natural that firms preferred to obtain foreign credit to finance their expansion, even if for the economy as a whole there was no need for additional finance of real resources transfers.

THE FINANCIAL REFORMS AND THE 'ECONOMIC MIRACLE'

The period 1967–73 was one of unprecedented economic growth for Brazil's economy. This period is characterised by an average yearly growth rate of real GNP and real GNP per capita of 11 per cent and 10 per cent respectively. Growth was led by industry, which grew at an average of 13 per cent per annum in the period, and specifically by the consumer durables and construction industries. This output performance was crowned by an almost steady decline of inflation from 38 per cent in 1966 to 15 per cent in 1973. Finally, the period was characterised by a fairly equilibrated balance of payments permitted by the steep rise in exports from US$1.6 billion in 1967 to US$6.2 billion in 1973. Given the extraordinary performance on both the internal and external fronts, the literature has designated 1967–73 the period of the economic 'miracle'.

How miraculous this economic boom was remains questionable. On the one hand, it must be borne in mind that this came after four years of economic slow-down, which had left high levels of idle capacity. This is confirmed by the fact that, even though there was no significant investment in the consumer durables sector, all of the durable items represented in Table 8.4 had average rates of growth superior to 10 per cent.

If the widespread idle capacity made it possible to stimulate growth by increasing demand, it was the mixture of exceptional external and internal conditions during the period and the government's looser monetary and credit policies which triggered the boom. On the external front, government implemented an aggressive policy, which included fiscal and credit subsidies to exports (Pereira 1974) after 1968. Further, the fast increase in reserves and the expansion of Banco do Brasil's loans generated an expansionary pressure on the monetary base which was not neutralised. The consequence of these factors was a significantly expansionist monetary policy, as Table 8.5 shows. Finally, the government also increased its investment from 1968 onwards (Table A.2.2 in the Appendix).

Thus the recovery could be seen as being triggered by classical expansionary monetary and fiscal instruments. However, the maintenance of growth and the subsequent boom cannot be totally explained by the initial determinants of expansion. The continuing widening of demand for consumer durables was determined by two main factors: (1) first, the high income concentration and stability of employment of white-collar workers associated with the increase in jobs generated by the expansion of government investment (including construction) in 1967; (2) second, the institutionalisation of hire purchase credit and the increased competition in this sector of the financial system, which created the credit facilities to meet increasing demand. Further, the new housing finance system rapidly increased the supply of funds available to construction, which also boomed in the period.

Therefore, the financial reforms contributed significantly to the 'economic miracle' for at least three reasons: first, the shifting of the operations of finance companies to consumer credit allowed the biggest consumer durables boom ever in Brazil (see Table 8.4). Second, the specialisation of investment banks in the financing of working capital provided the financial basis for the expansion of industrial sector operations. Finally, with the creation of the housing finance system it provided the mechanisms to finance the rapid growth of the construction sector.

Table 8.4 Sales of consumer durables: selected items (1967–73) (in thousands)

								Average yearly rates of growth		
	1967	*1968*	*1969*	*1970*	*1971*	*1972*	*1973*	*1967–70*	*1970–3*	*1967–73*
Refrigerators	385	503	539	525	680	829	1029	10.9	25.1	17.8
Air conditioners	32	35	64	59	101	110	152	22.6	37.1	29.7
TVs	467	678	746	816	958	1109	1345	20.4	18.1	19.3
Radios	884	1227	1547	1942	2238	2893	2777	30.0	12.7	21.0
Floor-waxing machines	175	179	244	221	240	297	329	8.1	14.2	11.1
Electric fans	118	100	171	157	220	225	389	10.0	35.3	22.0
Hoovers	42	71	57	54	74	89	99	8.7	22.4	15.4
Electric mixers	93	123	103	109	127	138	167	5.4	15.3	10.2
Exhausts	17	25	25	23	36	34	39	10.6	19.2	14.8
Blenders	337	381	424	443	554	642	744	9.5	18.9	14.1
Flat irons	242	274	282	302	354	433	545	7.7	21.7	14.5
Automobiles	132	161	237	250	342	409	451	23.7	21.7	22.7
Vans	62	71	70	124	131	148	207	26.2	18.7	22.4

Source: Galvêas 1985: 126–7

Table 8.5 Sources of expansion and contraction of the monetary liabilities of the monetary authorities (Cr$ billion) (1967–73)

Account	*1967*	*1968*	*1969*	*1970*	*1971*	*1972*	*1973*
Assets	1.8	6.1	7.6	4.4	8.2	14.8	26.4
Treasury operation	0.6	1.1	−0.7	−1.7	−1.8	−7.7	−5.3
Exchange currency operations	−0.1	1.6	4.5	2.5	2.2	1.4	1.5
Banco do Brasil (loans)	1.1	2.4	3.1	3.2	5.7	7.1	12.1
Re-discounts and loans to financial institutions	0.1	0.8	0.5	0.1	1.3	1.7	3.0
Buy/sell of agricultural products	0.1	0.3	0.3	0.3	0.9	−0.7	1.9
Liabilities	−0.1	−2.4	−4.2	−1.6	−2.1	−10.4	−13.3
Operations with coffee	−0.1	−0.9	−1.4	−1.2	−0.5	−0.4	0.2
Capital and reserves of the monetary authorities	−0.4	−1.1	−1.6	−3.0	−3.7	−0.6	−0.6
Other	0.4	−0.4	−1.2	2.6	+2.0	−0.4	−7.9
Monetary base	1.7	3.7	3.4	2.8	6.1	4.4	13.1

Source: Pereira 1974: 86

Notes: +, expansionary effect on the monetary base; −, contraction effect. Therefore an increase in the liabilities will have a negative sign (e.g. in 1967 the account 'Operations with coffee' had a surplus).

The role of the reformed financial sector is reflected in the data on loans to the private sector (see Table 4.2), which can be summarised as follows: (1) first, the loans of investment banks grew at a real average rate of 55 per cent, increasing their share of the total loans to the private sector (TLPS) from 4.8 per cent in 1967 to 12.7 per cent in 1973; (2) second, the loans of finance companies grew in real terms at an average 40.3 per cent, raising their portion of the TLPS from 10.4 per cent in 1967 to 15.1 per cent in 1973; and finally the housing finance system, represented by the National Housing Bank (BNH), savings and loan associations and Federal and State Savings Banks, saw their share of the TLPS more than double from 1967 (8.5 per cent) to 1973 (17.4 per cent). These three segments increased their joint participation in the loans to the private sector from 25 per cent in 1967 to 45 per cent in 1973.

It is important to stress that with the exception of the housing finance system, it was the failures of the reforms (as regards the operations of the finance companies and investment banks) which allowed the rapid expansion of lending associated with the 1967–73 boom. In other words, it was the enhancement of the private sector's short-term lending capacity which provided the liquidity required for the fast absorption of the productive capacity created in the 1950s. However, the intensity of this boom was such that the economy quickly approached full capacity in 1970; and it is then that the reformed financial structure showed its perverse shortcomings, hindering the continuance of growth. The analysis of the effects of such shortcomings on Brazil's development in 1974–83 is the topic of the next chapter; but before that, the dysfunctionalities that the new financial structure had already revealed by 1973 should be noted.

THE (DYS)FUNCTIONALITY OF THE REFORMED FINANCIAL SYSTEM

The financial system is functional for development if it has credit-creating capacity and this capacity is used to accommodate the additional demand for credit related to the *investment-finance motive* and to additional transactions demand; if it has funding capacity in order to reduce the increasing borrower's and lender's risks; and if it can maintain robustness throughout the process of growth, avoiding the possibility that increasing financial fragility might degenerate into financial instability. Given the particularities of the international financial structure, where the funding mechanism for loans to LDCs never emerged, it was also shown that a functional financial structure should limit the use of foreign loans to financing the transfer of real resources which complement internal accumulation.

The financial structure which emerged from the reforms of 1964–5 was highly dysfunctional in the process of development. First, regarding finance, even though the credit-creating capacity of the private financial structure was significantly enhanced, this was directed towards short-term operations. In addition, indexation did raise the rates of interest, which nevertheless did not deter the rapid rise of the indebtedness of firms and consumers. In other words, the financial fragility of the system increased. The system was only reasonably stable during the period from 1967 to 1973 because of relatively low inflation and the rapid increase of profits and employment.

Second, the mechanisms to fund investment never developed and indeed were discouraged by the increasingly speculative environment of the financial markets. The market for securities, for instance, suffered a considerable setback after the stock market crash in 1971. The issuing of other private long-term securities, such as debentures, never really took off. The organised financial markets in Brazil were never much more than money and quasi-money markets, whose development depended on speculation on government bonds.

Third, given the lack of funding mechanisms, the only source of long-term financing continued to be the State. This, however, increasingly linked its debt to operations to sterilise the expansion of liquidity caused by the flood of foreign loans permitted by Resolution 63 and Law 4131. Further, since nominal rates of interest were raised by indexation, the very cost of refinancing the roll-over of the public debt increased the need to expand such a debt.

Having mentioned the relationship between external and internal debts, the fourth dysfunctionality is related to the use of foreign finance. The reform permitted easier access to the international banking system at a time when this was experiencing a liquidity boom, whereas in Brazil the credit conditions remained very tight for firms. This caused an unprecedented rise in external debt which, to start with, had little to do with the need to finance the real resources gap or the current account of the balance of payments. In fact, the government had to strive to prevent the increasing levels of international reserves from neutralising its internal tight-money policy required to fight inflation. As the external debt rapidly increased, the cost of financing started to increase, making the external debt even less functional to Brazil's development.

As noted above, the shortcomings of this financial structure, crippled by speculation, were not clearly perceived at the time of the demand-led boom of 1967–73. It is only when *real* development, and therefore long-term investment, was resumed in 1974 that the problems showed their full extent. In the meantime, the reformers could claim to the world that the financial widening observed in 1964–73 was proof that the financial reform had been successful in increasing savings and the efficiency of its allocation.

SUMMING UP

The recession which began in the early 1960s showed the limitations of the financial system in supporting the extraordinary development of productive forces in the post-war period. Those limits were particularly: (1) the lack of medium-term finance, especially hire purchase credit; and (2) the lack of financing of private long-term physical capital.

The financial reforms, whose logic was based on the identification between finance and savings, did succeed in enhancing the sources of finance for government expenditure, consumption and residential construction. In this way, the financial reforms contributed to the economic boom from 1967 to 1973. However, the reforms also introduced some structural dysfunctionalities of the financial system, such as the tendency towards the short term, speculation and foreign indebtedness beyond the real needs for the development of the country. On top of these dysfunctionalities, the private mechanisms of investment finance and funding continued to be underdeveloped despite all the efforts to develop them during and after the reform.

In the period from 1970 onwards, the symptoms of the continuing structural deficiency of the financial structure were already visible. These took the form of increasing speculation and the accumulation of foreign indebtedness far above that needed to finance real resource transfers from abroad. But it was with the oil shock of 1973 and the decision of the Brazilian government to adjust to the shock by expanding the process of import substitution that the shortcomings of this system were revealed to their full extent. This is the topic of the next chapter.

Chapter 9

Towards the lost decade

The financial system in the imbalanced growth (1973–83)

INTRODUCTION

The year 1973 marked a new phase in Brazil's development, a phase in which the country had to face severe internal and external challenges to the continuance of its growth. On the internal front, the economy showed signs of the exhaustion of the boom begun in 1967, as industrial output reached full capacity, inflation began to rise and the demand for capital goods soared. On the external front, the fourfold increase in international oil prices caused a significant balance of payments problem, in an economy where 80 per cent of the oil needs were imported.

Two options were available to the Brazilian government then. One was to promote a severe adjustment programme in order to re-establish external equilibrium. This would almost inevitably cause recession, which was not politically bearable by the military government, as it was preparing for a transition to a civilian political system and wanted to guarantee that in this transition its political party (ARENA) remained in power. The second option, which was taken, was to deepen the process of import substitution so as to rapidly reduce Brazil's dependency on foreign resources. It implied heavy investment in technologically advanced basic input sectors and in the production of internally generated energy. This option took the form of the Second National Development Plan (the 1974 Plan), which raised the accumulation of the economy to levels which were unprecedented in Brazil's economic history.

In the implementation of the 1974 Plan, the government was split into two different (but not politically exclusive) orientations: one, led by the President and the Ministry of Planning, had a strongly interventionist view. The other, led by the Finance Ministry, continued to espouse the liberal approach to monetary policy and also favoured the maintenance of positive real interest rates in order to promote internal saving, to attract foreign saving and to maintain internal price stability. Given the inherited segmented financial structure, which had already shown inherent dysfunctionalities in 1973, the tension between these two approaches precipitated an environment in which capital gains could be obtained by speculating with government bonds and other indexed and non-indexed assets. As the public debt soared, and inflation rose, both the private financial sector and the big corporate sector engaged in such speculation. The result of such a perverse process was a financial disarray which contributed to the main macroeconomic imbalances of the period – i.e. high public and external debts, increasing inflation and menacing financial fragility. Ultimately, the financial trap into which the government led itself, left no choice but to step back in 1979 and to promote one of the stiffest recessions the country had ever experimented.

This chapter analyses in detail the evolution of the events which led Brazil from the economic 'miracle' in the 1970s to the lost decade in the 1980s. The emphasis is placed on the interrelation between (i) the macroeconomic imbalances of the period and (ii) the legacy of the financial reforms of 1964–6 and the monetary policies from the mid-1970s onwards. Following the method set up in Chapter 7, this part of our study begins by discussing the macroeconomic trends in the period, focusing on the pace of growth and the levels of accumulation. It then assesses the arrangements created to finance accumulation in the Second National Development Plan (1974–8) and discusses their limits. Finally, it discusses the inconsistencies of the government's overall financial strategy undertaken in the period, given the inherited financial structure, and indicates the effects of such inconsistencies to Brazil's vulnerable economic performance in the 1970s and 1980s.

GROWTH AND PACE OF ACCUMULATION IN THE PERIOD

After six years of demand-led economic boom, in 1973 Brazil's economic growth became increasingly threatened by both internal and external factors. The internal factors were three: first, the industrial sector was already facing full-capacity, which is indicated in Figure 9.1;[1] the demand for basic inputs and capital goods, for instance, was growing on average by 22.7 per cent a year since the 1970s (see Batista 1986: 4). Second, the indigenous capital goods sector was not sophisticated enough to provide the more technologically advanced investment goods required by this phase of growth. Third, the capacity of expansion of the

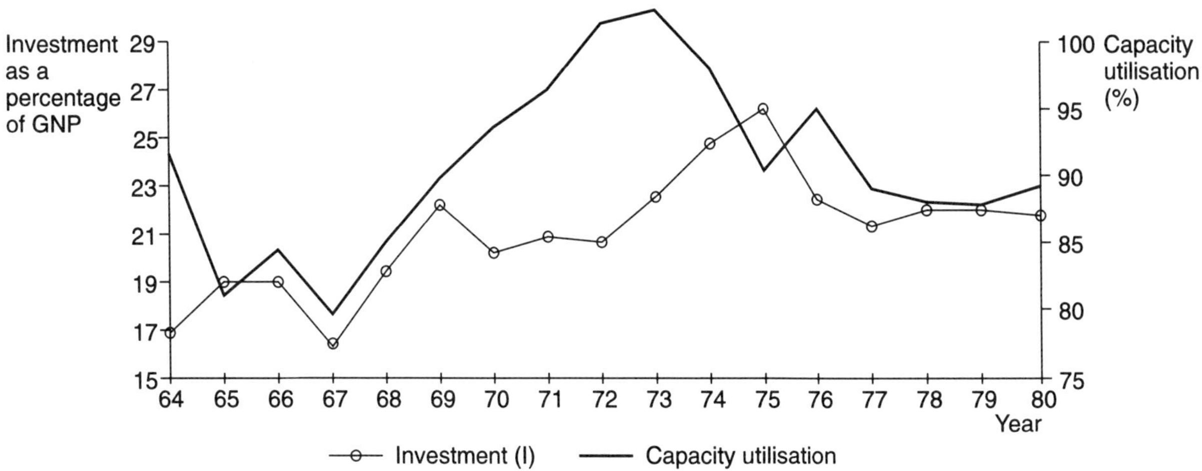

Figure 9.1
Source: See text

industrial sector was limited by the size of the market for consumer durables, especially after the rapid growth of their demand in the previous period. As noted in Chapter 8, the previous consumerist boom was based on the demand of the relatively small middle and upper classes. Because the income distribution was so poor and because it was not improved in the period of the 'miracle' (1967–73), the demand for these goods was inversely related to the stock of consumer durables already sold.[2]

As regards the external factors, the capacity to expand exports was limited by the recession in world trade (which began in 1974 and lasted until the first quarter of 1975). The need to do something about the external constraint was already clear in the three last years of the economic 'miracle': the imports of raw material from 1971 to 1973 had more than doubled; the demand for imported capital goods had expanded by 24.7 per cent on average between 1970 and 1973, despite the fact that domestic production rose rapidly. In addition, in 1973 this situation was aggravated by the first oil shock. Oil being the main source of energy in the industrial and transport sectors, and given that Brazil imported 80 per cent of its oil needs, the oil price shock represented a main source of disequilibrium in the trade balance.

Despite these constraints, in September 1974 the government launched its Second National Development Plan. This was a clear choice for growth and, further, to deepen the process of import-substitution from what was built in the 1950s. The choice for growth rather than conventional adjustment was – as it usually is – politically bounded. As Wells (1979) points out,

> [the] economic measures adopted during 1974 and afterwards need to be interpreted in the light of the President [Geisel]'s commitment, at least during the first half of the administration, to a series of steps leading to political democratisation: relatively free congressional elections (in 1974) and municipal election (in 1976) leading up to direct election for the state governorships in 1978 ... In order to try to insure that ARENA (the government party) was the main beneficiary of the electoral process, the government felt the need to sustain growth and was obliged to adopt certain measures of income redistribution.

Indeed the orthodox alternative – i.e. an attempt to equilibrate the external imbalances (caused by the rise of oil prices) and reduce inflation (through exchange devaluation and orthodox monetary and fiscal policies) – would be tremendously costly in terms of output and employment. Further, this would not cause a significant reversal of the trade deficit because of the low elasticity of the world demand for Brazil's exports caused by the international crisis and the inelasticity of the internal demand for oil (see Fishlow 1986; Castro and Souza 1985; and Batista 1986).

The political solution was then the Second National Development Plan. The stated objectives of the Plan were very ambitious: to maintain a 10 per cent economic growth in the period between 1974 and 1979; to produce a rapid import-substitution in the capital goods and basic inputs sector (heavy chemicals, iron and steel, ferrous and non-ferrous minerals); to expand rapidly the production and export of cellulose, iron, aluminium and steel; to develop infrastructure, specifically to increase rapidly the domestic production of oil and hydroelectric energy; to develop the railway and telecommunication systems; and to implement a vast programme of rural electrification, irrigation, agricultural goods warehouses etc.

For this the plan projected an accumulation ratio (investment/GNP) of 25 per cent in the four years of its implementation. Of the total projected investment in the period 1974–8, 22.8 per cent would concentrate in the manufacturing sector (18.3 per cent specifically in the basic inputs sector) and 15.0 per cent in the production of electricity (including both the expansion of hydroelectric power and the installation of nuclear power stations).

Despite the aforementioned constraints on growth, due to the 1974 Plan Brazil's macroeconomic performance in the period from 1974 to 1980 was surprisingly satisfactory, albeit nothing compared with the period from 1967 to 1973. For instance, real gross national product (GNP) grew 6.8 per cent, and per capita GNP 4.2 per cent, on average, from 1974 to 1980.[3] This growth was again led by the industrial sector, which expanded 7.0 per cent on average in the period.

In a way, when the Second National Development Plan was launched, the process of fast accumulation in fixed capital had already taken off, as Figure 9.1 indicates. The novelty introduced by this plan (in relation to the more *laissez-faire* approach thus far adopted by the military government) was the State's direct commitment to take the lead in the new phase of import-substitution, either through direct massive public investment or as a financier of the process. Indeed it is an irony that in the military government, which always pictured itself as the champion of liberalism, the role of government investment is high even in comparison with the period of the 'populist' Target Plan, as Figure 9.2 denotes.

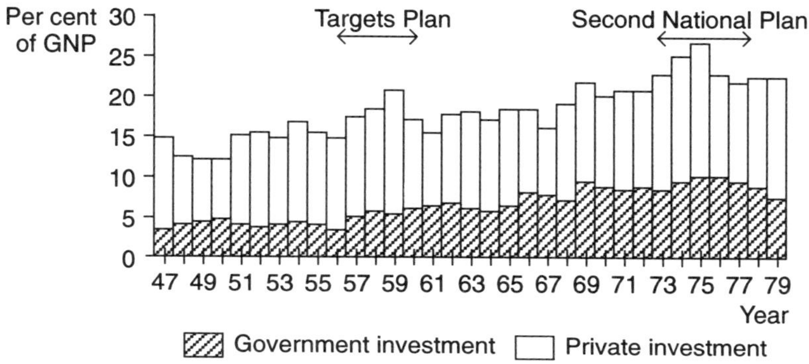

Figure 9.2
Source: Tables A.21 and A.22

The strategy behind the 1974 Plan was successful in maintaining a high growth and accumulation rates. The Plan also produced a considerable increase in production of capital goods, metallurgy and chemicals. As regards the import-substitution and export promotion, the import coefficient in the capital goods sector declined from 28.8 per cent in 1974 to 18.0 per cent in 1979, whereas the export coefficient rose from 5.3 per cent to 12.1 per cent in the same period. Similar results are found in the production of basic inputs. The Plan also produced a significant structural change within the productive (especially industrial) sector, as it reduced the dependency of Brazil's growth on imports of capital goods and basic inputs by promoting import-substitution in important industrial sectors and expanded the productive capacity of tradable goods (Table 9.1).[4]

If the 1974 Plan represented a successful development strategy, other indicators show that the economy was riding fast into macroeconomic and financial deterioration. On the one hand, despite the rise of investment, GNP growth fell from 8.8 per cent in 1976 to 4.6 per cent in 1977 and 4.8 per cent in 1978. This decline was especially severe in the manufacturing and agriculture sectors. On the other hand, inflation doubled from 1973 (22.6 per cent) to 1977 (46.2 per cent), declining only slightly in 1977 (38.7 per cent). Finally, the external debt rose from US$17 billion to over US$43 billion from 1973 to 1978.[5]

In 1979, the government was facing severe pressures from industrial sectors to accelerate growth, whereas its external debtors were pressing

Table 9.1 Indicators of the results of the Second National Development Plan

	1973	*1975*	*1977*	*1979*	*1981*
Ratio between imports and domestic production					
Intermediary products	0.22	0.12	0.13	0.11	0.08
Paper	0.16	0.10	0.05	0.03	0.01
Cellulose	0.76	0.34	0.38	0.15	0.02
Polyethylene	0.23	0.21	0.33	0.47	0.03
PVC	0.25	0.33	0.09	0.03	0.05
Steel	2.68	1.86	1.48	0.34	0.85
Fertiliser	0.58	0.68	0.62	0.37	0.14
Capital goods (to order)	0.66	0.65	0.46	0.37	0.40
Index of import ratio					
Total	100	111	88	90	74
Petroleum	100	93	88	97	77
Capital goods	100	144	70	64	57

Source: Fishlow 1986: 521
Note: The sectoral data was based on producers' estimate reported in *Revista Exame*, May 1983.

for the implementation of orthodox adjustment programmes. The reason for these pressures are rather straightforward: on the industrialists' side, the period of rapid accumulation (1974–9) had provided them with enhanced productive capacity, which they were anxious to use, if only to repay the debts obtained to finance their previous accumulation.[6] On the foreign debtors' side, the simple fact that the debt had risen to almost US$50 billion and over 327 per cent of the exports (see Table A.1.2 in the Appendix) was a matter of concern.

After two years when GNP growth fell consecutively, a change of government brought the man identified as the mentor of the economic 'miracle' (1967–73) back to power. Reversing the stop–go policy of his predecessor (Mario Henrique Simonsen), Delfim Netto promised in his inaugural speech to reproduce the 1967–73 economic boom. Delfim Netto's policy mixed orthodox with heterodox measures: the former included a 'corrective inflation' of prices of basic inputs and services produced by public enterprises, and a 30 per cent exchange devaluation. The latter involved selective price controls, a ceiling on the interest rates (which had been freely determined since 1976) and the pre-fixation of the monetary correction and exchange rates, breaking the rule, which had been followed for twelve years, of mini-devaluations according to the internal inflation and the inflation in the United States.

These measures caused significant impacts on both the real and the financial sides of the economy. To start with, the pre-fixed rates – of 40 per cent for monetary correction and 45 per cent for the exchange rate – were below any expected rate of inflation (55.6 per cent in 1979). The combination of cheap money, low rate of return on government bonds, over-valued currency and optimistic entrepreneurial expectations, provoked a speculative boom in the demand of basic inputs. Thus, whereas the internal demand for basic inputs is one of the main factors responsible for the growth in manufacturing in 1979 (Table 9.2), the speculative boom in demand for imported basic inputs represented an increase of those imports from US$4.5 billion to US$7 billion in 1980, adding to the already deteriorated trade balance (Table 9.3).

Contrary to the expectations of Delfim Netto, inflation proved persistent and, in fact, increased from 38.9 per cent to 91.8 per cent in the period from 1980 to 1981. On the external front, two factors were added to the speculative demand for basic inputs to provoke a fast deterioration of the balance of payments. First, the oil prices more than doubled (110 per cent growth from June 1979 to February 1980) and the terms of trade continued to fall after the deterioration begun in 1976. Second, the international interest rates rose substantially in the period – e.g. the average LIBOR rate increased steadily from under 6.4 per cent in 1977 to 14 per cent in 1980; deflated by the index of Brazil's terms

Table 9.2 Industrial production by categories of usage (1977–83)

			Consumer goods		
Year	*Capital goods*	*Intermediary goods*	*Total*	*Durable*	*Non-durable*
1977	−4.5	7.5	0.3	−0.1	0.3
1978	5.9	6.5	8.0	17.0	6.4
1979	5.6	8.6	4.9	7.7	4.4
1980	6.5	8.3	6.0	10.7	5.2
1981	−19.0	−10.6	−6.4	−26.3	−2.9
1982	−10.8	0.4	2.7	8.0	1.8
1983	−12.8	0.3	1.6	9.5	0.2

Source: Banco Central do Brasil, *Programa Econômico*, October 1983: 44

Table 9.3 Discrimination of imports: selected items (1971–80)

	1971	*1972*	*1973*	*1974*	*1975*	*1976*	*1977*	*1978*	*1979*	*1980*
In US$ million										
Oil	327	409	711	2,840	2,873	3,827	3,814	4,196	6,403	9,405
Capital goods	1,239	1,734	2,142	3,119	3,934	3,519	3,101	3,553	3,775	4,381
Raw materials	1,273	1,565	2,560	5,588	4,350	4,057	3,909	4,532	5,954	7,059
Grains	114	132	350	486	372	533	279	702	984	1,241
Basic inputs	1,045	1,291	1,993	4,664	3,595	3,140	3,202	3,286	4,160	5,010
Other	114	142	217	438	383	384	428	544	810	808
Consumption goods	358	464	721	826	866	932	1,116	1,582	1,315	989
As percentage of total imports										
Oil	10.1	9.7	11.5	22.5	23.5	30.9	31.7	30.7	35.4	41.0
Capital goods	38.2	40.9	34.6	24.7	32.2	28.4	25.8	26.0	20.9	19.1
Raw materials	39.2	37.0	41.3	44.2	35.6	32.8	32.5	33.1	32.9	30.8
Grains	3.5	3.1	5.7	3.8	3.0	4.3	2.3	5.1	5.4	5.4
Basic inputs	32.2	30.5	32.2	36.9	29.4	25.4	26.6	24.0	23.0	21.8
Other	3.5	3.4	3.5	3.5	3.1	3.1	3.6	4.0	4.5	3.5
Consumption goods	11.0	11.0	11.6	6.5	7.1	7.5	9.3	11.6	7.3	4.3

Sources: Banco Central do Brasil, *Boletim Mensal*, several issues; and Castro e Pires de Souza 1982: 182

of trade, this meant an increase in the real rates from 6.1 per cent in 1977 to 33.31 per cent in 1980.[7]

Already in the first semester of 1980, the government surrendered to the pressures for orthodox adjustment policies. Delfim Netto introduced strong quantitative ceilings on the expansion of bank credit and consumer credit; freed the rates of interest and (partially) prices from the government's monitoring; reduced investment of both the federal government and public enterprises; reduced government expenditures and subsidies; limited the re-adjustment of wages (causing a decline in the real wages); and increased the corporate income tax.

These measures provoked a reversal of the entrepreneurial expectations, causing a decline in industrial output of 8.2 per cent and in the real GNP of 3.4 per cent. The violence of the decline in the manufacturing industry has also to do with the speculative character of the recovery in 1979–80. In that period, as noted above, the firms rapidly increased their inventories of intermediary goods. Once the rate of interest rose and the expectations became gloomier, firms reduced their demand for basic inputs symmetrically to the expansion in the previous two years (see Table 9.3).

The combination of high interest rates and recession increased financial instability. This instability did not become a crisis because of the process of intensive financial restructuring that the private corporate sector engaged in and the generous financial assistance that the Central Bank provided to financial institutions in trouble. The cost of guaranteeing financial stability was high, as fragility was absorbed by the public sector in the form of a soaring public debt – both of the Treasury and of the public enterprises. That is, an old formula of the Latin American 'liberalism' was put into practice: to privatise the profits and socialise the losses. Before a detailed analysis of such processes is undertaken, a discussion of the reasons behind the failure of the financial strategy in the Second National Development Plan is in order.

THE FINANCIAL STRATEGY BEHIND THE SECOND NATIONAL DEVELOPMENT PLAN

In order to address the problems behind the financial strategy of the Second National Development Plan, one has to remember the (interrelated) limits imposed by the inherited financial structure. First, the financial system lacked private long-term financing, because of the 1964–5 reform's failure to develop investment banks and capital markets oriented towards long-term finance. With the co-existence of indexed and non-indexed assets and the process of financial conglomeration, the financial system became inherently speculative. Third, the links between the international banking system and the national private sector had been enhanced. Nonetheless, these links did not increase the supply of long-term funds when they were intermediated through the private banking system (through Resolution 63), as they were split into loans of smaller maturities to finance firms' working capital. In turn, during the whole period of 1967 to 1973 the rise of the external debt did not increase the transfer of real resources from abroad, but was largely used to pay the increasing costs of foreign capital and to accumulate idle international reserves.

Given these structural limits of the mechanisms to finance accumulation, and political will to grow and to deepen the process of import-substitution, it is understandable that the government had to find alternative or compensating structures to do the job. These will be examined below, so that their weaknesses can be addressed next.

Investment finance

The need for a rapid increase of supply of finance to new investment projects was evident from the projections made by the 1974 Plan, as all the investment projects were highly capital intensive and had a long horizon of maturation. Given the failure in 1964–73 to develop a long-term-oriented capital market, the impatience of the more interventionist sector within the government was growing. The solution found was similar to the one which existed before the reforms: to transfer public funds to finance investment. However, because of the 'liberal' orientation of the military government, these funds were directed to the private national enterprises, and not to public enterprises as before. Further, the government explicitly stimulated the allocation of such funds through private financial institutions. Take the case of the National Development Bank (BNDE).

The increase of BNDE's loans to the private sector took place through the creation of several specialised programmes which were created in the Bank's restructuring after the reforms of 1964–6. Already in 1966, the Fund for the Financing of Industrial Machines and Equipment (FINAME), created previously to finance the acquisition of internally produced capital goods by national producers, was transformed in a mixed-economy joint-stock company (with BNDE as the principal share-holder) and five other funds were also created within BNDE which directly financed research and development investments, investments in industrial modernisation and long-term working capital.[8] In 1974 two subsidiaries of the BNDE system were created: *Mecânica Brasileira S/A* (EMBRAMEC) and *Insumos Básicos S/A* (FIBASE), respectively to support investment in the machine tools and basic inputs sectors. Finally, in the same year, another subsidiary (*Investimentos Brasileiros S/A* (*IBRASA*)) was founded with the aim of promoting financial strengthening and underwriting of the issues of national private companies.

Even though the number of programmes to finance the private sector increased, until 1973 BNDE's loans had not significantly risen if compared with the needs of investment: using data provided by Zonisein (1984: 3), it can estimated that such loans never represented more than 5 per cent of total aggregate investment until 1973 (Figure 9.3).[9]

However, in 1974, two important funds, initially under the administration of the National Housing Bank, were transferred to the BNDE: the Program of Social Integration (PIS) and the Public Employees Financial Reserve (PASEP). The former was created in 1970 as a form of pension, based on the amount of tax paid and revenues from sales; the latter is similar to the PIS for the civil servants. These funds by themselves represented an enhancement of 0.6, 3.1 and 3.3 billion dollars in BNDE's funding respectively in 1974, 1975 and 1976, and came to represent over 60 per cent of the sources of BNDE's funds in the same years, as Figure 9.4 indicates.

Just to give some proportion of its role, the BNDE system administered financial applications equal to 41.2 billion cruzeiros in 1976,

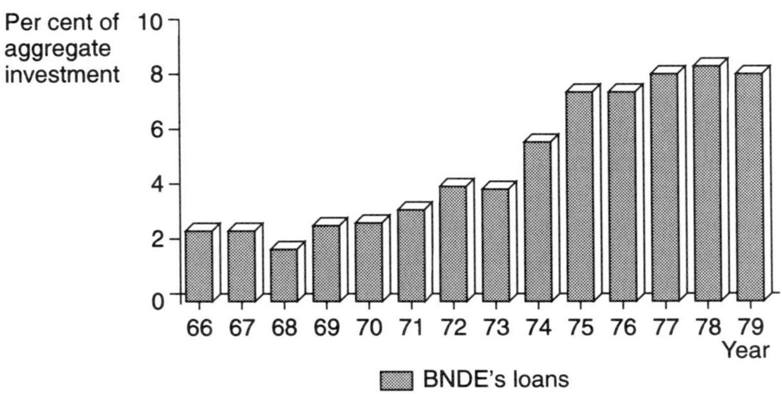

Figure 9.3
Source: Zonisein 1984: 3

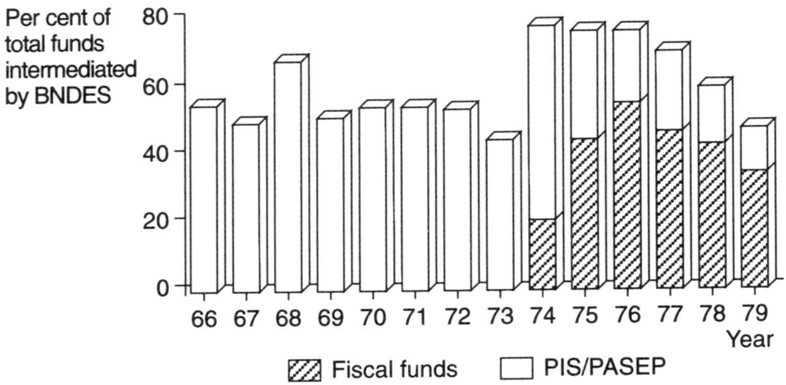

Figure 9.4
Source: Zonisein 1984: 41

equalling 72 per cent of the flow of compulsory savings in that year (Moura da Silva 1979: 46). Using these and other subsidised funds, BNDE rapidly restored its position as the centre of a system of long-term financing. In addition the orientation of its funds to finance private investment, another novelty in relation to the system previous to the 1964–6 reforms, was the fact that it used private investment banks, commercial banks and finance companies as 'intermediaries' of its loans, which in exchange charged a 'service fee' for what was virtually a riskless operation.

The BNDE was not the only institution to be privileged with a rapid enhancement of funds: the BNH and Banco do Brasil, respectively main suppliers of credit for construction and rural credit, also had their role expanded. Like the BNDE, the BNH's funds were significantly increased by the transfer of a special redundancy fund to it, the FGTS.[10] In addition, the central bank maintained a large number of special development programmes; and Banco do Brasil continued to provide loans to agricultural and industrial investment. Therefore, the whole of the medium and long-term financing became dependent on the transfer of fiscal and other public funds towards these three main public financial institutions. Table 9.4 summarises the flow of the main public funds earmarked to finance long-term investment projects.

To sum up, one may say that the expansion of long-term industrial finance in Brazil after 1964 is bound with the strengthening of the activities of the public financial system. This finance was provided by

Table 9.4 Three most important public sources of long-term financing of private investment (current Cr$ millions and as a percentage of total aggregate investment)[a] (1967–80)

Year	BNDE[b] (1)	*BNH*[c] (2)	*Central Bank*[b] (3)	*Total* (4)	*Column (4) as percentage of investment* (5)
1967	437	–	–	437	3.2
1968	467	1,422	–	1,889	8.6
1969	1,032	1,709	–	2,741	8.2
1970	1,443	2,749	1,708	5,900	14.8
1971	2,274	3,596	4,771	10,641	19.4
1972	3,755	4,368	4,776	12,899	17.5
1973	5,368	6,325	8,010	19,703	17.5
1974	11,219	13,442	13,344	38,005	21.0
1975	22,430	19,188	24,279	65,897	24.4
1976	32,733	39,586	43,200	115,519	30.7
1977	49,379	61,740	49,957	161,076	29.4
1978	74,063	94,761	5,828	174,652	21.4
1979	111,875	146,272	58,454	316,601	23.2
1980	175,467	359,145	135,441	670,053	23.6

Sources: col. 1, Zonisein 1984: 28; col. 2, Zini 1982: 350; col. 3, ibid.: 325.
Notes: [a] Banco do Brasil's loans were not included because most of them did not represent earmarked transfers from the monetary authorities, but credit-creation.
[b] Includes transfers to other financial institutions.
[c] Funds and programmes administered by the Central Bank of Brazil.

three basic mechanisms: (1) transfers of funds to private intermediaries; (2) direct lending (loans which could be convertible in equity), subscription of shares and underwriting; and (3) endorsement of loans in foreign currency. Not only did the public funds made available to finance (private) investment rise to proportions which were significantly higher than the period before the financial reforms, but also a complex system of transfers of funds from federal public institutions (the BNDE, the BNH and the Central Bank) to the private financial sector (and especially commercial, investment and state development banks) was established. This system allowed the private financial sector to participate (profitably, of course) in the process of investment financing.

It was as if, having given up the development of a long-term private capital market, the government had decided to leave the allocation of its own funds to private financial institutions. Whether this represented a show of ideological stubbornness or not, certainly the private financial conglomerates and their clients were the most favoured by the system. By 1976, more than 50 per cent of cruzeiro loans to the corporate sectors were either provided by public financial institutions (Banco do Brasil, BNDE, BNH, development banks) or through funds intermediated by the public sector to private financial institutions (savings and loans association, housing credit societies and savings banks (see Table A.3.4 in the Appendix).

The policy towards foreign capital inflows

On the external front, the government's policy was to stimulate the use of the abundant liquidity in the international financial system.[11] Among such incentives we may list: (1) the reduction of the minimum permitted foreign loan maturity from ten to five years;[12] (2) fiscal concessions over the payment of interest of external loans and income tax exemptions over financial operations (Resolutions 305/74 and 278/754); and (3) the maintenance of high levels of domestic interest rates through tight monetary policy.

The strategy also included forcing the public enterprises to borrow abroad. This was done by a sequence of measures. First, as noted above, long-term funds available to public enterprises were subsequently reduced, despite the central role of their investments in the Second National Development Plan. Second, these firms' self-financing capacity was diminished by the strict control of their prices and tariffs, a measure which was part of the anti-inflationary policy.[13] Finally, they suffered restrictions to their access to the internal credit market.

All these incentives would be fully justified if the external debt was actually required to permit the economy to proceed with its development. But this was not the case. First, it is important to acknowledge that the whole period is characterised by deficits in the real-resources-transfers account, as Figure 9.5 denotes.[14] This was due to the rise in the value of oil imports, precipitated by the successive increases in its prices and the increase in the import quantum caused by the continuance of growth, and the increase in the demand for imported basic inputs and capital goods.

However, only in the years 1974 and 1975 can the total volume of the capital inflows be justified by the rise in the above mentioned gap. From then on, as can be confirmed with the visual aid of Figure 9.5, an increasing part of the external borrowing was directed towards the accumulation of reserves. Further, if we look at the percentage of the

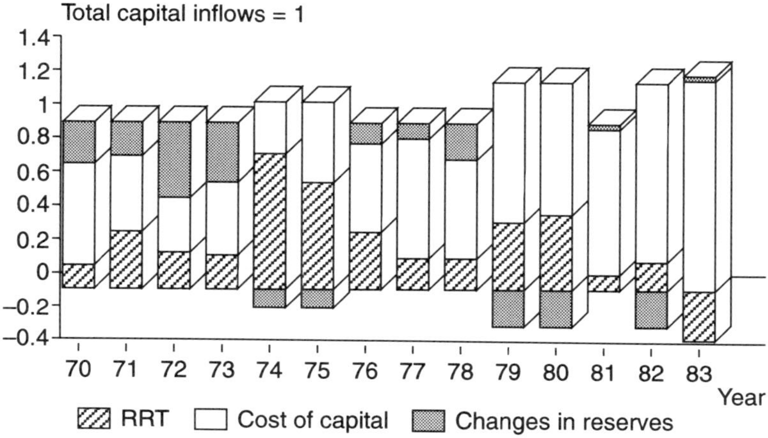

Figure 9.5
Source: Table A.7.2

capital inflows used to simply finance the servicing of the external debt, the picture becomes even more staggering (Figure 9.6). Already in 1974, when the oil shock was first felt in Brazil's balance-of-payments account, interest charges and amortisation of the external debt represented more than 30 per cent of the incoming external flows and, from then on, increased almost steadily to reach approximately 70 per cent in 1977.

From the analysis of Figures 9.5 and 9.6, one deducts that foreign indebtedness in the period was more a destabilising factor than one contributing effectively to economic development in Brazil. Even though the tendency to borrow above the financing requirements is a characteristic of the booming credit-based system, this tendency was amplified during the Second National Development Plan because of the high levels of internal interest rates and the incentives – in the case of the public enterprises, the economic pressure – to borrow in foreign currency above their needs for foreign real resources. It is true that the several external shocks imposed a significant stress upon the Brazilian economy. But this stress was amplified by the structural tendency, already observed throughout the country's post-war development process, to borrow beyond the country's need. This structural feature was then exacerbated by the inconsistency between the development and the financial strategies of 1974.

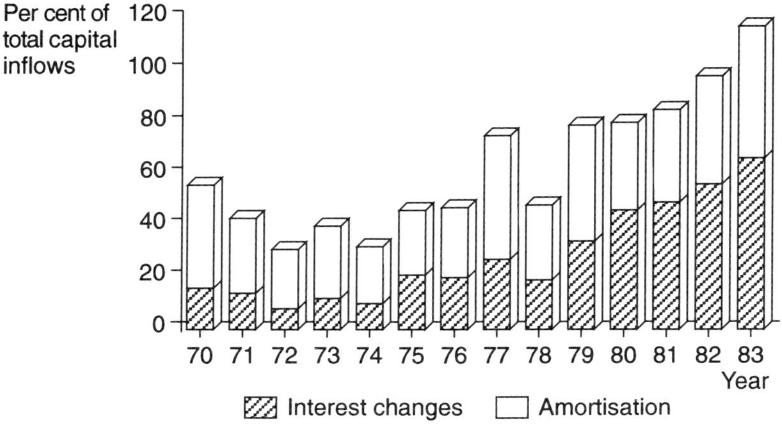

Figure 9.6
Source: Table A.7.2

Financial markets, orthodox monetary policies and the stimuli to speculation

The 1971 stock market crash seems to have destroyed what was left of the government's intentions to develop a private capital market. From then on the investment funds continued to exist, but their operations rapidly turned to applications in the secondary markets and in dealing with government bonds. The investment banks were incorporated into the financial conglomerates led by the old commercial banks, and increasingly reduced the maturities of their operations. Furthermore, their loans became increasingly dependent on the intermediation of foreign loans and transfers of public funds. Finally, they increasingly held government bonds as speculative balances (see Zini 1982: 278–92).

From our perspective, two most important results of the process described above must be stressed. Regarding the first consequence, it increased the systemic financial fragility of the Brazilian macroeconomy. In other words, as was noted in Chapter 7, an increase of finance without funding had two important consequences. First, a rapid increase of the financial fragility for lenders and borrowers, which was mitigated, however, from 1973 by the fact that a substantial part of the finance was directly provided by the subsided long-term loans of government agencies.[15] A second consequence is the inflationary bias that this type of finance has if production cannot keep up with the rise of loans to finance accumulation.

The government showed from the outset concern with the potential inflationary impact of the expansion of the monetary base, and much less with the signs of increasing financial fragility. The expansion of the monetary base was caused by the transformation of borrowed foreign currency to cruzeiros and expansion of the credit provided by the public agencies (Banco do Brasil, BNDE and BNH). The government's concern with such a problem was translated into a tight monetary policy basically by maintaining high interest rates on government bonds. The consequences, however, were disastrous: the tight monetary policy associated with the high levels of inflation caused an expected preference of surplus units for indexed assets (not only by households and firms, but also by financial intermediaries). This led to a dramatic situation, since these were either solely issued by government institutions (e.g. ORTNs) or with government backing (e.g. saving deposits).

Therefore, the system ended in the situation where, on the one hand, government financed accumulation with increasing foreign and internal debt, while, on the other hand, the monetary policy caused rapidly rising financial costs and damaged the government's own financial situation and financing capacity. Given that understanding such a process is crucial to assessing the financial side of Brazil's path to the 'lost decade', a detailed analysis of the shortcomings of the government's financial strategy is in order.

THE SHORTCOMINGS OF THE GOVERNMENT'S FINANCIAL STRATEGY

The financial strategy of the 1974 Plan was based on the government's increasing participation in the financing of accumulation and in the intermediation of foreign loans. This strategy naturally depended on the government's capacity to transfer funds to investing firms and the continuance of the inflows of foreign loan capital at reasonable conditions. These conditions were broken, partly because of the external shocks (especially the interest rate shocks), but also because of the monetary policy implemented since 1974 which, in our view, was inconsistent with the acceleration of accumulation in a credit-based financial system.

The vicious circle of the monetary policy

The period between 1974 and 1979 is characterised by a typical stop–go policy, but with a constantly strong control over monetary aggregates. The Minister of Finance, Mario H. Simonsen, was convinced that inflation was caused by excess demand – caused by the fast increase of government expenditures in the 1974 Plan and public (subsidised) credit – and the external price shocks.[16] Even though his view was not dominant in the government until 1976, the monetary policy was restricted since 1974, causing substantial rises in the rate of interest, as Table A.5.2 in the Appendix indicates.

In 1976, when inflation rose from 33 to 47 per cent, the view that inflation had to be controlled through monetary policy gained strength within the government. The monetary policy then started focusing on two objectives: to prevent inflation from rising and to attract foreign 'saving'. The tight monetary policy – associated with the expansion of demand caused by the investment boom, persistent inflation and a highly concentrated financial structure – maintained significant upward pressure on the interest rate. The whole extent of that pressure was felt when, in 1976, interest rates were freed from ceilings and had a rapid growth.[17]

The high levels of interest rates resulted in a rapid rise of the financial costs of productive firms and of the participation of the financial system in the GNP. Given the high level of concentration in the Brazilian economy and the high levels of indebtedness, this increase in financial costs was directly transmitted to prices. Higher inflation increased the impetus of the monetary authority to absorb the excessive liquidity by issuing government bonds (LTN) and thus raising interest rates. The vicious circle of monetary policy and public indebtedness, which is described in number by Table 9.5, was set.

Another perverse result of such a policy was the link between internal and external debt, to which we draw attention next.

The link between internal and external debt

The government's attempt, at the same time, to reduce aggregate demand and attract foreign loans through the maintenance of high levels of interest rate created a direct link between the external and internal debt. This link has two very perverse facets: one short run, the other long run.

The short-run facet is summarised in Figure 9.7.[18] In this figure, the bold

Table 9.5 Some indicators of the vicious circle of the monetary policy and the link between public and foreign debts (1967–83)

Year	*Net issues of LTN and ORTN* (1)	*Treasury deficit* (2)	*Financial cost over deficit* (3)	*(4) = (1)/(2)*	*ORTN*[b,c] (5)	*LTN*[b,c] (6)	*Total* (7)= (5)+(6)	*Foreign debt*[b] (8)	*(9)= (7)/(8)%*
1967	448	−1,225	...	0,37	0.96	n.a.	0.96	3.78	25.5
1968	93	−1,227	...	0,08	1.08	n.a.	1.08	4.40	24.5
1969	797	−756	...	1,05	1.48	n.a.	1.48	5.30	27.9
1970	2 282	−738	...	3,09	2.21	0.16	2.38	6.62	35.9
1971	2 987	−672	...	4,44	2.21	0.74	2.95	9.52	31.0
1972	6 826	−512	...	13,33	2.71	1.73	4.45	12.57	35.4
1973	5 757	295	...	19,52	3.43	2.85	6.27	17.17	36.5
1974	−2 595	3,382	...	0,77	4.91	2.21	7.12	21.17	33.6
1975	31 649	73	20.5	433,55	7.58	4.72	12.30	25.99	47.3
1976	10 814	423	30.1	25,57	8.05	6.62	14.67	32.04	45.8
1977	22 136	1,043	28.7	21,22	8.68	8.80	17.47	43.51	40.2
1978	9 359	4,872	30.7	1,92	9.24	11.02	20.26	49.90	40.6
1979	−4 037	2,296	31.1	1,76	9.85	10.59	20.44	53.85	38.0
1980	57 834	2,035	30.6	28,42	11.72	5.15	16.87	61.41	27.5
1981	912 002	615	41.0	1482,93	22.40	12.43	34.82	70.20	49.6
1982	666 457	331	51.1	2013,47	39.35	8.99	48.34	81.32	59.4
1983	256 000	6,596	63.4	38,81	38.78	8.82	47.60	91.09	52.3

Sources: cols 1–3, 1967–80, Zini 1982: 258; 1981–3, FUNDAP 1988: 209; col. 5–6: FUNDAP 1988: 212

Notes: [a] In current Cr$ million.
[b] In US$ billion.
[c] Deflated by the implicit rate of exchanges as in IBGE 1985: 525.
[d] i, less than 0.0005.

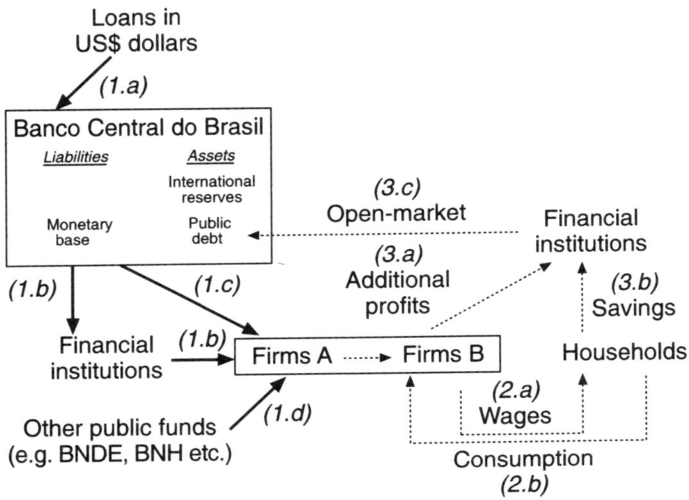

Figure 9.7

lines represent finance, the dotted lines describe the financial flows linked to the multiplier process and the broken lines symbolise the financial applications by the surplus units (firms and households); two firms are assumed: an investing firm A and a firm B which produces capital goods and wage-goods.[19] The causal links can be described as follows:

(1.a) A foreign loan is obtained either directly by a firm under Instruction 4131 (1.c in the figure) or by financial institutions under Resolution 63 (1.d in the figure).

(1.b) The money supply is expanded because of the increase in external debt beyond the requirements of the financing of balance of payments, resulting in accumulation of the international reserves; or (1.d) because of the expansion of subsidies and subsidised credit from public financial institutions in order to stimulate investments under the 1974 Plan.

(2) Such an expansion has a multiplier effect which ends up in additional profits, due to the high level of mark-up in Brazil's oligopolistic industries.

(3) In an attempt to reduce liquidity and thus the inflationary pressure the central bank increases interest rates in order to issue more government bonds. In turn, higher interest rates increase the financial costs due on the outstanding stock of debt.

The long-run facet is related to the fact that a significant part of the external debt incurred by public enterprises was used for expansion of the capacity to produce basic inputs. However, when such investment projects matured (by the end of the 1980s), these firms could not profit from their enhanced productive capacity as their prices were being controlled in the 1970s until 1983 as part of the government's anti-inflation policy. The result was that the government (through its enterprises) became the main external debtor, whereas the private sector was the main beneficiary from the externalities of public investment (see Werneck 1985: 564).

This schizophrenic long-term situation enhances the short-term perversity of the *ciranda financeira*, especially at the end of the 1970s and the beginning of the 1980s. Then the source of expansion of exports was mainly private enterprises whereas the foreign debt was in the hands of the public sector (see Castro and Souza 1985). In this case, the only way to repay the debt without further expanding the money supply was to accelerate the growth of internal debt and therefore promote the substitution of external public debt for internal public debt (Werneck 1985; and especially Cavalcanti 1988). This explains the increasing link between foreign and public debt (see Table 9.5).

Financial fragility

Even though the allocation of fiscal and para-fiscal funds to the non-financial private sector had significantly increased in the 1970s, this could not prevent the increase in financial fragility as the level of short-term corporate debt rose in the period from 1974 to 1979. The differences now, in relation to the period previous to the reforms of 1964–6, are twofold: first, a significant part of this debt was linked to obligations in foreign currency, either directly incurred by firms or intermediated by financial intermediaries. In both cases, however, the loans were based on floating interest rates, because of the conditions of credit in the 1970s international markets (on this, see, among others, Aglietta 1985). This created a direct link between the financial stability of the indigenous firms and the changes of monetary policies (and hence interest rates) in the Western economies – and especially in the United States.[20]

A second difference was the government's commitment to maintain high interest rates in the whole period between 1974 and 1979, rates which were liberalised in 1976.[21] Given the characteristics of the private lending institutions, which we have already discussed above, this liberalisation was likely to cause the explosion of the costs of borrowing for at least two reasons: first, the normally high mark-up maintained by banks which is linked to the basic rates, which, after indexation, were mainly determined by the rates on government indexed bonds; second, the tendency for this mark-up to rise with inflation, as the lender's risk increases.

The result of such an extraordinary conjunction of factors has been documented in several works on the financial behaviour of the non-financial firms in the 1970s and 1980s in Brazil.[22] Table 9.6 summarises some of the indicators of the increasing financial vulnerability of the productive sector in the 1970s and 1980s.

This table shows that neither the process of indebtedness in the 1970s nor the financial restructuring in the 1980s were equal for the private and public enterprises. This can be interpreted from what has been said above.

Let us take first the period of growth (roughly represented by the data from 1969 to 1977 in Table 9.6).[23] In this period, all firms increased their levels of indebtedness rapidly, as the rise of the debt–equity ratio (from 0.9 in 1969 to 1.3 in 1977) indicates (Figure 9.8). However, it is the private national enterprises which have the fastest increase in their debt ratios. This increase of indebtedness is closely followed by a rise in financial costs to all firms (from 3.9 per cent of their net operating income in 1969 to 6.9 per cent in 1977), but especially to the state enterprises (Figure 9.9). The reason for this disproportional increase of debt seems to be the fact that the size of these firms, and hence the need for financial levering, was smaller than foreign and public firms at the beginning of the Second National Development Plan. In turn, as pointed out above, the national firms had their sources of finance (public and foreign funds) significantly expanded after 1967. This contrasted with the public enterprises, which had their access to internal credit limited as part of the government's policy to capture 'foreign savings' using their firms for this purpose. Finally, as regards the foreign firms, their access to loans through Instruction 4131 provided a disguised form of foreign investment, but their role in the Second National Development Plan was much less prominent than that allotted to the public and national private enterprises.

In turn, the public enterprises were the group which had the fastest rise of their financial costs in relation to net operating income, a rise which was disproportionate to the performance of their debt–equity ratio. This has to do with two factors: first, the already mentioned fact that the government reduced the allocation of its subsidised credit to its

Table 9.6 Some indicators of the level of indebtedness and financial vulnerability of the corporate sector (by ownership of capital) (1969–83)

	1969	*1972*	*1975*	*1977*	*1978*	*1979*	*1980*	*1981*	*1982*	*1983*
Debt–equity ratios										
All firms	0.88	1.00	1.25	1.32	0.95	1.09	1.16	1.11	1.03	1.12
Private nationals	1.00	1.17	1.45	1.43	0.95	1.11	1.22	1.23	1.18	1.32
Foreign firms	0.82	1.17	1.45	1.43	0.93	0.96	0.93	0.83	0.72	0.68
State enterprises	0.80	0.82	0.91	1.15	0.96	1.09	1.16	1.11	1.03	1.12
Financial costs as percentage of the net operating income										
All firms	3.44	3.54	5.33	6.90	7.2	18.1	13.7	20.3	24.8	33.1
Private nationals	3.30	3.28	4.97	5.59	5.8	8.0	7.4	8.8	4.3	4.9
Foreign firms	3.57	3.43	5.10	6.78	5.2	7.0	5.7	7.9	9.1	12.1
State enterprises	4.22	7.32	10.75	18.16	10.5	37.9	26.3	39.4	49.3	64.1

Source: 1969–77, Zini 1984: 87; 1978–83, *Conjuntura Econômica*, April 1985: 70–3

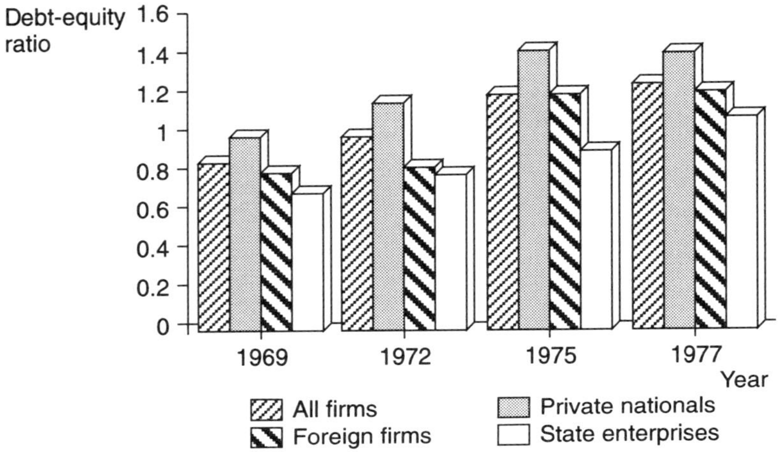

Figure 9.8
Source: Table 9.6

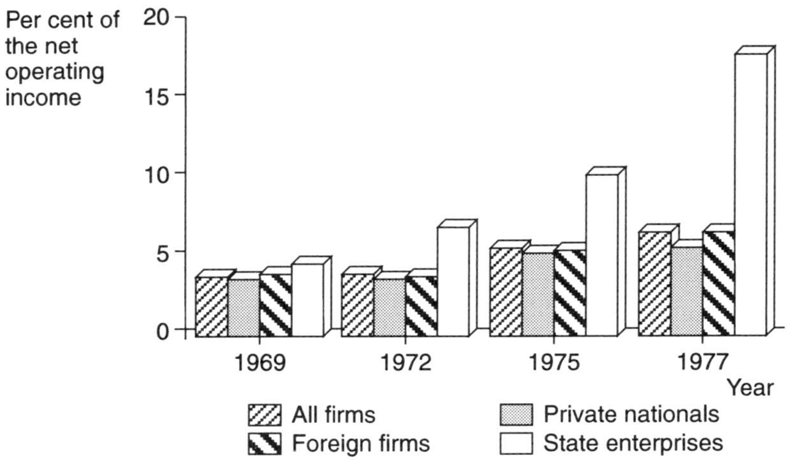

Figure 9.9
Source: Table 9.6

enterprises in favour of the private financial sector. The public firm was thus forced to finance its long-term investment by borrowing in much worse conditions than the private ones. Second, also already mentioned, these firms' capacity to increase prices was limited by the government's anti-inflationary policy.

At the beginning of the crisis in the early 1980s, Brazilian firms had very high levels of debt and were incurring further high levels of indebtedness. As was noted in Chapter 7, because of the degree of oligopoly of the corporate sector in Brazil, in periods of slow-down after an intensive accumulation, firms will attempt to reduce their financial vulnerability by increasing their prices so as to repay their outstanding debts. The period from 1978 to 1983 was no exception (Figures 9.10 and 9.11).

The differences in relation to the experience previous to 1964 are twofold: first, the process of financial restructuring implemented by the private non-financial sectors was very rapid, which avoided surges of financial instability. This rapid restructuring was made possible by the already mentioned mechanisms of financial speculation on the rising public debt, which meant higher interest rates for those firms which had sufficient mark-up power to create surplus amidst the crisis (see, for example, Almeida 1984). A second difference was the fact that the public enterprises' capacity to undertake their own financial restructuring was purposefully limited by the government's policies to reduce

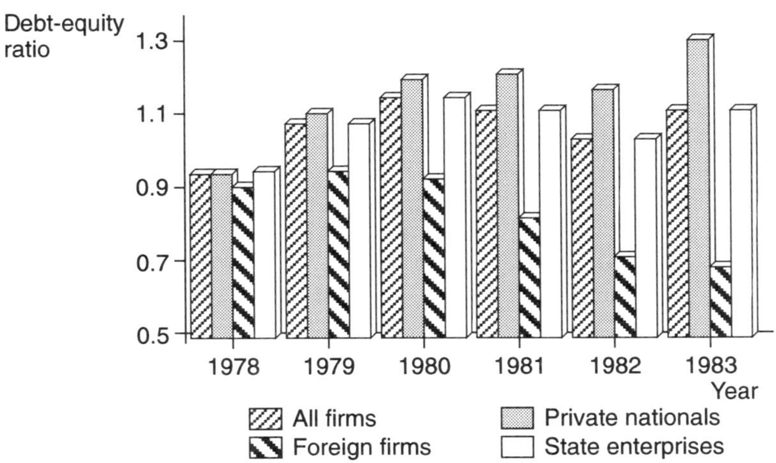

Figure 9.10
Source: Table 9.6

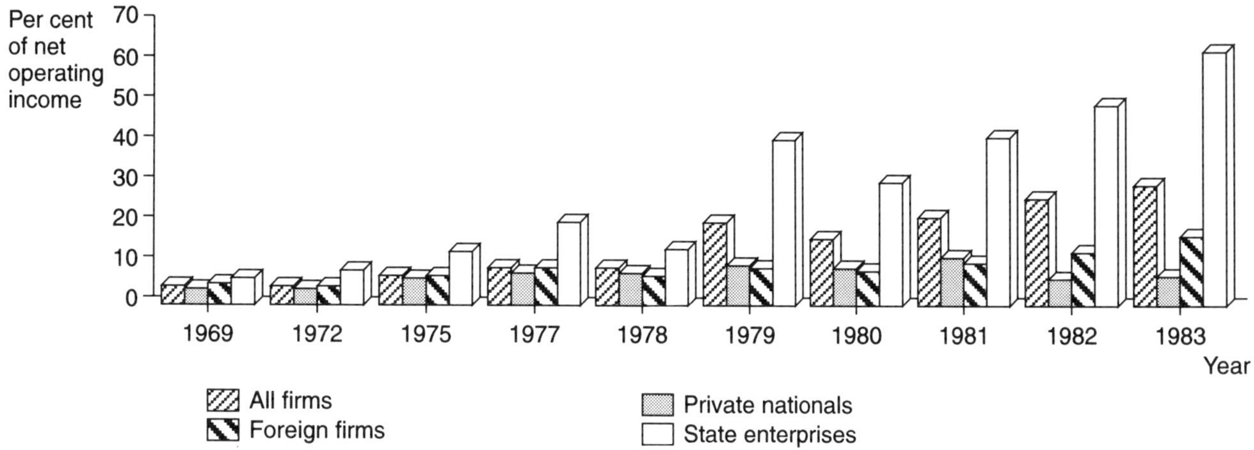

Figure 9.11
Source: Table 9.6

inflation and to attract foreign currency to finance the increasing costs of the external debt. As regards the policy to combat inflation, the public enterprises had their prices re-adjusted below the rate of inflation (see Werneck 1987). Given the increasing deficits of these firms, and the legal constraints imposed on them to obtain credit domestically, they were forced to borrow in foreign currency.

Thus, at the end of the 1970s Brazil's economy was in a process of deepening financial fragility. If this did not turn into financial instability, it was because firms were capable of restructuring financially, at the expense of transferring debts to both the central banks and the public enterprises. Not surprisingly, the main financial characteristic of the lost decade (i.e. the 1980s) was the disarray of the government's finance.

SUMMING UP

Brazil's 1964–6 financial reforms proved very successful in diversifying the financial structure of the country, especially in creating specialised institutions to deal with consumer and housing credit. This financial innovation increased the market for liquid assets by introducing short-term indexed assets which competed with non-indexed assets. It further provided the financial grounds for recovery and boom in the period 1967–73, mainly based on the use of the idle capacity accumulated after five years of recession between 1962 and 1966.

However, the reforms failed in one of their most important aspects: the development of private long-term financing mechanisms. In other words, the reforms created the basis for financial widening based on a competitive market of short-term financial assets, whose return depended basically on the indexed government bonds. But it failed to create the mechanisms to transform the enormous accumulation in financial wealth into funds which could support accumulation (i.e. long-term finance and funding of productive investment). The result was that an enormous financial wealth was accumulated at a much faster pace than the process of financing capital accumulation and with no direct link to capital accumulation. This created a highly speculative climate, which was enhanced by the orthodox monetary policy pursued from 1974 onwards.

As a consequence, when the limit of idle capacity was reached, and investment started increasing, the problem of financing long-term positions was even more acute than before the financial reform. The full extent of the constraint to growth imposed by the dysfunctional financial structure was only to be felt when accumulation accelerated in 1974, with the Second National Development Plan. Then the government had to rush in with *ad hoc* measures in order to increase the supply of finance to investment, including the hike of public funds intermediated by the private financial sector and the incentives for indigenous firms to become indebted in foreign currency. Despite the partial success in increasing these sources of finance, the government's monetary and external debt policies were never consistent with the attempt to accelerate accumulation given the financial structure inherited from the 1960s. With this structure, the mix of expansionary fiscal policy and conservative monetary policy ended up encouraging untenable external and internal debts and resulting in a highly speculative and financially fragile economy. The non-existence of internal private sources of funding created a system which was vulnerable to changes in the government's capacity to finance and to the credit conditions in the international financial markets. In addition to that, the process of financial deepening served only to increase the level of indebtedness within the private sector (based on consumer credit) and public debt, therefore increasing the susceptibility of the system to surges of financial instability.

Even though investment began to decelerate at the end of the 1970s, with the conclusion of many investment projects undertaken in the 1974 Plan, the significant recession of the beginning of the 1980s had to do with the government's desperate attempt to equilibrate the balance of payments in face of increasing external pressures for adjustment. The orthodox policies then adopted dragged the country into a financial trap, where the private and public firms, which had increased their productive capacity in the 1970s, could not benefit from the potential increase in profits. The only way a major surge of financial instability was avoided was to transfer the burden of the internal and external debts to government. Even though this was not seemingly a deliberate action, the transfer was permitted by government's policies from 1979 onwards. These included a monetary policy which raised the interest rates paid on the public debt, providing those firms with surpluses to obtain high capital gains through the speculation with government bonds; and a policy towards the public enterprises which reduced their relative prices and tariffs and forced them to borrow in foreign currency. The consequence was that the financial restructuring of the private sector took place to the detriment of the financial health of the government and its enterprises.

It must be stressed that the process of financial deterioration which has been described above is directly linked to the choices of development financing taken in the 1970s and the orthodox orientation of the government's policy, and not solely by the consecutive external oil and interest rate shocks (as the last military governments tried to establish). Finally, it cannot be forgotten that the Brazilian State has historically played an important leading role in Brazil's process of development, as we showed in the previous chapters and in this one. Therefore, the bankruptcy in which the State was left after 1983 is significantly responsible for the poor performance of the economy in the 'lost decade' and up to now.

Chapter 10

Conclusion

Every work in social science, theoretical or empirical, begins with a pre-scientific view of the subject under analysis. In our case, this view has been greatly influenced by Keynes's famous metaphor about the relation between investment and finance:

> The spectacle of modern investment markets has sometimes moved me towards the conclusion that to make the purchase of an investment permanent and indissoluble, like a marriage, except by reason of death or other grave cause, might be a useful remedy for our contemporary evils. For this would force the investor to direct his mind to the long-term prospects and to those only. But a little consideration of this expedient brings us up against a dilemma, and shows us how the liquidity of investment markets often facilitates, though it sometimes impedes, the course of new investment. For the fact that each individual investor flatters himself that his commitment is 'liquid' (though this cannot be true for all investors collectively) calms his nerves and makes him more willing to run a risk. If individual purchases of investments were rendered illiquid, this might seriously impede new investment, so long as *alternative ways* in which to hold his savings are available to the individual. This is the dilemma. So long as it is open to the individual to employ his wealth in hoarding or lending *money*, the alternative of purchasing actual capital assets cannot be rendered sufficiently attractive (especially to the man who does not manage the capital assets and knows very little about them), except by organising markets wherein these assets can be realised for money.
>
> (Keynes 1936: 161)

In this conclusion, Keynes's metaphor can be used to explain the view that guided this thesis. As Keynes noted, in an early stage of capitalism the act of investing was inseparable from the act of saving. This double act was performed by one entrepreneur or a group of entrepreneurs whose animal spirits prompted them to accumulate beyond the wealth previously obtained. Investment represented a long-term, financial and personal commitment for the entrepreneur which, as in marriage, was irrevocable.

This changed fundamentally with the development of the financial structure. To start with, the creation of banks with credit-creating capacity permitted investment projects to be undertaken independently of and prior to the accumulation of savings. This form of finance substantially increased the capitalist system's capacity to accumulate. In turn, this meant that, at least in its first stages, the marriage between finance and investment had to have the blessing of a bank. The bank's credit policy becomes the second most important causal agent in the dynamics of accumulation of capitalism.

A second important innovation which occurred in some countries (e.g. the United States and England) was the organisation of markets for shares and long-term securities. This innovation produced a further enhancement of banks' capacity to finance accumulation, as it opened up the possibility of mitigating the risk of long-term financial commitment. That is, now entrepreneurs could borrow short from banks with the prospect of funding their short-term debt by later issuing shares or long-term securities. For wealth-owners, the development of organised markets and the continuous trading in the secondary markets permitted them to hold equities without having to commit themselves to the marriage between finance and investment. In other words, with the existence of organised markets for securities, banks still had to give their blessing for the wedding, but now they could count on the mechanisms of funding to restrict the scope of their obligations of keeping the marriage together.

Despite Keynes's warnings that the 'prior-saving' assumption is a fallacious foundation to understand the financial sphere of capitalist economies, this view has become an established assumption in development economics. To use the above-mentioned metaphor, the mainstream view assumes that savers continue to be the bride in the marriage between finance and investment in an economy with a developed banking system. The financial systems have the important, though ancillary, role of arranging the wedding place (market) and acting as marriage-brokers, providing the information to both groom and bride so that they can evaluate the prospects of their marriage. Failures to achieve optimal levels of marriages must be only due to either lack of information or financial repression or both.

In our opinion, the problem with such an approach is neither the realism of the assumptions which lead to the view of long-term neutrality of money, nor the internal consistency of the models (this is hardly a good front of attack against neoclassical models). A more appropriate attack must fall on the paradigm used to depict modern capitalist economies which completely disregards the fundamental changes of the dynamics of accumulation which have been introduced by institutional evolution as regards the way such an accumulation is financed. In other words, it disregards the fact that with a credit-creating banking system, it is banks, and not savers, which finance investment. It is the bankers' decisions to finance and the entrepreneurial long-term expectations which are now the main determinants in the process of accumulation. Because it wrongly identifies the real source of finance, the prior-saving argument is misleading, and can be quite dangerous when used as a basis for policy.

We used Keynes's concept of a monetary-production economy as a paradigm on which to base our view on finance and growth. For Keynes, a market economy is better described as one in which the means of production are privately owned and output is organised by a profit-seeking class of entrepreneurs. Production decisions are necessarily forward-looking, and therefore entrepreneurial expectations are the main determinants of output and employment. Among those expectations, long-term expectations are the most volatile as the gap between the entrepreneur's decision to invest and the return on such an investment is more uncertain. This potential volatility is one of the two reasons which permitted Keynes to single it out as the *causa causans* in the dynamics of a market economy. The second one is the fact that, unlike other sources of demand (such as consumption), investment finance is independent of previous saving or current income.[1]

Having established the paradigm on which our analysis is based, we presented our view on the role of banks and financial markets in the determination of investment and growth. First, a stocks and flows model was used to confirm conclusively Keynes's and the post-Keynesians' assumption that banks, and not savers, are the main actors in the process of financing investment. Second, we showed that even though bank credit is essential to growth, the liability structure of banks does not normally allow long-term finance to be provided to investors. This means that, for the economy as a whole, credit permits the accumulation of illiquid assets, which are financed by a revolving fund of liquid assets. Third, we show that this type of financing tends to increase lender's and borrower's risk and the degree of systemic financial fragility. This can halt growth for microeconomic as well as for macroeconomic reasons: as regards the former, both banks and entrepreneurs may fear to expand even further their financial vulnerability; as regards the latter, financial fragility may deteriorate into financial instability as liquidity preferences of the lending institutions and borrowers rise. This is where the question of funding (i.e. the transformation of short-term debt into long-term position by issuing securities or equities) becomes so fundamental. It is funding which re-establishes the conditions for the marriage between the maturities of finance and investment, and therefore permits a more financially stable growth.

Because of the inherent uncertainty of real-life economies, savers are normally interested in acquiring financial assets as *liquidity time machines* (Davidson 1978) and not as a long-term commitment. Thus the above-mentioned marriage can only take place if the acquisition of long-term securities does not eliminate its holder's power of disposal. It is here that financial markets play an important role, as the continuous trading in the secondary markets allow the holding of assets which are illiquid for the community as a whole to be 'liquid' for the individual. Holdings of these assets represent saving: saving funds accumulation. Thus we established, from a post-Keynesian perspective, the role of saving and financial markets in supporting growth. This positive role, however, must be balanced with the potentially destabilising effects of speculation in those markets – which is the dilemma to which Keynes refers to in the quotation above. Having defined the roles of banks and financial markets in the process of growth, we offered the concept of functionality as a criterion to analyse financial markets as a counterpart to the neoclassical concept of efficiency. Functionality exists if, independently of its specific institutional characteristics, the financial system

1 has credit-creating capacity and this capacity is used to accommodate the additional demand for credit related to investment finance motive and to additional transactions demand;
2 has funding capacity which will reduce the increasing borrower's and lender's risks and reduce the risk of financial fragility which is inherent in the process of growth;
3 can maintain robustness throughout the process of growth, ensuring that increasing financial fragility does not degenerate into financial instability;
4 can avoid over-borrowing in foreign currency, reducing to the

minimum required the financial vulnerability of the economy to changes in credit conditions abroad.

Having established the theoretical reasons for the differentiation between finance and saving for a closed economy, we showed that this distinction must also be made in the analysis of the role of foreign capital flows in the financing of internal accumulation.

This story thus far depicts the basic institutional background with which Keynes developed his views on the finance and funding of accumulation in a developed market economy. This also allowed him to indicate the weakness of such a system through his theory of speculation. More recently, Minsky and others have used this institutional background to indicate the shortcomings of the financial basis of capitalist accumulation, which is inherently financially fragile. However, history shows that many other forms of organising the financial system can enhance the functionality of credit-based financial systems. For that, compensating structures or a consistent financial policy, or preferably both, must exist. This was our next topic.

Zysman's (1983) classification of a financial system into credit-based and capital-market-based structures was used to point out (from the post-Keynesian perspective developed thus far) the weaknesses and strengths of different financial structures. Further, we indicated that a fast-developing economy will tend to develop a credit-based financial system for three reasons. First, growth depends on additional credit, whatever the existing type of financial structure. Second, if growth is high, then even if the marginal propensity to buy placements out of households' saving is high enough, long-term funds will not be available to fund all existing outstanding short-term debt. Third, if development creates constant excess demand for financing short-term operations (working capital, for instance), financial institutions (especially banks) will have no competitive stimulus to finance long-term investment or to promote funding. Credit-based financial systems cannot support high levels of growth unless other financial arrangements are created to overcome the lack of mechanisms to fund investment and the increasing financial fragility inherent in growing economies. In many less developed countries (LDCs) the process of growth and structural change proceeds faster than one can expect the financial structure to develop, especially as regards the capacity to fund ongoing investments. This means that, unless other arrangements to overcome the gap between financial and economic development exist, growth will be constantly constrained by the lack of sources for financing or by surges of financial instability.

As regards our case study again it is possible to use Keynes's metaphor quoted at the beginning of this chapter to understand what happened in Brazil in the period under analysis. In the 1950s, private mechanisms to finance accumulation did not exist. The development of such mechanisms is definitely linked to the State's increasing role in leading the process of industrialisation. In this period then, it is the State which promoted the flirting between its own banking system and development agencies with private and public investment. The flirting never developed into marriage because the need to develop a proper mechanism to fund the investment was neglected. Public enterprises had access to long-term financing and finance was never a problem to foreign firms, but national private firms had to finance their investment through inflationary mechanisms. As a consequence, the mechanisms to finance accumulation were dependent on inflation not rising above a certain level and, especially, on the government's capacity to continue expanding its investment.

With the conclusion of the main investment projects of the Target Plan (1955–60), the above-mentioned mechanisms revealed their shortcomings. As investment was reduced, the highly indebted firms attempted to increase their liquidity positions by raising their mark-ups, which led to an acceleration of inflation. As inflation rose and the level of activity declined, the public deficit became chronic, which increased the already eminent pressure on government for stabilisation. The adjustment programme introduced by the government in 1962–6 increased, rather than reduced the problem.

The financial reforms introduced by the military *junta* from 1964 to 1966 represented the neoclassical response to the need to restructure the financial system. The State again intervened in order to promote the marriage between the financial system and the productive sector, so that accumulation could be resumed. However, unlike in the 1950s, the neoclassical reformers were misguided to choose individual saving as the bride, and the private financial sector as the best man. In order to stimulate the bride to make a commitment, the government offered high interest rates through the indexation of its own assets and opened up the access of indigenous firms to finance in foreign currency. Because the decision to finance lies, not on the individual saver, but on the lending institutions, indexation did not expand the private sources of finance. In contrast, the increase of the rates of interest augmented both lenders' and borrowers' risks, as the financial operation within the private sector became more speculative and more oriented to the short term.

As the bride did not show an intention to commit, the increasing impatience of the interventionist groups within the government led to the increase of the public financial system's role as financier of both public and private accumulation. When the need to resume the process of import-substitution arose in 1973, it is again the State which completely assumes that role, even though the Ministry of Finance remained convinced of the correctness of maintaining high interest rates to stimulate internal saving, to guarantee inflows of 'external saving' and to maintain price stability. The conjunction of high interest rates and increasing inflation and uncertainty stimulated even further speculation, in which both wealth-holders and the private financial system engaged. Now the bride chosen by the government became an evil mistress, exploiting every opportunity to gain financially from the financial disarray of the State. Because the State has for so long played the leading role in the process of development in Brazil, its imminent bankruptcy dragged the whole economy into the 'lost decade' of the 1980s. The financial system still seems to represent a major obstacle to the reassumption of development in Brazil. The fact that other problems (e.g. fighting inflation and restructuring the external debt) are now priority should not stop us from outlining a reform which could enhance the functionality of Brazil's financial system.

Hence, what lessons can be drawn from the Brazilian case? First, we must conclude that policy towards enhancing the functionality of the financial system for economic development should focus as much on an appropriate financial policy as on institutional development. As regards financial policy, it must be remembered that in a fast-growing economy, with constant pressure on finance, private financial institutions can profitably grow simply by providing short-run finance to credit-thirsty enterprises. Neither private banks nor other financial institutions will have the competitive stimulus to finance long-term positions. In this case, in order to grow firms will have to resort to short-term credit, self-finance or foreign indebtedness in order to implement their investment projects.

Second, we also conclude that it is naïve to expect that financial liberalisation and positive real rates of interest in themselves will be sufficient to solve the problem of the lack of long-term finance (and it may even prevent the solution of the problem). In fact, our analysis points out that, in a credit-based financial system, ceilings on interest rates may be rational mechanisms to avoid financial instability.

Third, with regard to institutional development, our conclusion is that this must be a long-term policy. Thin financial markets, which are the rule in LDCs, tend to be highly speculative and manipulated by a few big 'insiders'. This creates a comprehensive mistrust amongst most small savers and even some potential institutional investors (e.g. pension funds). Therefore, such development must be carried out with careful regulation by the authorities – regulation which can be loosened according to the development of such markets. It is unlikely though that complete deregulation will ever be compatible with financially stable growth.

Finally, it is important to remember that in countries where financial markets did not develop sufficiently to support financially stable growth, compensating structures were created – such as, for example, a strong commitment on the part of private banks (e.g. the German universal banks), the development of financial/corporate conglomerates (e.g. the Japanese financial/corporate conglomerates) or close government intervention such as the creation of development banks and the use of a regulated selective credit mechanism (e.g. the South Korean case). It seems that LDCs, and perhaps multilateral development agencies, have more to learn from these experiences than from the 'capital-market-based' paradigm of an efficient financial structure.

Notes

2 FINANCE AND ECONOMIC DEVELOPMENT

1 In Chick's (1983: 190) words: 'The ideological importance of this view of investment *resulting* from saving is clear enough: savers determined the rate of capital accumulation. The choices of households control the firms: consumer sovereignty determines current output and saving determines future output.'
2 For an analysis of the theory of saving and investment in economic history until Keynes, see Schumpeter (1954: 322–54).
3 On this, see Cameron *et al.* (1967) and below.
4 Chick's hypothesis that the proposition that investment precedes saving depends on the stage of development reached by the banks was already raised in her *Macroeconomics after Keynes* (1983: 190). This was certainly the main inspiration of her theory of the stages of the development of the banking system (Chick 1986). More on this theory in Chapter 3.
5 It is worth noting that although sharing the postulate of the long-term neutrality of money the theoretical agenda of the classical and neoclassical schools are different:

> in classical political economy the laws of motion are all proposed as a result of the interaction between elements such as the surplus rate, the organic composition of capital, real wages and so on. The central proposition of neoclassical theory refers to the reconciliation between limited availability of resources and the consumers' preferences obtained by the system of relative (real) prices. Money cannot influence the basic choices to be made, except to the extent that it can obscure the informational content of market prices. In the long run, when all erratic influences are cancelled out and agents learn to separate information from noise (created by monetary disturbance), all that matters is real variables.
>
> (Carvalho 1992: 32)

6 The neoclassical labour market can be described as follows. The labour supply schedule is upward sloping in the real-wage/employment space, so as to reflect the decline of marginal disutility of labour (as opposed to

leisure) as work hours increase. The labour demand curve is derived from the production function: assuming that capital is fixed (the Marshallian short period) and diminishing returns, the marginal productivity of labour declines with employment. Equilibrium in the goods market is achieved at the point where the real wage equals the marginal productivity of labour. Therefore, full employment – here defined as the non-existence of involuntary unemployment – is guaranteed as long as real wage flexibility prevails.

7 Of course, the assumption of short-run neutrality of money will depend on the pace of re-adjustment in the labour market after a change in money supply. Ever since the Phelps–Friedman reinterpretation of the Phillips curve (the expectations-augmented Phillips curve), the pace of adjustment has become a matter of how workers and firms adapt their expectations to changes in money supply. In the long run, however, Friedman (1968) established and most mainstream economists accepted that the Phillips curve is vertical. Finally, the rational expectations revolution restricted even further the scope for non-neutral money by claiming that not even in the short run did the trade-off between inflation and unemployment exist if some strong-form of rational expectations is assumed. For an extensive review, see Amadeo (1982).

8 If saving were not totally channelled to investment, aggregate demand would be inferior to aggregate supply. Then an increase of money supply to finance investment could increase the level of output.

9 The competitive capital market is one where information is freely available and there is no constraint on the price mechanisms and competition. For instance, the efficient markets hypothesis suggests that the prices of shares are the best available estimates of their 'real value' because information is made available in competitive stock markets – which implies that savers can count on past prices as a good guide for the actual value of a firm (weak-form efficiency) or that share prices fully reflect all publicly available information (strong-form efficiency). It is further implicit in financial models that if allocation is efficient at the microeconomic level it will be optimal at the macroeconomic level because a high return on the capital saved will mean a high productivity of the capital invested. Any fallacy of composition is assumed away.

10 On this see, for example, Leijonhufvud (1968), Robinson (1972), Davidson (1978), Chick (1983) and Carvalho (1992).

11 In Hicks's (1937) notation M is money, I is income, I_x is investment, C is the marginal efficiency of capital schedule, i is the interest rate and S is saving.

12 More on Keynes's liquidity preference theory of the interest rate in the next chapter.

13 In this framework it is argued, for instance, that an active monetary policy can stimulate growth by reducing the perceived return on money and thus forcing the substitution of money for capital in the portfolio of the agents (Tobin 1965). The effectiveness of monetary policy will then depend on (1) the expectations of savers/wealth-holders and (2) the degree of substitutability between assets.

14 The other front, as we mentioned in note 7, was the Phillips curve and the

effectiveness of monetary policy.

15 In this case, and with adaptive expectation as common ground, Keynesians would naturally assume that only financial assets and physical capital are close substitutes so that this monetary illusion would take the form of a higher propensity to invest. In contrast, monetarists would assume that other goods should also be included, so that the excess money would increase nominal demand and inflate prices. Monetary economics then became the analysis of short-term departures from equilibrium, which are caused by exogenous changes of money supply.

16 A detailed examination of the rational expectations macroeconomics is beyond the scope of the present chapter. For this, see, for example, Rogers (1989: ch. 3).

17 Blanchard and Fisher (1989) represents an extensive survey of the New Keynesian economics.

18 See Blanchard and Fisher (1989: 478–89) for a survey of New Keynesian models of credit rationing based on the theory of imperfect information.

19 Credit-worthiness here is defined, accordingly, as the capacity to repay which in the long run is associated with the return of the borrower's investment project. A recent application of this view that financial institutions are 'social accountants and screening devices for the allocation of credit' is found in Stiglitz and Weiss (1988).

20 Gertler (1988: 560, my emphasis). Most of such models stress the credit-rationing aspect of asymmetric information, whereas the financial markets are still seen as efficient allocators of resources. The exception, which will be discussed later, is the case of adverse selection which may have perverse allocative results.

21 See Stiglitz and Weiss (1981). See also Lewis (1992) for a review of contemporary mainstream theory on the banking firm under the assumption of asymmetric information.

22 In particular banks are seen as mere 'social accountants and screening devices for the allocation of credit' (Stiglitz and Weiss 1988) or 'delegated monitors of borrowers on behalf of the depositors' (Diamond 1984). Asymmetric information only reduces, but does not change, this 'essential' role of banks as intermediaries between savers and investors.

23 This identification between saving and finance has led to very awkward results in the attempts to introduce money explicitly into growth analysis. In neoclassical growth models it is assumed that is the relative rates of return that regulate the allocation of wealth into the several existing assets. Usually two assets are considered: physical capital and money balances. Hence, as we have shown above, growth can be speeded up by decreasing the rate of return on money in relation to the rate of return on capital (e.g. Tobin 1965; Johnson 1967; Patinkin and Levhari 1968). The same sort of argument has led to the theoretical conclusion that growth is faster in a barter economy (where money is not a choice in the allocation of wealth and saving is always channelled towards investment) than in a monetary economy. Therefore financial development is seen as a deterrent to growth.

24 Actually, there is no independent investment function in Solow's model either.

25 For a discussion of the evolution of growth theory see Sen (1970) and Simonsen (1991).

26 In their own words:

> The portfolios of surplus spending units deteriorate, as bonds or illiquid assets gain relative to liquidity in money form. This decline in the liquidity index of their portfolios may induce surplus units to express a *diversification demand* for additional money balances that does not depend on speculative and precautionary considerations of the Keynesian short-run liquidity preference. With the money supply given, the diversification demand may bring about a rise in interest rates that can depress national income below its initial level ... Because of debt accumulation, equilibrium at the given level of income is threatened. Just as investment may add to output capacity and so jeopardize the level of national income, the issue of debt through the channels of direct finance may have its deflationary impact through the responses of both deficit and surplus units.
>
> (Gurley and Shaw 1955: 515–6; their emphasis)

27 As Cameron remarked once, 'stimulating and perceptive though it is, the financial institutions are considered [by Gurley and Shaw] to be mere automatons, appearing to supply the demand for financial assets mechanically' (Cameron *et al.* 1967: 7).

28 In a similar vein, recently the World Bank and the IMF expressed concerns about the shortage of world savings and its impact on LDC's growth. On this, see Lal (1991).

29 The two-gap model was initially developed by Chenery and his associates, culminating in Chenery and Strout's (1966) classic article. The article was reviewed by Fei and Ranis (1968), who also provided a simplified version of Chenery and Strout's two-gap models. We have used Fei and Ranis's simplified version here, only changing the symbols V (GNP) for Y and E (export) for X, as used in the rest of this book.

30 Notice that either of the two implies the other, i.e. if $X_0 = M_0$ then $kr = m'$.

31 For a summary of the three-fold process of development in the Chenery–Strout model see Fei and Ranis (1968). The latter also strongly criticise what they call the *ad hoc* mechanical character of those stages (1968: 907) and the empirical analysis found in the Chenery–Strout model. For a reply see Chenery and Strout (1968).

32 See for instance the World Bank (1989) report on development and financial structure.

33 Other liberalising recommendations that also commonly follow from this framework are directed towards reducing government's 'overcrowding' in the capital markets by tightening fiscal and monetary policies and liberalising exchange rates. These are meant to re-establish the sovereignty of prices in the allocation of resources.

34 This 'institution-less' approach contrasts even with the seminal work of McKinnon (1973), much of which is devoted to institutional analysis.

35 For alternative models within the same framework see Galbis (1977), Mathieson (1980) and Cho (1986). Fry (1989) presents a good survey of some other models based on the Shaw–McKinnon framework.

36 For a review of McKinnon's hypothesis of money–capital complementarity

within a three period life-cycle model, see Molho (1986).

37 In reality, in Kumar's (1983: 22) model this 'private saving' corresponds to the real aggregate profit – i.e. it is equal to the total income minus the wage costs (as usual other costs are ignored).

38 In Kumar's model, aggregate saving is defined as the 'social propensity to save out of income' ($s = s' + [d/dt(M/P)]/Y - G/Y$) multiplied by current income (Y).

39 The model presented below assumes a closed economy and all variables (except M and P, obviously) are expressed in real terms.

40 For instance, the technological disparity between modern and traditional sectors in LDCs is commonly associated with selective credit policies which encourage the choice of capital-intensive technologies, despite the existence of abundant labour. Since non-priority sectors do not receive subsidised credit, the technological gap would tend to widen with financial repression (Fry 1989: *passim*).

3 DEPARTING FROM THE PRIOR-SAVING ARGUMENT

1 This is not the place to make a restatement of the philosophical meaning of such an approach, as here we are only concerned with the consequences of such an alternative view of the way market economies operate. Shackle (e.g. 1955) is the most eminent post-Keynesian theorist on the role of uncertainty in economic modelling from a post-Keynesian. For a concise, but precise, discussion of the Shacklean approach, see Dixon (1986).

2 Tony Lawson (1985) 'Uncertainty and economic analysis', *Economic Journal* 95, December: 914; as quoted in Davidson (1978: 333).

3 Money is demanded for two basic reasons: as a medium of exchange and as a store of wealth. Even though the store-of-wealth function of money is singled out by most mainstream monetary economic textbooks, only in an uncertain (non-ergodic) world does it makes sense to hold money as a store of wealth:

> Money, it is well known, serves two principal purposes. By acting as a money of account it facilitates exchanges without its being necessary that it should ever itself come into picture as being a substantive object. In this respect it is a convenience which is devoid of significance or real influence. In the second place, it is a store of wealth. So are we told, without a smile on the face. But in the [ergodic] world of the classical economic, what an insane use to put it! For it is a recognised characteristic of money as a store of wealth that it is barren; whereas practically every other form of storing wealth yields some interest or profit. Why should anyone outside a lunatic asylum wish to use money as a store of wealth?
>
> (1937a: 116)

4 Money is also important because it provides its holder with the ability to postpone consumption or investment decisions. More on this later.

5 For a detailed examination see Amadeo (1991).

6 In this respect, as Amadeo (1991: 11) rightly points out, the similarity of

Keynes's refutation of Say's law (i.e. his principle of effective demand) is staggeringly similar to Marx's criticism of Ricardo:

> Marx argued that when money is introduced and the separation of the acts of selling and buying is recognized, the possibility of a breakdown in the 'metamorphosis of commodity' – the circular flow of income – becomes evident. The possibility of crisis is even stronger in a capitalist economy, continues Marx's argument, where the motivation to produce is not the production of use values but the creation and realization of surplus value.

7 As Chick (1983: 65–6) points out, three assumptions are required to obtained the *Z* curve of Figure 3.1: (i) atomistic firms; (ii) labour is the only variable factor of production to be taken into account; and (iii) the composition of output and demand does not change with the overall volume of output, *Q*.

8 In his text *The general theory of employment* Keynes is explicit about his assumption on short-term expectations:

> We assume that the *existing* state of opinion as expressed in prices and the character of existing is based on a *correct* summing up of future prospects, so that we can accept it as such unless and until something new and relevant comes into the picture.
>
> (1937a: 115)

9 In Keynes's words:

> our basis of knowledge for estimating the yields ten years hence of a railway, a copper mine, a textile factory, the goodwill of a patient's medicine, an Atlantic liner, a building in the City of London amounts to little and sometimes nothing; or even five years hence. In fact, those who seriously attempt to make any such estimate are often so much in minority that their behaviour does not govern the market.
>
> (1936: 149–50)

10 'Asset' here is defined broadly, i.e. it can be either a physical asset (consumption or investment) or a financial asset.

11 Following Carvalho (1992: 89) the variable *r* replaces Keynes's *l* as the measurement of risk (which, as that author reminds us, should not be confused with probability risk) ascertained for each asset according to the expected losses in money terms involved in its conversion into a means of payment. With this amendment, the starting point of the ascending scale is the return on the most liquid asset.

12 As Carvalho (1992: 100–1) points out, even spot transactions involve a contract by which one party is committed to the immediate delivery of a certain good/service and the other to the immediate payment. See also Keynes (1930: 4).

13 Keynes himself explicitly corroborated this interpretation in his discussion of the finance motive (e.g. Keynes 1939: 283–4).

14 On this see also Schumpeter (1934).

15 This of course is even more true in an overdraft system, where banks must

accommodate any level of their clients' demand for credit within pre-arranged credit (or overdraft) limits. However, one may imagine that even in a lend-over-the-counter system, a bank's refusal of a good client's demand for additional credit can cost it the loss of clientele, especially in times of expansion.

16 Of course the level of voluntary reserves in the form of cash that banks hold is also influenced by the stage of development of financial markets. In a very developed financial market (such as in Chick's stage 5) bank loans become themselves marketable securities, so that the level of reserves can be dramatically reduced.

17 In this vein, securitisation can be seen as one of many other innovations created by banks to reduce the risk of holding non-marketable assets.

18 See also Winnet (1992) and Carvalho (1992).

19 See, among others, Moore (1989) and Heise (1992). In a perfectly competitive environment with no uncertainty, in the long run the profit-maximizing lending rate r_l would be set according to the average deposit rate r_d and the reserves ratio τ: $r_l = r_d/(1 - \tau)$.

20 Notice that the bank's 'liquidity' is only one sign of change of uncertain expectations. Inflation is also likely to provoke a wide *m*, because uncertainty increases (see Frenkel 1979). More on this in Chapter 8.

21 This is the case when capital markets are underdeveloped or non-existent. For reasons that will be discussed in the next chapter, in this case lender's and borrower's risks will be greater. In turn, banks will restrain from financing long-term positions and borrowers will search for alternative sources of finance.

4 SAVING AND FINANCIAL MARKETS IN ECONOMIC GROWTH

1 See Keynes (1936; 1937b, c; 1938; 1939), Robertson (1937a, b) and Ohlin (1937a, b).

2 Uncertainty in portfolio choice decisions, which represents a crucial aspect of Keynes's theory, will be addressed later.

3 Banks' liquidity can be measured by the difference between the turnover of their assets in relation to the turnover of their liabilities. However, assuming that all deposits are demand deposits, the reserve ratio/deposit (row 15 of Table 4.1) may be used as a measure of banks' liquidity.

4 This should not be confused with the identity between saving and investment. At any point aggregate saving will correspond to the non-consumed income, which is held either in a definite form (securities) or in the form of additional transactions balances (deposits). On this see Chick (1984).

5 Keynes (*C.W.* XXIX: 222).

6 The other possibility is to borrow from the international banking system, even though this demand for finance may not be directly related to the acquisition of a capital good from abroad. In this case, the additional supply of finance will come from the central banks' conversion of the loans into national currency, which is exactly as if the monetary authority had decided

to accommodate the additional demand for money by expanding the monetary base. This possibility will be analysed below in more detail.

7 As Keynes pointed out:

> The rate of prior saving only tells us how much of the current investment can find a permanent home beforehand without upsetting the liquidity position and the long-term rate of interest, and without time lag. Subject to these conditions, the *increment* of current investment over prior investment (or saving) can only be cared for *permanently* out of the increment of *current* saving; and the period during which current savings are kept liquid by their owners must be bridged by an increase in the revolving fund of 'finance', i.e., of liquid funds provided by the banking system or by dehoarding. It is the rôle of the credit system to provide the liquid funds which are required first of all by the entrepreneur during the period before his actual expenditure, and then by the recipients of this expenditure during the period before they have decided how to employ it.
>
> (Keynes 1939: 284–5, my emphasis)

8 Minsky gives another more trivial example of *Ponzi finance* which is a current part of business in market economies, i.e. a firm in a highly seasonal industry that pays equal quarterly dividends through the year, even though it does not earn enough to meet its dividends (1986: 340). Another example, to which we shall return later, is the rapid increase of LDCs' indebtedness after the so-called first oil shock. In that period, most LDCs faced severe balance-of-payment crises which could be reversed in the short run. If there was any rationality in the lending of that rising mountain of credit, it lied on the expectations that, in the long run, LDCs could restructure their productive sector and increase their exports, reversing the flow of capital towards the repayment of their external debts. Whether these expectations could ever be fulfilled is debatable; the fact is that the sharp rise of interest, especially after 1979, degenerated the speculative and Ponzi character of the financing of LDCs into the debt crisis of the 1980s.

9 In this same vein, persistent inflation will increase the liquidity preference of the banking firm because this increases the lender's risk. This will, accordingly, result either in credit rationing or in a preference for shorter-term loans, or both. The application of such an adaptation of Minsky's model to the analysis of the behaviour of the banking firm under inflationary circumstances will be seen in Chapters 6–8, which analyse the Brazilian experience.

10 The underwriter bears the responsibility for the acquisition of the securities which are not absorbed by the market after the price offered reaches a pre-established minimum. So the institution must be prepared to take up shares if called upon to do so, and therefore it must have access to cash when this occurs. This access can be provided by credit lines with banks, but it may also be necessary to sell some of its assets. Since its assets are likely to primarily be securities, then secondary markets are obviously useful to provide the underwriter with cash when it is required.

5 FINANCIAL STRUCTURES, FINANCIAL DEVELOPMENT AND ECONOMIC DEVELOPMENT

1 See Gerschenkron (1962), Cameron *et al.* (1967) and Kennedy (1987).
2 This explains why the proportion of banks' assets in national income grew so fast: in 1775, 1800, 1825 and 1844 the ratios were respectively 15.2, 27.9, 29.6 and 34.4 per cent (Cameron *et al.* 1967).
3 Indeed, personal thrift was also a very important source of finance. For instance: 'The usual practice among English industrialists, especially in the early days of the Industrial Revolution, was to allow themselves 5 per cent on their invested capital for living expenses. Only the net income in excess of that amount was called profit, and it was usually reinvested in the business' (Cameron *et al.* 1967: 39).
4 Data from Phyllis Deane's 'Capital formation in Britain before the railway age', *Economic and Cultural Change* IX (April, 1961); quoted in Cameron *et al.* (1967: 17).
5 In fact Pollard (1964: 301–2) showed a range of numerical examples where the ratio of fixed capital to stocks varied from 8 to 12 per cent.
6 See Table 5.2 for the pace of growth and accumulation in the recent experiences of development.
7 Up until now although the banking system is mostly private, it depends strongly on the central bank for access to supplementary deposits. In all these cases government sets interest rates and limits on collateral requirements (Wade 1989: 133).
8 In fact, our analysis points out that, in a credit-based financial system, ceilings on interest rates may be rational mechanisms to avoid financial instability. This conclusion has been stressed by many neo-structuralist economists. See, for example, Taylor (1991: 111–24) and Dutt (1990–1).

6 FROM THEORY TO EVIDENCE

1 The BNDE was created in 1952 to finance investment made by public enterprises, using public funds and other transfers for this purpose. Only in the 1970s did the BNDE begin to finance national private companies as well.
2 This was indeed the case of Brazil after the 1964–6 financial reforms. That is, a rapid process of financial deepening is observed, but this process served more to stimulate financial speculation and much less to increase the supply of loanable funds to finance working capital and investment. But more on this later.

7 FINANCIAL SYSTEM AND INDUSTRIALISATION IN BRAZIL, 1947–66

1 In 1940 31.2 per cent of Brazil's population lived in the urban areas; already in 1950 this proportion had risen to 36.2 per cent; and in the 1960s, 44.9 per cent (Ludwick, 1978: 57–8).
2 See Lessa (1982). In the 1950s and 1960s this interventionist approach to

development was shared by most international development agencies, such as the United Nations agencies (especially the ECLA) and even by the American government. On this see FitzGerald and Vos (1989).

3 During the war, Brazil became a main supplier of primary goods to the belligerent nations. In addition to the forced decline in imports, this caused a fast accumulation of international reserves of US$9,399.0 million. However, a significant part of these reserves were not convertible (Malan *et al.* 1980: 394) and most of them were quickly depleted with the end of conflict. This quick depletion was due to three main factors. First, the demand for consumer and capital goods was very repressed during the whole war period. Second, after the fall of the Vargas dictatorship government, the provisional Dutra government assumed a liberal exchange policy by abolishing the official exchange market (Instruction 17 of 1947) and an 'open door' policy to imports. This policy stimulated imports significantly: the exchange rate of Cr$18.50/US$ was fixed until 1953 (despite the average annual inflation of 15 per cent) and taxation on exports was almost absent (see Lessa 1982: 16–17). Third, 'allied countries', such as the English, used their political influence to force the Brazilian government to accept physical assets in the country (such as railways) in the repayment of outstanding debts (see Pereira 1983: 22–3).

4 The political background of the American commitment to the industrial development in Brazil can be found in the deepening of the 'cold war' and the fear that the political tensions created by a frustrated process of development would open ways to the 'red threat'. The solution was to enhance a market development, based on private enterprise. On this see FitzGerald (1989).

5 Unless otherwise stated, all macroeconomic data quoted in this chapter are drawn from the statistical appendix.

6 See Lessa (1982) for detailed data on growth of specific productive sectors in this period.

7 This partly explains the emergence and rapid growth of the market for discounting bills of exchange in the beginning of the 1960s. This market was to become the only private source of medium-term credit in Brazil. More on the development of this market below.

8 Investment over GNP declined steadily from 20.6 per cent in 1959 to 15.1 per cent in 1961 and the decline of accumulation was more intense in the private sector, whose investment decreased in real terms by 19.1 per cent and 12.1 per cent, respectively in 1960 and 1961; government investment continued to grow (19.3 per cent and 12.8 per cent respectively in 1960 and 1961). The growth of GNP declined from an average 7.6 per cent in the period 1947–61 to 1.1 per cent in 1961, and then a further decline of 0.6 per cent in 1962; though this affected all the productive sectors, it was the industrial sector which had the greatest reduction in the rate of growth, contracting by 4.7 per cent in 1965.

9 Even at the beginning of the economic slow-down, the political demands on the government became polarised, with some sectors demanding stabilisation and resumption of growth and others demanding structural reforms, which included land reform and income redistribution. The

existence of such divergent demands was a direct result of the characteristics of the industrialisation of the previous period, which accelerated the process of urbanisation and 'proletarisation' of the working class without attempting to reduce the income distribution gap between different economic strata.

10 A summary of these reforms can be found in Moura da Silva (1979: 10–11). Two are worth mentioning here: (1) the introduction of monetary correction for fiscal debts, which reduced the stimulus for postponing payment as inflation grew; (2) the centralisation of the fiscal administration in the federal government and prevention of Congress raising the total government expenditure in the federal government budget.

11 According to Resende (1982) the real minimum wage in Rio de Janeiro in March 1967 was only 83 per cent of its correspondent in January 1952. Even though the decline of the real minimum wage began in 1959, it is in the period 1964–6 that it suffered its heaviest loss. The indices of the real minimum wage from Resende (1982: 779) were

Period	1/52	6/54	7/56	1/59	10/60	1/63	3/64	3/65	3/66	3/67
Index	100	127	135	146	136	122	126	103	91	83

12 As Sochaczewski (1980: 25) points out, until slavery was abolished (in 1888), the demand for long-term finance came mainly from producers wanting to acquire slaves; this was usually supplied by the slave traders themselves. Working capital needs for the extensive agriculture practised then (especially coffee) were low, since there were almost no wage costs and the raw material consisted basically of seeds saved for production. It is only when the slave trade was abolished that working capital needs increased (in order to pay wages to the immigrant workers) at the same time, as the main source of collateral for loans (slaves) disapeared. Not surprisingly, in 1888 banking regulation forced the banks to make rural loans and the parliamentary Decree which abolished slavery was followed by the determination that Banco do Brasil would provide grants to support former slave owners.

13 Indeed the role of the stock market was so limited that stock exchange indexes only appeared in 1954 (*Conjuntura Econômica*, November 1972: 49–52).

14 Estimates from MiniPlan (1965: 59).

15 There were two main legal ceilings on deposit and loan rates: the usury law and the gold clause. The usury law (Decree 22.262 of 1933) limited nominal interest rates on almost all financial transactions to 12 per cent, whilst the loan rate to agriculture was further limited to 6 per cent. The gold clause (Decree 23.501 of 1933) declared null any contract denominated in gold or foreign currency, so that any kind of indexation was legally prohibited.

16 On this see Tavares (1972: 146).

17 This hypothesis is further analysed in Chapter 8 when the effects of introducing indexation following the financial reforms of 1964–6 are discussed.

18 These figures do not include the expenditures with the construction of Brasilia. According to Sochaczewski (1980: 113), the majority of the financing of the new federal capital actually came from public funds in the

following amounts (in constant 1961 thousand cruzeiros): 1957, 8,000; 1958, 11,000; 1959, 23,000; 1960, 35,300; 1961, 16,300. Leff (1968: 39) claims that if those expenditures were included, the government's share in the total capital formation would be the following: 1957, 51.2 per cent; 1958, 46.5 per cent; 1959, 58.8 per cent.

19 This tax was created in 1951 by Law 1518 of 24 November 1951 and was valid until 26 November 1966. The additional rate was 15 per cent on personal income and retained profits. The tax was partially refunded after five years with 25 per cent additional bonus in special government bonds and its total amount could be claimed in twenty annual instalments.

20 In qualitative terms, however, it represented a great support especially for public enterprises, to which 90 per cent of its funds were allocated. Also the BNDE was, and has remained, not merely a development bank but a development agency and a research institution as well.

21 Interestingly, this financial arrangement also provided the private sector with sources for its own investment, an issue that is discussed below.

22 This is not a purely technical requirement, since, as we have seen, external finance was not such an important variable in the overall financing of internal accumulation. However, this was an important political factor, for once the stock of external debt becomes significant, if refinancing is not forthcoming, repayments become conditional on a drain of internal real resources (i.e. an inversion of the RRT). In the latter case, the limits on the capacity to expand exports rapidly enough may force the government to adopt stabilisation programmes which, following the recipe dictated by the orthodoxy of the international financial institutions, may reduce government investment, creating a reduction of overall demand which discourages private investment. This was indeed the case in 1961.

23 As Tavares (1972) and Serra (1982) point out, productive capacity in many investment projects in the capital goods and consumer durables sectors was oversized. Serra (1982: 83) explains the three main reasons behind this phenomenon: the requirement of a minimum scale of production in the face of a limited market size, competition for market shares between transnational enterprises (leading to the creation of entry barriers) and the need to guarantee a future share of the market.

8 THE FINANCIAL REFORMS AND THE 'ECONOMIC MIRACLE'

1 The following passage from an official document, which presents the government's stabilisation policy, gives the liberal tone which would guide the reforms: 'The government action in the democratic political systems must be oriented towards the establishment of the conditions which warrant maximum efficiency to the functioning of the free-market economies. In this context, the economic planning will implement measures that will create the order in which the market forces will function ...' (MiniPlan 1965, quoted in Almeida 1984: 5).

2 The logic behind the new wage policy was exactly the opposite of the logic applied to the reform of the financial market: whereas in the latter market

inefficiency had been caused by excessive regulation (e.g. usury law, gold clause and the unfair competition of official banks) in the labour market inefficiency was caused by the excessive populism of the previous government, which allowed wages to rise beyond the increase of labour productivity. Therefore, the new wage policy redefined the method of re-adjusting wages (the minimum wage, wages of public servants and of workers in the private sector), which became pegged to an official index. Since this index was repeatedly below inflation, this procedure significantly compressed the real wage in a short period of time.

3 See, for example, MiniPlan (1965: 77). This position is also indicated by an interview given by Bulhões Pedreira (BP) and Teixeira da Costa (TC), two of those mainly responsible for the drafting and implementing of the Capital Market Reform, to Maria Conceição Tavares (MCT) in the *Bulletin*, Instituto de Economia Industrial, Universidade Federal de Rio de Janeiro, no. 14, June 1980. For the sake of making the position of the reformers clear, it is worth reproducing a part of this interview:

MCT: According to the logic of the 1964 Capital Market Reform, who would be the saver? Would it be the small saver?

BP: ... The guideline of the reform was the following: in order to organise a market a brokerage system is required ... ; if this system exists, it will, by itself, look for investors. The simple fact that shares are issued also helps to create saving. If there is no share in which to invest, the saver will end up spending. If there is a broker after you, you might buy ...

...

MCT: I insist on the question, because it is not clear to me who would be the saver in this market. Was it thought, for instance, that the multinationals, which have sufficient retained profits to finance their investment projects and to maintain surplus balances, could be interested in acquiring shares ... [For,] unless you could suppose so ... I do not see how one could develop a stock market [based on households' savings ...]

BP: There was no intention to create the whole market from scratch. First of all, before 1965 ... there already existed a stock market in which shares were issued. It is true that by the end of the 1950s inflation and the emergence of the market in bills of exchange made the development of the stock market difficult. The intention was [then] to create an institutional framework for a brokerage system; it was not assumed that there was enough saving to finance all investment, but there was a need to stimulate saving. However one obvious fact existed: some savings were being invested in real estate. Therefore there were indeed some savings [being unproductively used ...]. ... the development of the stock market required then the execution of the law, the creation of the brokerage system, in the shifting of savings from real estate to other forms of [productive] investment. ... It is obvious that, [because] real estate investment in Brazil has so many fiscal incentives, it is difficult to convince the individual investor to opt for shares ... The aim of the

> reform was to improve the institutional framework so as to make such changes possible [i.e. the shifting of saving towards productive investment] . . .

In the interview with Teixeira da Costa a similar argument is reproduced:

MCT: . . . what I am asking is whether you ever wondered whether previous 'savings' were available, ready to be re-shifted . . . I have never learned of a case of a stock market being developed by putting brokers after individual savers. Why did one not think from the start of insurance companies [as institutional savers]?

TC: I confess that I am part of the group that romantically thought that, in order to have a really capitalist society, there need be an individual participation in the market, independent from the institutional environment . . .

4 For an extended description of the government's view on the question of the need of external saving and of the logic behind the policy implemented in the period from 1967 to 1973, see Banco Central do Brasil (1973: 11–39).

5 Law 4131 of 24 October 1962.

6 Respectively through SUMOC's Instruction 289 of 24 January 1965, and Resolutions 63 of 21 August 1964 and 64 of 23 August 1967.

7 On this link, see Chapter 6.

8 There is a clear circularity in this argument, but this did not seem to bother the reformers.

9 The other was the creation of investment banks, as will be seen later.

10 That is, loans which were not funded by transfers of public funds or foreign borrowing.

11 In fact, the cost of borrowing through Resolution 63 in real terms was not smaller than borrowing from any commercial banks or finance companies. But the maturities of the loans were in general longer for Resolution 63 loans.

12 Resolution 45 of 30 December.

13 For instance, (1) tax exemption on dividend payments for joint-stock companies (whereas all other companies would have to pay 5 per cent tax on dividends); (2) lower direct taxation for joint-stock companies' shareholders; (3) tax exemption on capital gains due to the differential between market stock prices and declared value of capital (Article 58 of Law 1728).

14 That is, the big investors such as big corporations and financial institutions themselves, who have the time and the money to establish financial departments with the specific task of making capital gains with such financial transactions. The small investor remained dependent on financial intermediaries and generally invested in financial assets as a form of hedge against inflation.

9 TOWARDS THE LOST DECADE

1 In this figure, the data on utilisation of productive capacity in the industrial sector (CU) was obtained from Serra (1982: 102). We estimated the level of potential output in the period from 1964 to 1973 by applying the average

capital output ratio (COR) to the series of capital stock. From 1974 on, because of the investments in capital-intensive sectors of the 1974 Plan, we assume that the COR is rising at a geometric average rate, so that CU was estimated as follows:

$$CU_{1974+t} = \left(\frac{COR_{1984}}{COR_{1980}}\right)^{t/4} CU_{1974}$$

Needless to say, this is a rough estimate; but it is nonetheless consistent with other data on the path of growth in industrial output and investment.

2 This is a dynamic problem in any demand-led growth, but especially in the Brazilian economic model, which has always excluded a significant part of the population from the progress achieved in the productive sectors. This contrasts, for instance, with the process of economic development in the United States, where the above-mentioned dynamic problem could be solved by widening the market for consumption goods, as with the Taylorist mass-consumption model.

3 Unless otherwise stated, all macroeconomic data related to growth, inflation and the external sector are summarised in Tables A.1.2 and A.2.2 in the Appendix.

4 For more detailed data, see Castro and Souza (1985) and Batista (1986).

5 It is common to blame the external shocks for such imbalances. In contrast, and without neglecting the destabilising effects of such shocks, we maintain that the financial structure inherited from the reforms of 1964–6 and the orthodox policies in the mid-1970s are responsible for much of this macroeconomic imbalance. More on this below.

6 The increase of indebtedness was a characteristic of the period of the implementation of the 1974 Plan. This was expected in the light of the approach so far embraced: i.e. in economies with a credit-based system an increase of accumulation tends to be closely linked to the debt of the corporate sector. The growth of such indebtedness and its consequences for the financial instability of Brazil's economy after the 1974 Plan will be analysed from page 157.

7 See Table A.7 in the Appendix for detailed data.

8 These were the Fund for Technical and Scientific Development (FIPEME); a fund responsible for viability studies (FUNTEC); the Fund for Industrial Modernisation and Reorganisation (FMRI); and the FUNGIRO, a fund for financing of medium- and long-term industrial working capital.

9 Before making international comparisons, the reader must bear in mind that the BNDE is the only source of long-term finance in Brazil. Thus, even though a participation of 5 per cent in the total financing of investment may not seem so small for some readers, it is in such a context.

10 This fund, created in 1966, is financed by an 8 per cent contribution of the employer payroll and it bore monetary correction and interest fixed at 3 per cent.

11 As mentioned earlier, the logic behind this option was the view that the acceleration of accumulation because of the 1974 Plan would cause an increased demand for external resources, whose financing could not count,

at least in the medium term, on the increase in exports.

12 Central Bank's Resolution 305 of 1974. Notice that this measure reversed the trend in 1967–73, where the monetary authorities continuously extended the allowed minimum maturity in order to slow down borrowing in foreign currency.

13 On this see Werneck (1985).

14 The method of analysis of the causes of the external debt is identical to the one used in Chapters 7 and 8. That is, we divide the balance of payments into real resources transfers (RRT), costs of capital (CC) and capital inflows (CI). RRT comprises the trade balance and non-factor payments; CC includes interest charges, amortisation of outstanding foreign debt and profit remittances (the first two corresponding to the great part of CC). CI represents the net foreign capital inflows, which in the period of analysis are principally composed of foreign loans. Given that CI roughly represents the yearly additional debt and that the sum of RRT, CC and CI is equal to the changes in international reserves (RES), then the causes of increase of the foreign debt can be analysed by the ratios of RRT, CC and RES over CI.

15 Nonetheless, this does not apply to the foreign loans obtained through Resolution 63. But this will be discussed in detail below.

16 Simonsen's main concern was only made public after he left the post in 1979. In 1984 he would state that

> strong inflationary pressures were created in 1973, when M_1 expanded 47 per cent, output grew far faster than its tendency and the OPEC quadruplicated the oil prices. However, the Medici government was strongly committed to the maintenance of inflation at 12 per cent and, with strict controls of prices and subsidies, the general price index was *repressed* at 15.7 per cent.
>
> (quoted in Fishlow 1986: 51)

17 This was done through the National Monetary Council Resolution 361 of 12 March 1967, which permitted finance companies and investment banks to determine their loan rates freely. Resolution 389 of 15 September 1976 did the same for commercial banks.

18 The interrelation between external and foreign debts in Brazil had already been pointed out by Pereira (1974). However, it was Tavares (1978) who fully described this macroeconomic process, which she named the financial 'ring-around-a-rosy' (*ciranda financeira*). This metaphor was used to emphasise the merely circular character of the interrelation mentioned above. See text for more detail.

19 This is a very unorthodox division, but certainly is suitable for the graphic exposition of Figure 9.7. A more complete division, like in Kalecki (1971), would divide the sectors in industries producing, respectively, investment and intermediary goods, capitalist goods and wage-goods.

20 There is an extensive literature on the effects of the change of US monetary policy in 1979 and its role in the triggering of the Third World Debt crisis. See, for example, FitzGerald (1989).

21 The reasons for this commitment, which have been discussed above, were

related to the government's policies to combat inflation and to attract 'foreign savings'.

22 See *inter alia* Calabi *et al.* (1981), Zini (1984), Almeida (1987, 1988) and Almeida and Ortega (1987).

23 It is important to observe that the data presented in this table are only compatible (in what concerns the size of sample and coverage) within the periods 1969–77 and 1978–83. The data for the period 1969–77 cover a sample of 3,790 obtained from the archives of the *Secretaria da Receita Federal* (Treasury) of corporate tax declarations; even though the data was summarised in Zini (1984); see Zini (1982) for the methodology of estimation of the data. The data for the period from 1978 to 1983 cover samples of the biggest corporate firms within their sectors, and the sizes of the samples are: private national firms, 793; foreign firms, 88; state enterprises, 119; total, 1000; the methodology of aggregation of such data is found in *Conjuntura Economica* (op. cit.: 68–9).

10 CONCLUSION

1 The existence of consumer credit facilities nowadays does not invalidate the causality proposed by Keynes, for the first criterion – i.e. the dependency on more volatile long-term expectations – is still valid for investment and not for consumption.

Statistical appendix

Table A.1.1 Macroeconomic indicators of growth, inflation and the external sector (1947–66)

	Growth (%)				Inflation (%)		External sector (%)			
Year	GNP (1)	Per capita GNP (2)	Industry (3)	Agriculture (4)	GNP deflator (5)	WPI [a] (6)	M/GNP (7)	X/GNP (8)	Debt/GNP (9)	Debt/X (10)
1947–61	7.0	4.2	8.7	4.1	14.8	15.8	6.5	7.5	7.9	123.6
1962–6	5.0	1.0	4.9	4.4	82.5	81.9	4.5	5.4	15.7	291.8
1947	2.4	–	–	–	–	11.8	10.7	12.0	6.5	54.0
1948	9.6	7.0	11.3	6.9	5.9	7.0	8.1	10.6	5.3	50.5
1949	7.9	5.4	10.3	4.5	8.1	6.8	7.3	8.4	4.6	54.6
1950	6.6	4.1	11.3	1.5	9.2	11.5	6.1	8.9	3.7	41.1
1951	4.6	1.7	6.4	0.7	18.4	16.5	9.1	9.4	3.0	32.2
1952	7.6	4.5	5.0	13.0	9.3	11.8	7.7	6.4	2.9	45.1
1953	4.8	1.9	8.7	−3.3	13.8	14.5	4.6	6.3	4.7	75.3
1954	7.9	4.8	8.7	7.9	27.1	27.2	6.5	7.1	6.0	84.5
1955	8.5	5.4	10.6	7.7	11.8	16.3	5.7	7.3	7.5	101.8
1956	3.0	0.0	6.8	−2.4	22.6	19.9	4.9	7.0	12.6	181.7
1957	7.7	4.6	5.8	9.3	12.7	14.2	5.3	5.7	10.9	190.9
1958	10.7	7.5	16.2	2.0	12.4	13.0	4.9	5.1	12.7	246.7
1959	9.8	6.5	11.9	5.3	35.9	37.9	5.3	5.6	14.9	264.6
1960	9.4	6.2	9.6	4.9	25.4	29.1	5.2	5.1	15.7	307.6
1961	8.5	5.1	10.6	7.6	34.7	37.2	5.3	5.7	15.4	268.5
1962	6.7	3.5	7.8	5.5	50.1	51.9	5.3	5.0	16.4	331.3
1963	0.6	−2.5	0.2	1.0	78.4	73.7	4.5	4.8	13.7	283.5
1964	3.2	0.0	5.2	1.3	89.9	90.7	3.7	4.9	13.3	270.9
1965	2.9	−0.3	−4.7	13.8	58.2	57.1	3.4	5.8	17.2	298.1
1966	6.7	3.4	11.7	−3.2	37.9	38.5	4.5	6.1	18.1	298.4

Sources: cols 1–4, 6–10 as in Table 6.1; col. 5: IBGE 1987: 111; col. 6, ibid. 189–93; cols 7–8: ibid: 536–7; cols 9–10, ibid.: 543
Note: [a]Wholesale price index.

Table A.1.2 Macroeconomic indicators of growth, inflation and the external sector (1967–83)

Year	Growth (annual real rate, %)				Inflation (annual rate, %)		External sector (%)			
	GNP (1)	Per capita GNP (2)	Industry (3)	Agriculture (4)	GNP deflator 5)	WPI [a] (6)	M/GNP (7)	X/GNP (8)	Debt/GNP (9)	Debt/X (10)
1967–73	11.2	8.5	13.5	4.9	20.9	19.4	6.0	6.1	12.8	208.3
1974–80	6.8	4.2	7.0	5.4	51.2	49.2	8.5	6.9	18.7	274.2
1981–3	−0.8	−3.1	−3.4	−0.1	120.4	123.0	7.2	8.4	27.5	327.6
1967	4.2	1.0	3.0	5.7	26.5	28.6	4.5	5.1	10.5	203.9
1968	9.8	7.2	15.5	1.4	26.7	24.2	5.2	5.3	10.6	201.0
1969	9.5	6.9	12.1	3.8	20.1	20.1	5.2	6.1	10.6	190.5
1970	10.3	7.7	10.4	10.3	16.4	19.8	5.5	6.0	11.6	193.3
1971	11.3	8.6	11.8	10.2	20.4	20.0	6.5	5.8	13.3	228.0
1972	12.1	9.4	14.2	4.0	19.4	17.3	7.2	6.7	16.1	238.6
1973	14.0	11.2	17.0	0.0	22.6	14.9	7.8	7.8	15.8	202.8
1974	9.0	6.4	8.6	1.0	34.4	28.7	11.9	7.5	16.1	215.9
1975	5.2	2.6	4.9	7.2	33.9	27.9	9.6	6.8	16.7	244.2
1976	9.8	7.1	11.8	2.4	47.4	41.2	8.0	6.5	16.7	256.6
1977	4.6	2.1	3.3	12.1	46.2	42.7	6.6	6.7	17.7	264.3
1978	4.8	2.3	6.5	−3.0	38.9	38.7	6.7	6.2	21.2	343.7
1979	7.2	4.6	6.7	4.9	55.6	54.0	7.6	6.4	21.1	327.4
1980	9.1	6.5	9.2	9.6	91.8	100.2	9.1	8.0	21.4	267.5
1981	−3.4	−5.6	−9.2	6.1	102.6	109.9	7.9	8.3	22.0	263.6
1982	0.9	−1.4	−0.1	−1.9	92.9	95.5	6.6	6.8	23.7	347.9
1983	−2.5	−4.8	−6.6	1.8	151.8	154.5	7.0	9.9	36.8	371.3

Sources: cols 1–4, 6–10 as in Table 6.1; col. 5: IBGE 1987: 111; col. 6, ibid.: 189–93; cols 7–8, ibid.: 536–7; cols 9–10, ibid.: 543
Note: [a]Wholesale price index.

Table A.2.1 Investment indicators (1947–66)

	Total investment [a]		*Private investment*		*Government investment* [c]	
Year	*Percentage of GNP* (1)	*Real growth* [b] *(%)* (2)	*Percentage of total investment* (3)	*Real growth* [b] *(%)* (4)	*Percentage of total investment* (5)	*Real growth* [b] *(%)* (6)
1947–61	15.4	9.5	73.4	6.7	26.6	12.0
1962–6	17.4	6.6	65.5	15.0	34.5	12.6
1947	14.7	–	79.8	–	20.2	–
1948	12.6	−5.9	69.7	−17.8	30.3	41.1
1949	12.3	5.2	65.0	−1.8	35.0	21.4
1950	12.3	6.6	64.1	5.2	35.9	9.4
1951	14.8	26.1	75.3	47.9	24.7	−13.0
1952	15.2	10.0	78.2	14.3	21.8	−3.1
1953	14.6	0.7	76.2	−1.9	23.8	9.9
1954	16.7	23.3	76.6	23.9	23.4	21.3
1955	15.2	−0.9	77.9	0.8	22.1	−6.5
1956	14.4	−2.3	79.4	−0.5	20.6	−8.7
1957	17.4	29.5	73.4	19.8	26.6	67.0
1958	18.2	15.9	69.7	10.1	30.3	32.0
1959	20.6	24.2	74.8	33.3	25.2	3.3
1960	17.0	−9.5	66.8	−19.1	33.2	19.3
1961	15.1	−3.9	61.0	−12.1	39.0	12.8
1962	17.7	25.4	65.4	34.4	34.6	11.2
1963	18.0	2.6	70.0	9.7	30.0	−10.9

Table A.2.1 continued

Year	Total investment [a]		Private investment		Government investment [c]	
	Percentage of GNP (1)	Real growth [b] (%) (2)	Percentage of total investment (3)	Real growth [b] (%) (4)	Percentage of total investment (5)	Real growth [b] (%) (6)
1964	16.9	−3.6	70.2	−3.2	29.8	−4.3
1965	18.4	12.4	68.4	9.5	31.6	19.4
1966	18.4	6.8	58.0	11.9	42.0	41.9

Sources: As in Table 7.1
Notes: [a]Total investment includes changes in inventories.
[b]From 1947 to 1966 real total investment was obtained by deflating nominal values by GNP implicit deflator (from Table 7.1, col. 6).
[c]Includes investment of government-owned enterprises.
[d]Simple average of the period.

Table A.2.2 Investment indicators (1967–83)

	Total investment [a,b]		*Private investment*		*Government investment* [c]	
Year	*Percentage of GNP* (1)	*Real growth* [b] *(%)* (2)	*Percentage of total investment* (3)	*Real growth* [b] *(%)* (4)	*Percentage of total investment* (5)	*Real growth* [b] *(%)* (6)
1967–73	20.5	17.9	42.5	14.3	57.5	21.2
1974–80	23.6	6.4	39.3	3.5	60.7	6.2
1981–3	19.5	−11.9	36.8	−16.2	63.2	−8.5
1967	16.3	−8.1	46.9	2.7	53.1	−15.8
1968	19.0	28.1	38.0	3.8	62.0	49.6
1969	22.0	27.0	44.0	47.0	56.0	14.7
1970	20.5	1.5	44.1	3.1	55.9	2.7
1971	21.1	15.3	42.5	11.2	57.5	18.6
1972	21.1	16.7	43.5	19.5	56.5	14.7
1973	23.2	21.0	38.3	6.5	61.7	32.1
1974	25.4	13.3	39.0	15.3	61.0	12.0
1975	26.8	9.7	39.0	9.7	61.0	9.7
1976	23.1	6.8	45.4	24.3	54.6	−4.4
1977	22.0	−1.4	44.6	−3.2	55.4	0.0
1978	22.6	3.1	39.5	−8.7	60.5	12.6
1979	22.5	4.7	32.1	−14.9	67.9	17.5
1980	22.4	8.5	35.4	19.6	64.6	3.2
1981	22.3	−13.3	39.2	−3.9	60.8	−18.4
1982	20.6	−5.4	36.0	−13.1	64.0	−0.4
1983	15.7	−17.0	35.1	−19.1	64.9	−15.8

Sources: As in Table 7.1

Notes: [a]Total investment includes changes in inventories.

[b]From 1966 to 1969 real total investment was obtained by deflating nominal values by GNP implicit deflator; data for 1970–83 obtained from IBGE 1987: 126.

[c]Includes investment of government-owned enterprises.

[d]Simple average of the period.

Table A.3.1 Financial assets: 1967 cruzeiros and growth rates

	Monetary assets (MA) [a]				Non-monetary assets (NMA) [a]			
		Demand deposits						
Year	Currency	Banco do Brasil	Other [b]	Total MA	Time deposits	Government bonds	Total NMA	Total assets (FA)
Averge yearly growth rates (%)								
1947–55	2.3	0.3	8.9	5.7	−5.0	−11.3	−7.6	2.6
1956–61	3.8	21.8	7.6	8.0	−11.2	18.2	4.6	7.6
1962–6	−4.9	−1.4	−4.6	−4.2	−5.3	−46.6	24.9	−0.7
In constant 1967 million cruzeiros								
1947	2.5	0.8	3.2	6.5	1.6	1.5	3.0	9.5
1948	2.5	0.8	3.2	6.5	1.5	1.4	2.9	9.4
1949	2.5	0.9	3.7	7.2	1.7	1.3	3.0	10.2
1950	3.0	0.7	4.8	8.5	1.7	1.2	2.9	11.3
1951	3.0	0.8	6.2	9.8	1.6	1.0	2.7	12.5
1952	2.8	0.9	6.4	10.1	1.5	0.9	2.4	12.5
1953	3.0	0.8	6.6	10.5	1.4	0.8	2.2	12.7
1954	3.0	0.9	6.2	10.1	1.2	0.6	1.9	12.0
1955	3.0	0.8	6.3	10.1	1.0	0.6	1.6	11.7
1956	2.9	0.8	6.4	10.1	0.9	0.5	1.4	11.6
1957	3.2	1.0	7.5	11.7	1.0	0.4	1.4	13.0
1958	3.5	1.1	8.2	12.7	0.9	0.4	1.3	14.0
1959	3.2	1.1	8.6	12.8	0.7	0.3	1.0	13.9
1960	3.3	1.4	9.0	13.7	0.6	0.4	1.2	14.9
1961	3.6	2.1	9.2	15.0	0.5	1.1	1.8	16.7

Sources: Banco Central do Brasil, *Boletim Mensal* 10 (1), January 1974: 4–11.
Notes: [a] Deflated by the general price index.
[b] Includes all other commercial banks and federal and state savings banks.

Table A.3.2 Financial assets: 1967 million cruzeiros and growth rates

	Monetary assets (MA)[a]				Non-monetary assets (NMA)[a]								
		Demand deposits							Government bonds				
Year	Currency	Banco do Brasil	Other[b]	Total MA	Time deposits	Passbook savings	Bills of exchange	Housing bonds	ORTN	LTN	Other	Total NMA	Total (FA)[a]
Average yearly growth rates (%)													
1967–73	11.6	14.4	13.4	13.2	52.7	96.1	33.7	40.7	19.5	–	157.9	44.8	26.1
1974–80	6.1	−7.2	1.1	0.8	11.7	32.6	−12.5	−63.8	12.9	12.2	25.9	11.5	7.3
1981–3	−15.0	−13.4	−21.4	−19.2	33.1	21.7	38.0	−6.3	44.8	−7.3	14.0	26.4	15.7
In constant 1967 million cruzeiros													
1967	2.9	2.3	10.2	15.4	0.7	0.1	2.1	0.3	2.5	n.a	0.0	5.7	21.1
1968	3.3	2.6	11.2	17.1	1.2	0.3	3.7	0.5	2.8	n.a	0.0	8.5	25.6
1969	3.6	3.0	12.3	18.9	1.4	0.6	4.1	0.8	3.9	n.a	0.0	10.9	29.8
1970	3.8	3.0	13.0	19.8	2.5	1.2	5.5	1.1	5.3	0.4	0.7	16.6	36.4
1971	4.0	3.6	14.0	21.6	4.4	1.8	6.7	1.5	5.4	1.8	0.7	22.3	43.8
1972	4.6	3.8	17.0	25.4	6.8	3.1	8.3	2.0	6.3	4.1	0.7	31.2	56.6
1973	5.7	5.1	21.7	32.5	8.9	4.9	12.0	2.3	7.2	6.0	11.2	52.5	85.0
1974	5.6	5.6	22.5	33.6	9.0	7.8	11.5	2.2	8.9	4.0	1.5	44.8	78.4
1975	6.5	5.8	25.4	37.7	11.5	11.6	11.7	1.9	12.6	7.9	2.9	60.1	97.8
1976	6.9	5.5	24.6	37.0	10.9	16.0	10.2	1.5	12.6	10.3	3.5	64.9	101.8
1977	6.8	4.7	24.2	35.7	13.9	18.5	8.5	1.1	12.5	12.6	3.3	70.5	106.2
1978	7.1	4.7	24.6	36.3	17.0	21.7	9.8	0.8	12.3	14.6	3.5	79.8	116.1
1979	8.2	5.5	27.2	40.9	17.7	25.6	9.1	0.6	12.3	13.2	4.1	82.6	123.5
1980	7.1	4.1	23.5	34.7	14.0	24.0	6.7	0.0	14.4	6.3	3.7	69.1	103.9
1981	6.1	3.4	21.4	30.9	5.9	28.9	5.7	0.0	23.1	12.8	4.8	81.3	112.2
1982	6.0	2.9	17.3	26.2	7.9	34.0	10.6	0.0	38.1	8.7	6.2	105.5	131.7
1983	4.4	2.6	13.2	20.2	10.5	42.8	10.9	0.0	48.4	11.0	6.2	129.9	150.0

Sources: 1964–72, Banco Central do Brasil, *Boletim Mensal* 10 (1), January 1974: 4–11; 1973–9, ibid., 16 (11), November 1980: 82–3; 1980–3, ibid., 20 (2), February 1984: 74–7

Notes: [a]Deflated by the wholesale price index as in Table 7.1 (IGP-DI).
[b]Includes all other commercial banks and federal and state savings banks.

Table A.3.3 Financial assets: percentage of total assets and of GNP (1947–61)

	Monetary assets				*Non-monetary assets*					*Assets as a percentage of GNP*		
		Demand deposits										
Year	*Currency*	*Banco do Brasil*	*Other*	*Total*	*Time deposits*	*Passbook savings*	*Bills of exchange*	*Government bonds*	*Total*	*MA*	*NMA*	*Total*
1947	26.5	8.2	33.3	68.0	16.6	n.a	n.a	15.4	32.0	24.7	12.5	37.2
1948	26.3	8.9	34.0	69.1	16.2	n.a	n.a	14.7	30.9	20.9	9.8	30.7
1949	25.0	8.9	36.7	70.6	16.5	n.a	n.a	12.9	29.4	19.3	8.6	27.9
1950	26.1	6.2	42.3	74.7	14.8	n.a	n.a	10.5	25.3	19.5	8.1	27.6
1951	22.9	6.2	49.4	78.5	13.1	n.a	n.a	8.4	21.5	20.6	7.0	27.6
1952	22.7	6.8	51.1	80.7	11.8	n.a	n.a	7.6	19.3	23.7	6.5	30.2
1953	23.6	6.7	52.3	82.6	10.9	n.a	n.a	6.5	17.4	22.9	5.5	28.3
1954	25.3	7.4	51.5	84.2	10.4	n.a	n.a	5.4	15.8	19.8	4.2	24.0
1955	25.9	6.8	53.5	86.2	9.0	n.a	n.a	4.8	13.8	20.0	3.8	23.8
1956	25.8	6.9	55.1	87.8	8.1	n.a	n.a	4.1	12.2	18.5	3.0	21.4
1957	24.2	7.5	57.8	89.5	7.3	n.a	n.a	3.2	10.5	18.4	2.5	20.9
1958	24.5	7.6	58.6	90.7	6.5	n.a	n.a	2.7	9.3	19.3	2.3	21.6
1959	22.9	8.0	61.7	92.6	5.2	n.a	0.2	2.0	7.4	15.9	1.6	17.5
1960	22.0	9.5	60.3	91.8	4.3	n.a	0.8	3.1	8.2	16.2	1.3	17.5
1961	21.5	12.8	55.2	89.4	3.1	n.a	1.0	6.5	10.6	15.2	1.4	16.6

Source: Table A.3.1.

Table A.3.4 Financial assets: percentage of total assets

	Monetary								Government bonds				% GNP			% Total	
		Deposit deposits															
Year	*Currency*	*Banco do Brasil*	*Other*	*Total*	*Time deposits*	*Passbook savings*	*Bills of exchange*	*Housing bonds*	*ORTN*	*LTN*	*Other*	*Total*	*MA*	NMA	*Total*	*Indexed*	*Fixed yield*
1966	17.8	12.0	49.6	79.4	2.4	0.1	6.9	0.4	10.6	n.a	0.3	20.6	14.5	2.3	16.7	11.4	88.6
1967	13.9	10.7	48.4	73.0	3.3	0.4	10.0	1.4	11.8	n.a	0.2	27.0	12.7	3.3	15.9	13.7	86.3
1968	12.8	10.3	43.8	67.0	4.5	1.0	14.3	2.0	11.0	n.a	0.1	33.0	13.4	5.0	18.3	14.2	85.8
1969	12.1	10.2	41.2	63.5	4.7	2.0	13.9	2.7	13.2	n.a	0.0	36.5	14.1	6.9	21.0	17.9	82.1
1970	10.3	8.4	35.8	54.5	6.8	3.3	15.0	3.1	14.5	1.1	1.8	45.5	14.5	8.4	22.9	22.6	77.4
1971	9.1	8.2	31.9	49.2	10.1	4.1	15.3	3.3	12.3	4.1	1.6	50.8	13.6	11.4	25.0	21.3	78.7
1972	8.1	6.7	30.0	44.8	11.9	5.4	14.7	3.5	11.2	7.2	1.2	55.2	13.3	13.7	27.0	21.4	78.6
1973	6.7	6.0	25.5	38.2	10.5	5.7	14.2	2.7	8.5	7.1	13.2	61.8	13.1	16.1	29.2	30.1	69.9
1974	7.1	7.1	28.7	42.9	11.5	9.9	14.6	2.8	11.3	5.1	1.9	57.1	13.2	21.3	34.4	25.9	74.1
1975	6.7	5.9	26.0	38.5	11.7	11.9	12.0	1.9	12.9	8.0	3.0	61.5	12.5	16.6	29.0	29.7	70.3
1976	6.8	5.4	24.2	36.3	10.7	15.7	10.0	1.4	12.3	10.1	3.4	63.7	11.0	17.6	28.6	32.9	67.1
1977	6.4	4.4	22.8	33.6	13.1	17.4	8.0	1.1	11.7	11.9	3.1	66.4	10.0	17.5	27.5	33.3	66.7
1978	6.1	4.0	21.2	31.3	14.7	18.7	8.5	0.7	10.6	12.6	3.0	68.7	9.5	18.7	28.1	33.0	67.0
1979	6.6	4.5	22.0	33.1	14.3	20.7	7.4	0.5	9.9	10.7	3.3	66.9	8.0	17.6	25.6	34.5	65.5
1980	6.8	4.0	22.6	33.4	13.5	23.1	6.4	0.0	13.8	6.1	3.5	66.6	6.6	13.4	20.0	40.6	59.4
1981	5.4	3.1	19.0	27.5	5.3	25.8	5.1	0.0	20.6	11.4	4.3	72.5	5.8	11.5	17.2	50.6	49.4
1982	4.6	2.2	13.1	19.9	6.0	25.8	8.1	0.0	28.9	6.6	4.7	80.1	5.5	14.5	20.0	59.4	40.6
1983	2.9	1.7	8.8	13.4	7.0	28.5	7.3	0.0	32.3	7.3	4.2	86.6	3.7	15.0	18.7	64.9	35.1

Source: Table A.3.2.

Table A.4.1 Loans to the household and corporate sectors (including public enterprises) (1951–66)

	Banking system [a]			*Non-banking system* [a]							*Banking system* [b]				
Year	*Banco do Brasil*	*Other commercial banks*	*Total*	*Finance companies*	*BNH*	*Savings banks*	*BNDE*	*BNCC*	*Total*	*Total* [a]	*Banco do Brasil*	*Other commercial banks*	*Total*	*OFI* [b]	*Total* [b]
1951	99.9	246.3	346.2	n.a.	n.a.	36.4	–	0.8	73.7	419.9	n.a.	n.a.	n.a.	n.a.	n.a.
1952	124.0	245.5	369.6	n.a.	n.a.	40.0	–	0.6	40.6	410.2	24.2	−0.3	6.8	−44.9	−2.3
1953	127.6	252.6	380.2	n.a.	n.a.	41.6	–	0.6	42.2	422.4	2.9	2.9	2.9	3.8	3.0
1954	142.5	235.4	377.9	n.a.	n.a.	39.5	–	0.6	40.1	417.9	11.7	−6.8	−0.6	−5.0	−1.1
1955	138.7	227.1	365.8	n.a.	n.a.	42.2	7.1	0.6	59.4	425.2	−2.7	−3.5	−3.2	48.2	1.7
1956	133.7	231.9	365.5	n.a.	n.a.	42.5	10.3	0.5	66.7	432.2	−3.7	2.1	−0.1	12.3	1.7
1957	143.1	253.6	396.7	n.a.	n.a.	44.2	17.0	1.2	82.4	479.0	7.1	9.4	8.5	23.5	10.8
1958	159.9	269.5	429.5	n.a.	n.a.	46.1	22.9	1.1	95.9	525.4	11.8	6.3	8.3	16.5	9.7
1959	134.4	266.5	400.9	1.0	n.a.	38.9	28.6	1.3	100.8	501.7	−16.0	−1.1	−6.7	5.1	−4.5
1960	141.4	296.1	437.6	4.8	n.a.	36.7	32.5	1.1	109.4	546.9	5.2	11.1	9.1	8.5	9.0
1961	157.9	283.1	441.0	6.6	n.a.	35.0	30.2	0.9	104.5	545.5	11.6	−4.4	0.8	−4.5	−0.3
1962	178.2	288.0	466.2	16.4	n.a.	34.3	31.7	0.7	120.5	586.7	12.9	1.7	5.7	15.3	7.6
1963	157.2	258.8	416.0	15.6	n.a.	27.7	29.3	0.5	103.7	519.7	−11.8	−10.1	−10.8	−14.0	−11.4
1964	143.4	249.9	393.2	25.8	n.a.	21.8	21.2	0.7	93.4	486.6	−8.8	−3.5	−5.5	−9.9	−6.4
1965	113.0	281.2	394.2	51.0	1.4	25.9	17.6	1.1	119.9	514.1	−21.2	12.6	0.3	28.3	5.6
1966	128.0	252.4	380.4	54.0	3.8	31.7	15.8	1.2	131.6	511.9	13.3	−10.2	−3.5	9.7	−0.4

Sources: Banco Central do Brasil, *Boletim Mensal* 10 (1), January 1974; finance companies from 1959–63, Banco Central do Brasil, *Boletim Mensal* 10 (1), January 1974; *Conjuntura Econômica*, December 1972: 56

Notes: OFI, other financial institutions.

[a] Million cruzeiros, 1959.

[b] Yearly growth rates, %.

Table A.4.2 Loans to the private sector: 1967 billion cruzeiros and growth rates (1967–83)

	Banking system			Non-banking system											
Year	Banco do Brasil	Other commercial banks	Total	Finance companies	Investment banks	BNH[b]	HCC	SLA	CE	BNDE(S)[b]	BDE	PIS	BNCC	Total	Total
Average yearly growth rates (%)															
1967–73	28.8	21.2	23.7	40.3	55.0	42.6	72.2	104.3	37.7	26.2	89.8	–	12.5	49.5	34.8
1974–80	5.3	6.3	5.9	−5.8	6.5	−16.4	9.8	19.8	13.1	14.6	14.0	−21.8	21.0	10.3	8.6
1981–3	−18.3	0.4	−5.9	29.1	−9.2	27.7	19.5	−17.8	11.3	17.0	4.2	−19.2	13.9	10.0	2.9
In constant 1967 million cruzeiros															
1970	8.5	13.6	22.1	3.7	3.1	0.1	1.3	0.2	2.4	1.5	0.4	n.a	0.0	2.0	44.1
1971	10.5	16.4	26.9	6.0	4.5	2.7	1.9	0.3	3.1	1.3	0.5	0.0	0.0	0.7	56.5
1972	12.0	20.4	32.4	7.9	7.7	2.4	3.5	0.6	4.0	1.3	0.9	0.3	0.1	41.6	74.0
1973	15.7	25.6	41.3	12.4	10.5	2.5	5.1	0.9	5.7	1.7	1.4	0.9	0.1	9.8	101.1
1974	21.7	29.3	51.0	12.1	10.9	2.5	6.4	1.3	7.8	4.2	2.1	1.4	0.1	74.2	125.1
1975	27.9	34.6	62.5	12.6	13.3	2.5	7.2	1.7	11.5	6.6	3.0	1.0	0.3	94.3	156.8
1976	31.9	36.8	68.7	11.5	13.7	2.5	8.5	2.4	15.3	8.5	4.1	0.9	0.3	120.1	181.4
1977	33.2	39.3	72.5	10.3	14.8	3.0	9.8	13.0	16.2	9.5	4.6	0.7	0.3	125.6	198.1
1978	33.0	44.5	77.4	12.0	16.0	3.6	10.1	3.5	17.3	10.8	5.1	0.6	0.3	141.6	219.0
1979	35.2	49.3	84.5	11.6	18.0	4.1	11.6	4.0	17.2	11.4	5.4	0.5	0.4	151.4	235.9
1980	29.5	42.4	71.9	8.5	15.9	0.8	11.3	3.8	16.3	9.5	4.7	0.3	0.5	133.7	205.6
1981	23.5	41.5	65.1	7.7	15.5	0.9	13.6	4.2	18.0	9.9	5.2	0.2	0.2	75.4	140.5
1982	20.5	42.2	62.7	13.6	14.1	1.4	17.2	3.4	21.7	12.4	5.7	0.2	0.4	90.2	152.9
1983	15.7	41.9	57.6	12.8	12.8	1.5	19.4	2833	22.2	13.6	5.6	0.1	0.3	91.2	148.8

Sources: 1966–72, Banco Central do Brasil, *Boletim Mensal* 10 (1), January 1974; 1973–9, ibid., 16 (1); 1980–3, ibid., 20 (2), February 1984

Notes: BNH, National Housing Bank; CE, savings banks; BNDE(S), National Social and Economic Development Bank; BNCC, National Agricultural Credit Bank.

[a]Includes loans to public enterprises (as in the statistics of Brazil's central bank).

[b]Net lending which equal total lending minus funds intermediated to other financial institutions.

Table A.4.3 Loans to the household and corporate sectors (including public enterprises): participation of each lending institution and of loans to GNP (1951–66)

Year	Banking system [a]			Other financial institutions [a]									
						Savings banks							
	Banco do Brasil	Other commercial banks	Total	Finance companies	BNH	Federal (CEF)	State (CEE)	BNDE	BNCC	Total	Banking [b] system	Non-banking [b] system	Total [b]
1951	23.8	58.7	82.4	0.0	0.0	7.3	1.4	0.0	0.2	17.6	24.5	5.0	29.6
1952	30.2	59.9	90.1	0.0	0.0	7.5	2.2	0.0	0.2	9.9	24.9	2.4	27.3
1953	30.2	59.8	90.0	0.0	0.0	7.5	2.3	0.0	0.1	10.0	24.6	2.0	26.6
1954	34.1	56.3	90.4	0.0	0.0	7.0	2.5	0.0	0.1	9.6	22.7	1.4	24.1
1955	32.6	53.4	86.0	0.0	0.0	7.4	2.5	1.7	0.1	14.0	21.0	1.7	22.8
1956	30.9	53.6	84.6	0.0	0.0	7.3	2.5	2.4	0.1	15.4	20.0	1.5	21.5
1957	29.9	52.9	82.8	0.0	0.0	6.8	2.4	3.6	0.3	17.2	20.4	1.4	21.7
1958	30.4	51.3	81.7	0.0	0.0	6.6	2.2	4.3	0.2	18.3	20.0	1.2	21.2
1959	26.8	53.1	79.9	0.2	0.0	5.5	2.3	5.7	0.3	20.1	17.3	0.9	18.1
1960	25.9	54.1	80.0	0.9	0.0	4.6	2.1	5.9	0.2	20.0	17.8	0.6	18.4
1961	28.9	51.9	80.8	1.2	0.0	4.0	2.4	5.5	0.2	19.2	16.8	0.4	17.2
1962	30.4	49.1	79.5	2.8	0.0	3.7	2.2	5.4	0.1	20.5	16.8	0.3	17.1
1963	30.3	49.8	80.0	3.0	0.0	3.5	1.8	5.6	0.1	20.0	14.5	0.1	14.7
1964	29.5	51.3	80.8	5.3	0.0	2.7	1.8	4.3	0.2	19.2	13.4	0.1	13.4
1965	22.0	54.7	76.7	9.9	0.3	2.9	2.1	3.4	0.2	23.3	12.9	0.1	13.0
1966	25.0	49.3	74.3	10.6	0.7	4.0	2.2	3.1	0.2	25.7	11.7	0.0	11.8

Source: As in Table A.4.2

Notes: [a] Per cent of total loans.

[b] Per cent of GNP.

Table A.5.1 Assets, loan rates and rate spreads (%) (1947–66)

	Asset rates[a]										Loan rates[a]				Rate spreads[b]	
	Discount rates		Time deposits Banks		Government bonds		Bills of exchange		Savings deposits (CEF)		Bank loan rates working capital		Finance company working capital		Banks	Finance companies
	Nominal	Real	Nominal	Real	Nominal	Real	Nominal	Real	Nominal	Real	Nominal	Real	Nominal	Real		
Year	(1)		(2)		(3)		(4)			(5)	(6)			(7)	(8)	(9)
1947	6.0	–	–	–	–	–	n.a.	n.a.	n.a.	n.a.	–	–	n.a.	n.a.	–	–
1948	6.0	−0.9	–	–	–	–	n.a.	n.a.	n.a.	n.a.	–	–	n.a.	n.a.	–	–
1949	6.0	−0.8	–	–	–	–	n.a.	n.a.	n.a.	n.a.	–	–	n.a.	n.a.	–	–
1950	6.0	−5.0	–	–	7.3	−3.8	n.a.	n.a.	n.a.	n.a.	–	–	n.a.	n.a.	–	–
1951	6.0	−9.0	4.7	−10.1	–	–	n.a.	n.a.	n.a.	n.a.	14.3	−1.9	n.a.	n.a.	14.3	–
1952	6.0	−5.2	4.4	−6.6	–	–	n.a.	n.a.	n.a.	n.a.	14.1	2.0	n.a.	n.a.	14.1	–
1953	6.0	−7.4	4.7	−8.6	–	–	n.a.	n.a.	n.a.	n.a.	13.0	−1.3	n.a.	n.a.	13.0	–
1954	6.0	−16.7	4.9	−17.5	–	–	n.a.	n.a.	n.a.	n.a.	13.0	−11.2	n.a.	n.a.	13.0	–
1955	6.0	−8.9	4.4	−10.3	–	–	n.a.	n.a.	n.a.	n.a.	13.8	−2.2	n.a.	n.a.	13.8	–
1956	6.0	−11.6	4.2	−13.1	–	–	n.a.	n.a.	n.a.	n.a.	14.5	−4.5	n.a.	n.a.	14.5	–
1957	6.0	−7.2	4.2	−8.7	–	–	n.a.	n.a.	–	–	15.1	0.8	n.a.	n.a.	15.1	–
1958	6.0	−6.2	4.7	−7.4	–	–	n.a.	n.a.	–	–	16.0	2.6	n.a.	n.a.	16.0	–
1959	6.0	−23.1	4.0	−24.6	–	–	n.a.	n.a.	–	–	17.5	−14.8	n.a.	n.a.	17.5	–
1960	8.0	−16.4	4.0	−19.5	6.4	−17.6	21.0	−11.8	–	–	18.6	−8.2	42.0	10.0	18.6	42.0
1961	8.0	−21.3	4.0	−24.2	–	–	26.3	−5.6	–	–	19.6	−12.8	52.0	10.8	19.6	52.0
1962	8.0	−28.9	3.8	−31.6	–	–	29.5	−11.1	–	–	22.3	−19.5	60.0	5.4	22.3	60.0
1963	8.0	−37.8	3.6	−40.4	–	–	35.0	−17.2	–	–	25.1	−28.0	70.6	−1.8	25.1	70.6
1964	8.0	−43.4	3.4	−45.8	–	–	43.9	−28.7	67.7	−12.1	30.5	−31.6	81.2	−5.0	30.5	81.2
1965	10.0	−30.0	2.0	−35.1	69.0	7.6	36.0	−13.4	43.6	−8.6	33.3	−15.1	79.0	14.0	33.3	19.0
1966	12.0	−19.1	1.9	−26.4	45.2	4.9	30.4	−5.8	42.1	2.7	34.7	−2.7	71.5	23.9	34.7	71.5

Sources: col. 1, Goldsmith 1986: 417; col. 2, Banco Central do Brasil, *Boletim Mensal* 13 (3), March 1977: 96–7; cols 3–6, Banco Central do Brasil, ibid.: 96–7

Notes: [a] Real rates deflated by the general price index (IGP–DI) as in Table 7.1.

[b] Data for the savings deposits in the federal savings bank (*Caixa Economica Federal*).

[c] Rates paid on time deposits by banks and associated investment banks.

Table A.5.2 Asset rates (%) (1967–83)

Year	Non-indexed assets[a]								Indexed rates[a]			
	Discount rates		Time deposits banks		Treasury bills (LTN)		Bills of exchange		Savings deposits[b]		Treasury bonds (ORTN)	
	Nominal	Real	Nominal	Real	Nominal	Real	Nominal	Real	Nominal	Real	Nominal	Real
	(1)		(2)		(3)		(4)		(5)		(6)	
1967	17.0	−9.0	1.7	−20.9	n.a.	n.a.	31.3	2.1	29.6	0.8	29.2	0.5
1968	22.0	−1.8	3.7	−16.5	n.a.	n.a.	29.6	4.4	29.6	4.4	31.0	5.5
1969	21.0	0.7	4.3	−13.2	n.a.	n.a.	28.4	6.9	26.0	4.9	24.5	3.7
1970	20.0	0.2	24.3	3.8	n.a.	n.a.	28.8	7.5	26.9	5.9	25.6	4.9
1971	20.0	0.0	24.3	3.6	18.0	−1.7	28.0	6.6	27.6	6.3	28.7	7.2
1972	20.0	2.3	24.0	5.7	15.9	−1.2	24.2	5.8	20.8	3.0	21.3	3.4
1973	19.0	3.6	21.0	5.3	13.9	−0.9	22.0	6.2	26.2	9.8	18.8	3.4
1974	18.0	−8.3	27.4	−1.0	16.2	−9.7	27.0	−1.3	38.1	7.3	39.3	8.3
1975	18.0	−7.7	27.1	−0.6	18.4	−7.4	26.6	−1.1	36.0	6.4	30.2	1.8
1976	23.0	−12.9	33.5	−5.5	29.4	−8.4	39.2	−1.4	41.9	0.5	43.2	1.4
1977	29.0	−9.6	45.9	2.3	31.9	−7.5	42.9	0.2	43.0	0.3	36.1	−4.6
1978	31.5	−5.2	45.9	5.2	34.1	−3.3	47.8	6.5	41.5	2.0	42.2	2.5
1979	33.0	−13.6	51.2	−1.8	23.4	−19.8	49.9	−2.6	49.9	−2.7	53.2	−0.5
1980	35.5	−32.3	56.9	−21.6	47.5	−26.3	82.3	−9.0	64.0	−18.1	56.8	−21.7
1981	70.0	−19.0	94.3	−7.4	71.2	−18.4	84.6	−12.0	98.0	−5.7	89.7	−9.6
1982	80.0	−7.9	103.6	4.2	79.2	−8.3	110.5	7.7	105.1	4.9	120.7	12.9
1983	100.0	−21.4	152.9	−0.6	104.1	−19.8	180.0	10.0	172.5	7.1	196.6	16.5

Sources: col. 1, Goldsmith 1986: 417; col. 2, Banco Central do Brasil, *Boletim Mensal* 13(3), March 1977: 96–7; cols 3–6, Banco Central do Brasil, ibid.: 96–7

Notes: [a] Real rates deflated by the general price index (IGP–DI) as in Table 6.1.
[b] Data for the savings deposits in the federal savings bank (*Caixa Econômica Federal*).
[c] Rates paid on time deposits by banks and associated investment banks.

Table A.5.3 Loan rates and spreads between lending and borrowing rates (%)[a] (1967–83)

	Working capital		*Discount of firms' bonds (desconto de duplicatas)*		*Resolution 63*		*Subsidised loans to small and medium enterprises*		*Finance companies* [b]		*Spreads* [c]	
Year	*Nominal*	*Real*	*Nominal*	*Real*	*Nominal*	*Real*	*Nominal*	*Real*	*Nominal*	*Real*	*Banks*	*Finance companies*
1967	34.9	4.9	–	–	40.2	9.0	n.a	n.a	60.3	24.7	32.6	22.1
1968	34.1	8.0	–	–	60.2	29.0	n.a	n.a	56.4	25.9	29.3	20.7
1969	33.7	11.3	–	–	34.2	11.7	n.a	n.a	53.2	27.5	28.2	19.3
1970	30.9	9.3	–	–	30.7	9.1	n.a	n.a	54.5	29.0	5.3	20.0
1971	31.0	9.1	–	–	46.5	22.1	n.a	n.a	53.6	28.0	5.4	20.0
1972	32.0	12.5	–	–	32.4	12.9	n.a	n.a	49.0	27.0	6.5	20.0
1973	34.0	16.6	28.4	11.7	34.6	17.1	21.7	5.9	44.6	25.8	10.7	18.5
1974	38.5	7.6	32.9	3.3	49.9	16.5	21.7	−5.4	47.6	14.7	8.7	16.3
1975	39.7	9.2	43.9	12.5	57.0	22.7	21.7	−4.9	44.4	12.9	9.9	14.1
1976	52.9	8.3	57.7	11.7	56.8	11.0	21.7	−13.8	65.5	17.2	14.5	18.9
1977	59.7	11.9	63.7	14.7	49.4	4.7	21.7	−14.7	71.5	20.2	9.5	20.0
1978	70.4	22.8	69.7	22.3	68.5	21.5	21.7	−12.3	76.5	27.2	16.8	19.4
1979	83.5	19.2	87.6	21.9	187.1	86.5	21.7	−20.9	79.5	16.6	21.4	19.7
1980	88.0	−6.1	110.0	4.9	105.9	2.8	29.9	−35.1	92.9	−3.7	19.8	5.8
1981	141.7	15.2	160.1	23.9	162.4	25.0	50.8	−28.1	176.3	31.7	24.4	49.7
1982	160.3	33.2	223.9	65.7	248.9	78.5	72.2	−11.9	234.6	71.2	27.8	59.0
1983	266.8	44.1	279.7	49.2	333.2	70.2	160.3	2.3	270.4	45.5	45.0	32.3

Sources: cols 1–3, Banco Central do Brasil, *Boletim Mensal* 12 (4), April 1976; col. 4, *Revista Cenarios*, October 1990; Resolution 63 loan rates were estimated from 1971 to 1972 using nominal LIBOR rate (r_L), the rate of change of the implicit exchange rates (e), the rate of inflation in Brazil (p) and the average of the spreads from 1967 to 1970 (s) where $r_{63} = [(1 + r_L)(1 + p)(1 + e)(1 + s)] - 1$; col. 5, 1964–6, Christoffersen 1968: 50; from 1967 onwards, Banco Central do Brasil, op. cit.

Notes: [a]Real rates obtained by deflating nominal rates by the general price index (IGP–DI).

[b]Until 1970 loans to working capital; from then on, consumer credit rates.

[c]Obtained as follows: $r = [(1 + r_l)/(1 + r_d)] - 1$ where r_l stands for the loan rate and r_d for the deposit rate.

Table A.6 Some indicators of the stock markets in the 1950s/1960s

Year	*Issues by new companies*	*Issues by existing companies*		*Index of column (2)*[b] *1950=100*	*Column (2) as percentage of total investment*	*Assets transacted in stock markets (%)*			*Rate of growth of the share index*[b,c]	*Share turnover*
		Subscription in cash	*Other*[a]			*Shares*	*Bills of exchange*	*Public bonds*		
	(1)	(2)	(3)	(4)	(5)	(6)	(7)	(8)	(9)	(10)
1950	19.3	48.3	32.4	100.0	6.34	–	–	–	16.9	0.11
1951	18.2	42.9	38.9	176.6	9.11	–	–	–	−7.8	0.13
1952	13.5	49.5	37.0	263.8	12.75	–	–	–	−13.3	0.10
1953	15.7	46.7	37.6	226.1	10.99	–	–	–	−13.3	0.23
1954	25.8	40.7	33.5	267.5	10.33	–	–	–	−14.4	0.12
1955	16.6	46.0	37.4	279.7	11.67	54.0	–	46.0	−9.1	0.07
1956	6.8	26.6	66.5	363.1	15.42	68.8	–	31.2	6.7	0.08
1957	10.8	50.8	38.4	433.2	14.44	54.9	–	45.1	−2.5	0.07
1958	13.5	66.3	20.2	455.9	13.35	51.1	–	48.9	18.3	0.11
1959	8.1	55.8	36.1	570.5	13.68	49.7	–	50.3	28.5	0.16
1960	15.2	50.0	34.8	460.6	13.22	60.0	17.5	22.5	10.4	0.12
1961	8.4	43.2	48.4	354.2	11.01	29.8	60.7	9.4	−2.7	0.14
1962	10.1	51.5	38.4	534.8	13.32	31.3	63.2	5.5	102.3	0.25
1963	7.0	42.8	50.2	420.6	10.04	45.7	50.5	3.8	−36.8	0.41
1964	3.4	16.5	80.1	361.1	8.54	22.9	74.4	2.7	−41.2	0.28
1965	0.2	18.3	81.5	707.5	14.43	24.0	69.3	6.8	–	–
1966	2.0	27.3	70.7	737.4	14.38	17.7	72.7	9.6	−13.3	–

Sources: cols 1–5, *Anuarios APEC* 1970, Table D-1; cols 6–10, Goldsmith 1986: 275

Notes: [a]Includes incorporation of reserves, asset revaluations, fiscal incentives and other operations.
[b]Deflated by general price index as in Table 7.1.
[c]Rio de Janeiro stock exchange (index = IBV-RJ).

Table A.7.1 Some indicators of the use of external funds to finance internal accumulation (1948–66)

Average value in US$ billion	*1948–55*	*1956–61*	*1962–6*
Current account	−0.21	−0.55	−0.37
1 Real resources transfers (RRT)	−0.05	−0.13	0.10
1.1 Trade balance	0.19	0.13	0.29
Imports	−1.23	−1.22	−1.19
Exports	1.42	1.35	1.48
1.2 Non-factors-services (NFT)[a]	−0.26	−0.26	−0.19
2 Cost of capital (CC)	−0.16	−0.43	−0.47
Interest	−0.03	−0.09	−0.13
Amortisation	−0.08	−0.31	−0.32
Profits & dividends	−0.05	−0.03	−0.02
3 Net capital inflows (CI)	0.15	0.52	0.47
Transfers	−0.01	0.00	0.06
Net FDI	0.01	0.11	0.05
MLT loans	0.05	0.38	0.33
ST loans	−0.02	0.00	0.00
Other	0.11	0.03	0.02
4 Superavit/deficit	−0.06	−0.03	0.10
5 Changes in reserves (Res)	0.06	0.03	−0.10
Some indexes (%)			
RRT/GNP	0.92	2.71	−1.74
CC/GNP	6.58	10.53	9.38
FDI/INV	0.59	2.78	1.10
Res/GNP	−2.36	−0.22	2.01
CI/GNP	5.14	13.01	9.65
External debt/GNP	4.72	13.70	15.74
RRT/CI	0.02	0.20	−0.32
CC/CI	1.57	0.86	1.04
Res/CI	−0.59	−0.06	0.28

Sources: IBGE 1987: 536–8; external debt from ibid., p. 543

Notes: INV, total investment; GNP, gross national product; dollar values deflated by implicit exchange rate as in IBGE (1987).

Table A.7.2 Some indicators of the use of external funds to finance internal accumulation (1967–83)

	Current account [a]						Capital inflows [a]										
		Cost of capital						Financial flows									
Year	RRT	Interest	Amortis- ation	π & dividends	Total	Total	Transfers	FDI	MLT	ST	Other	Total	Res [a]	RRT/ GNP	RRT/CI	CC/CI	Res/CI
1967	−0.06	−0.18	−0.44	−0.07	−0.70	−0.76	0.08	0.08	0.53	−0.01	−0.20	0.47	0.29	1.1	0.1	1.5	−0.61
1968	−0.30	−0.14	−0.48	−0.08	−0.71	−1.01	0.02	0.06	0.58	0.00	0.37	1.03	−0.02	4.5	0.3	0.7	0.02
1969	−0.05	−0.18	−0.49	−0.08	−0.76	−0.81	0.03	0.18	1.02	0.18	−0.06	1.35	−0.55	0.6	0.0	0.6	0.41
1970	−0.23	−0.23	−0.67	−0.12	−1.03	−1.26	0.02	0.13	1.43	0.08	−0.03	1.63	−0.38	2.4	0.1	0.6	0.23
1971	−0.90	−0.30	−0.85	−0.12	−1.27	−2.17	0.01	0.17	2.04	0.49	−0.05	2.65	−0.48	8.6	0.3	0.5	0.18
1972	−0.97	−0.36	−1.20	−0.16	−1.72	−2.70	0.01	0.32	4.30	0.02	0.42	5.07	−2.37	7.8	0.2	0.3	0.47
1973	−1.00	−0.51	−1.67	−0.20	−2.38	−3.39	0.03	0.94	4.50	−0.20	0.27	5.53	−2.15	5.4	0.2	0.4	0.39
1974	−6.22	−0.65	−1.92	−0.25	−2.82	−9.04	0.00	0.89	6.89	0.46	−0.15	8.10	0.95	23.0	0.8	0.3	−0.12
1975	−4.97	−1.50	−2.17	−0.23	−3.90	−8.87	0.00	0.89	5.93	1.55	−0.44	7.93	0.94	14.6	0.6	0.5	−0.12
1976	−3.83	−1.81	−2.99	−0.38	−5.18	−9.00	0.00	0.96	7.77	1.11	0.30	10.14	−1.14	10.7	0.4	0.5	0.11
1977	−1.48	−2.10	−4.06	−0.46	−6.62	−8.10	0.00	0.81	8.42	0.30	−0.83	8.71	−0.61	3.7	0.2	0.8	0.07
1978	−2.83	−2.70	−5.32	−1.54	−9.56	−12.38	0.07	2.05	13.81	1.58	−0.85	16.66	−4.28	6.1	0.2	0.6	0.26
1979	−5.22	−4.19	−6.38	−1.36	−11.93	−17.14	0.02	2.21	11.23	0.76	−0.40	13.82	3.32	9.8	0.4	0.9	−0.24
1980	−5.94	−6.31	−5.01	−0.72	−12.04	−17.99	0.17	1.53	10.60	2.72	−0.54	14.48	3.51	10.5	0.4	0.8	−0.24
1981	−1.66	−9.16	−6.24	−1.11	−16.51	−18.17	0.20	2.33	15.55	1.23	−0.48	18.82	−0.65	2.7	0.1	0.9	0.03
1982	−2.81	−11.35	−6.95	−2.14	−20.45	−23.25	−0.01	2.55	12.52	−0.06	3.99	18.98	4.27	4.6	0.1	1.1	−0.23
1983	4.06	−9.56	−6.86	−1.45	−17.87	−13.81	0.11	1.36	6.71	1.07	5.12	14.36	−0.55	−11.7	−0.3	1.2	0.04

Source: Balance-of-payments data, IBGE 1987: 539; external debt: ibid., 543–4

Notes: RRT, real resources transfers, which includes trade balance and net payments of non-factors; π & dividends, profits and dividends (net); FDI, foreign direct investment (ne medium and long-term loans; ST, short-term loans; CI, capital inflows; CC, capital costs; Res, changes in the international reserves held by the central bank.

[a]Billion current dollars.

Table A.8 The international rates of interest and the terms of trade (1967–85)

Year	*LIBOR*	*Real LIBOR*			Prime	*Real 'Prime'*			Terms of trade
		US WPI	*US CPI*	*Terms of trade*		*US WPI*	*US CPI*	*Terms of trade*	
1967	5.5	5.2	2.6	7.8	5.6	5.4	2.7	7.9	135.1
1968	6.4	3.8	2.1	11.1	6.3	3.7	2.0	11.0	128.7
1969	9.8	5.6	4.1	5.1	8.0	3.9	2.4	3.3	134.7
1970	8.8	5.0	2.7	−1.1	7.9	4.2	1.9	−2.0	148.0
1971	7.0	3.5	2.5	13.5	5.7	2.3	1.4	12.3	138.3
1972	6.0	1.5	2.6	5.1	5.2	0.8	1.9	4.4	139.5
1973	9.3	−3.3	3.0	−1.7	8.0	−4.5	1.7	−3.0	154.9
1974	11.2	−6.4	0.2	27.9	10.8	−6.7	−0.2	27.5	129.0
1975	7.8	−1.3	−1.2	10.3	7.9	−1.2	−1.1	10.4	125.7
1976	6.2	1.6	0.4	−5.9	6.8	2.1	1.0	−5.3	141.0
1977	6.4	0.3	−0.1	−6.5	6.9	0.8	0.4	−6.1	159.3
1978	9.2	1.3	1.4	23.7	9.1	1.2	1.4	23.6	136.1
1979	12.2	−0.3	0.8	19.3	12.7	0.1	1.2	19.8	126.4
1980	14.0	−0.1	0.4	32.1	15.2	1.0	1.5	33.3	103.6
1981	16.8	7.0	5.8	32.9	18.8	8.9	7.6	35.0	86.8
1982	13.6	11.4	6.9	15.3	14.8	12.6	8.1	16.6	85.3
1983	9.9	8.5	−32.7	9.9	10.8	9.4	−32.1	10.8	85.3
1984	11.2	8.6	6.6	2.3	12.1	9.4	7.4	3.1	92.9
1985	8.7	9.1	5.0	15.2	9.9	10.4	6.2	16.5	86.8

Source: Cavalcanti 1988 : 24
Notes: US WPI, nominal rate deflated by the US wholesale price index; US CPI, deflated by the US general price index.

Bibliography

Aglietta, M. (1985) 'The creation of liquidity', in L. Tsoukalis (ed.) *The Political Economy of International Money: In Search of a New Order*, London: Royal Institute of International Affairs.

Akerlof, G. (1970) 'The market for "lemons": qualitative uncertainty and the market mechanism', *Quarterly Journal of Economics* 84 (3): 488–500.

Almeida, J.S.G. (1980) 'As financeiras na reforma do mercado de capitais: o descaminho do projeto liberal', unpublished M.A. thesis, Universidade Estadual de Campinas.

—— (1984) 'As reformas financeiras de 1964–65: objetivos, rumos e desvios', *Texto para Discussão* 59, Rio de Janeiro: Universidade Federal do Rio de Janeiro, Instituto de Economia Industrial.

—— (1987) 'O ajuste financeiro das empresas produtivas na crise', *Texto para Discussão* 112, Rio de Janeiro: Instituto de Economia Industrial, Universidade Federal do Rio de Janeiro.

—— (1988) 'Instabilidade da economia e estrutura financeira das empresas no Brasil no ajustamento recessivo', *Texto para Discussão* 178, Rio de Janeiro: Instituto de Economia Industrial, Universidade Federal do Rio de Janeiro.

Almeida, J.S.G. and Ortega, J.A. (1987) 'Financiamento e desempenho financeiro das empresas industriais no Brasil', *Texto para Discussão* 81, Rio de Janeiro: Instituto de Economia Industrial, Universidade Federal do Rio de Janeiro.

Amadeo, E.J. (1982) *Desemprego, Salários e Preços: Um Estudo Comparativo de Keynes e do Pensamento Macroeconômico da Década de 1970*, Rio de Janeiro: BNDES.

—— (1991) *Keynes's Principle of Effective Demand*, Aldershot: Edward Elgar.

Amadeo, E.J. and Franco, G.H.B. (1989) 'Entre Keynes e Robertson: finance, poupança e investimento', *Pesquisa e Planejamento Econômico* 19(2): 379–86.

Amsden, A.H. and Euh, Y. (1990) 'Republic of South Korea's financial reform: what are the lessons', *UNCTAD Staff papers* 30.

Andersen, T.B. (1983–4) 'Some implications of the efficient capital markets hypothesis', *Journal of Post Keynesian Economics* 6 (2): 281–94.

Andrade, J.P. (1988) 'Motivo financas ou motivo poupança: o papel transitório do crédito em Kalecki', in *Ensaios de Teoria Pós-Keynesiana*, Ceará: Universidade Federal do Ceará.

Asimakopulos, A. (1983) 'Kalecki and Keynes on finance, investment and saving', *Cambridge Journal of Economics* 7 (3–4): 221–34.

Bain, A.D. (1981) *Economics of the Financial System*, Oxford: Martin Robertson.

Banco Central do Brasil (1973) 'Setor externo e desenvolvimento da economia', *Boletim*, Anexo Especial II.

Batista, J.C. (1986) 'Brazil's second national plan and its growth-*cum*-debt strategy', *Texto para Discussão* 93, Rio de Janeiro: Institute de Economia Industrial, Universidade Federal do Rio de Janeiro.

Becker, B.K. and Egler, A.G. (1992) *Brazil: a New Regional Power in the World-Economy*, Cambridge: Cambridge University Press.

Beckerman, P. (1983) 'Non-positive market-clearing real rates of interest', *Journal of Post Keynesian Economics* 6 (1): 53–63.

Blanchard, J.O. and Fisher, S. (1989) *Lectures on Macroeconomics*, Cambridge Mass.: The MIT Press.

Calabi, A., Reiss, G.D. and Levy, P.M. (1981) *Geração de Poupanças e Estrutura de Capital da Empresas no Brasil*, São Paulo: Universidade de São Paulo, Instituto de Pesquisas Econômicas.

Cameron, R. (ed.) (1972) *Banking and Economic Development: Some Lessons of History*, New York: Oxford University Press.

Cameron, R., Crisp, O., Patrick, H.T. and Tilly, R. (eds) (1967) *Banking in the Early Stages of Industrialization: a Study in Comparative Economic History*, New York: Oxford University Press; reprinted, 1972.

Carvalho, F.J.C. (1986) 'Inflation and indexation in a post keynesian model of asset-choice', unpublished Ph.D. thesis, Rutgers University, New Jersey.

——— (1992) *Mr. Keynes and the Post Keynesians: Principles of Macroeconomics for a Monetary Production Economy*, Aldershot: Edward Elgar.

Castro, A.B. and Souza, F.E.P. (1985) *A Economia Brasileira em Marcha Forçada*, Rio de Janeiro: Paz e Terra.

Cavalcanti, C.B. (1988) *Transferência de Recursos ao Exterior e Substituição de Dívida Externa por Dívida Interna*, Rio de Janeiro: BNDES.

Cencini, A. (1988) *Money, Income and Time*, London: Pinter.

Chenery, H.B. and Strout, A. (1966) 'Foreign assistance and economic development', *American Economic Review* 56 (4): 679–733.

——— and ——— (1968) 'Foreign assistance and economic development: reply', *American Economic Review* 58 (4): 912–16.

Chick, V. (1983) *Macroeconomics after Keynes*, Oxford: Philip Allan.

——— (1984) 'Monetary increases and their consequences: streams, backwaters and floods', in A. Ingham and A.M. Ulph (eds) *Demand, Equilibrium and Trade: Essays in Honour of Ivor F. Pearce*, London: Macmillan. Reprinted in P. Arestis and S.C. Dow (eds) *Money, Method and Keynes: Selected Essays of Victoria Chick*, London: Macmillan, pp. 167–79.

——— (1985) 'Time and the wage-unit in the method of the *General Theory*: history and equilibrium', in T. Lawson and H. Pesaram (eds) *Keynes's Economics: Methodological Issues*, London and Sydney: Croom Helm.

——— (1986) 'The evolution of the banking system and the theory of saving, investment and interest', *Economie et Societés (Cahiers de l'ISMEA Serie*

Monnaie et Production, 3). Reprinted in P. Arestis and S.C. Dow (eds) *Money, Method and Keynes: Selected Essays of Victoria Chick*, London: Macmillan.

——— (1990) 'Some methodological issues in the theory of speculation', in D.E. Moggridge (ed.) *Perspectives on the History of Economic Thought* 4. Reprinted in P. Arestis and S.C. Dow (eds) *Money, Method and Keynes: Selected Essays of Victoria Chick*, London: Macmillan.

Chick, V. (1992) *Money, Method and Keynes*. London: Macmillan.

Chick, V. and Dow, S. (1988) 'A Post-Keynesian perspective on the relation between banking and regional development', *Thames Papers in Political Economy*, Thames and North East London Polytechnic, spring.

Cho, Y.J. (1986) 'Inefficiencies from financial liberalization in the absence of well-functioning equity markets', *Journal of Money, Credit and Banking* 18 (2): 191–9.

Christoffersen, L.E. (1968) 'Interest rates and the structure of a commercial banking system under inflationary conditions: a case study of Brazil', *Working Paper* 26, Washington, DC: World Bank Economics Department.

Corbo, V. and De Melo, J. (1987) 'Lessons from the Southern Cone policy reforms', *Research Observer*, Washington, DC: World Bank, pp. 111–35.

Coutinho, L.G. and Belluzo, L.G. (1983) 'Estado, sistema financeiro e formas de manifestação da crise: 1929–1975', in L.G.M. Belluzzo and R. Coutinho (eds) *Desenvolvimento Capitalista no Brasil: Ensaios sobre a Crise*, São Paulo: Ed. Brasiliense.

Cysne, R.P., Lees, F. and Botts, J.B. (1990) *Banking and Financial Deepening in Brazil*, Basingstoke: Macmillan.

Darity, W. and Horn, B.L. (1990) 'Some repressed aspects of the case for financial reform in LDCs', Department of Economics, Barnard College, Columbia University, July, mimeo.

Davidoff Cruz, P. (1984) *Dívida Externa e Política Econômica*, São Paulo: Brasiliense.

Davidson, P. (1978) *Money and the Real World*, Basingstoke, Hampshire: Macmillan.

——— (1986) 'Finance, funding, saving and investment', *Journal of Post Keynesian Economics* 9 (1): 101–10.

——— (1988) 'A technical definition of uncertainty and the long-run non-neutrality of money', *Cambridge Journal of Economics* 12 (3): 329–37.

De Meza, D. and Webb, D.C. (1987) 'Too much investment: a problem of asymmetric information', *Quarterly Journal of Economics* CII (2): 281–92.

Deane, P. (1961) 'Capital formation in Britain before the Railway Age', *Economic Development and Cultural Change* IX.

Diamond, D.W. (1984) 'Financial intermediation and delegated monitoring', *Review of Economic Studies* 51 (3): 393–414.

Díaz-Alejandro, C. (1985) 'Good-bye financial repression, hello financial crash', *Journal of Development Economics* 19 (1–2): 1–24.

Dismoor, J. (1990) *Brazil: Responses to the Debt Crisis*, Washington, DC: Inter-American Development Bank.

Dixon, R. (1986) 'Uncertainty, unobstructedness and power', *Journal of Post Keynesian Economics* 8 (4): 585–90.

Dow, S. (1985) *Macroeconomic Thought: A Methodological Approach*, Oxford and Cambridge: Basil Blackwell.

——— (1990) *Financial Markets and Regional Economic Development*, Aldershot: Avebury.

Dow, S. and Earl, P.E. (1982) *Money Matters*, Oxford: Martin Robertson.

Dreifuss, R. (1984) *1964: A Retomada do Poder*, Petrópolis: Vozes.

Dutt, A.K. (1990–1) 'Interest rate policies in LDCs: a Post Keynesian view', *Journal of Post Keynesian Economics* 13 (2): 211–32.

Dymski, G.A. (1989) 'Keynesian versus credit theories of money and banking: a reply to Wray', *Journal of Post Keynesian Economics* 12 (1): 157–67.

Edwards, S. (1988) 'Financial deregulation and segmented capital markets: the case of Korea', *World Development* 16 (12): 185–94.

Fei, J.C.H. and Ranis, G. (1968) 'Foreign assistance and economic development: comment', *American Economic Review* 78: 897–912.

Felix, D. and Caskey, J.P. (1990) 'The road to default: an assessment of debt crisis management in Latin America', in D. Felix (ed.) *Debt and Transfiguration? Prospects for Latin America's Economic Revival*, New York and London: M.E. Sharpe.

Fisher, I. (1933) 'The debt-deflation theory of great depression', *Econometrica* 1: 337–57.

Fishlow, A. (1972) 'Some reflections on the post-1964 economic policy', in A. Stepan (ed.) *Authoritarian Brazil*, New Haven: Yale University Press.

——— (1986) 'A economia política do ajustamento brasileiro aos choques do petróleo: uma nota sobre o período 1974/84', *Pesquisa e Planejamento Econômico* 16 (3), Rio de Janeiro: IPEA.

FitzGerald, E.V.K. (1990) 'Kalecki on financing development: an approach to the macroeconomics of the semi-industrialised economy', *Cambridge Journal of Economics* 14 (2): 183–203.

FitzGerald, E.V.K. and Vos, R. (1989) *Financing Economic Development: an Approach to Economic Development*, Aldershot: Gower.

Foley, D. and Lazonick, W. (1986) *Finance, Growth and Stagnation*, mimeo.

Frenkel, R. (1979) 'Decisiones de precio en alta inflacion', Buenos Aires: Estudioes CEDES nu. 6.

Friedman, M. (1968) 'The role of monetary policy', *American Economic Review* 58 (March): 1–17.

Fry, M. (1989) *Money, Interest, and Banking in Economic Development*, Baltimore and London: The Johns Hopkins University Press.

FUNDAP (Fundação do Desenvolvimento Administrativo) (1988) 'Déficit e endividamento do setor público', *Relatório de Pesquisa* 5, São Paulo: FUNDAP.

Galbis, V. (1977) 'Financial intermediation and economic growth in less developed countries: a theoretical approach', *Journal of Development Studies* 13 (2): 58–72.

Galvêas, E. (1985) *Sistema Financeiro e Mercado de Capitais*, Rio de Janeiro: Instituto Brasileiro de Mercado de Capitais.

Gatti, D.D. and Gallegatti, M. (1990) 'Financial instability, income distribution, and the stock market', *Journal of Post Keynesian Economics* 12 (3): 356–74.

Gerschenkron, A. (1962) *Economic Backwardness in Historical Perspective: a*

Book of Essays, Cambridge, Mass.: Belknap Press of Harvard University Press.

Gersovitz, M. (1988–9) 'Saving and development', in H.B. Chenery and T.N. Srivasan (eds) *Handbook of Development Economics*, Amsterdam: North-Holland.

Gertler, M. (1988) 'Financial structure and aggregate economic activity: an overview', *Journal of Money, Credit, and Banking* 20 (3): 559–87.

Godley, W.A.H. and Cripps, F. (1985) *Macroeconomics*, London: Fontana.

Goldsmith, R.W. (1969) *Financial Structure and Development*, New Haven: Yale University Press.

——— (1986) *Brasil 1850-1984: Desenvolvimento Financeiro um Século de Inflação*, São Paulo: Harper & Row.

Goodhart, C.A.E. (1975) *Money, Information and Uncertainty*, London: Macmillan; revised edition,1989.

——— (1989) 'Has Moore become too horizontal?', *Journal of Post Keynesian Economics* 12 (1): 29–34.

Gurley, J. and Shaw, E.S. (1955) 'Financial aspects of economic development', *American Economic Review* 45 (4): 515–38.

——— and ——— (1960) *Money in a Theory of Finance*, Washington, DC: Brookings Institution.

Hahn, F.H. (1981) *Money and Inflation*, Cambridge, Mass.: MIT Press.

Harrod, R.F. (1939) 'An essay on dynamic theory', *Economic Journal* 49: 14–33.

——— (1956) *Towards a Dynamic Economics*, London: Macmillan.

Heise, A. (1992) 'Commercial banks in macroeconomic theory', *Journal of Post Keynesian Economics* 14 (13): 285–96.

Hicks, J.R. (1937) 'Mr. Keynes and the classics: a suggested interpretation', *Econometrica* 5. Reprinted in *Critical Essays in Monetary Theory*, New York, Oxford University Press.

——— (1985) *Methods of Dynamic Economics*, Oxford: Caledon Press.

Hilferding, R. (1910) *Finance Capital: A Study of the Latest Phase of Capitalist Development*, London: Routledge & Kegan Paul; reprinted 1981.

Hirschman, A.O. (1970) *Exit, Voice and Loyalty: Responses to Decline in Firms, Organisations and States*, London: Harvard University Press.

IBGE (Instituto Brasileiro de Geografia e Estatística) (1987) *Séries Estatísticas Retrospectivas* 3, Rio de Janeiro: IBGE.

Johnson, H.G. (1967) 'Money in a neo-classical one-sector growth model', in *Essays in Monetary Economics*, 2nd edn, London: George Allen & Unwin, pp. 141–78.

——— (1976) 'Destabilizing speculation: a general equilibrium approach', *Journal of Political Economy* 84 (1): 101–8.

Kaldor, R. (1985) *Economics without Equilibrium*, New York: M.E. Sharpe.

Kalecki, M. (1971) *Selected Essays on the Dynamics of the Capitalist Economy: 1933–1970*, Cambridge: Cambridge University Press.

Kennedy, W.P. (1987) *Industrial Structure, Capital Markets and the Origins of British Economic Decline*, Cambridge: Cambridge University Press.

Keynes, J.M. *Collected Writings* (*CWJMK*), D.E. Moggridge (ed.), London: Macmillan for the Royal Economic Society, various dates from 1971.

——— (1930a) *The Treatise on Money: The Pure Theory of Money*, 2 vols,

London: Macmillan, 1930. Republished in *CWJMK* as vol. V.

——— (1930b) *The Treatise on Money: The Pure Theory of Money*, 2 vols, London: Macmillan, 1930. Republished in *CWJMK* as vol. VI.

——— (1936) *The General Theory of Employment, Interest and Money*, London: Macmillan, 1947.

——— (1937a) 'The general theory of employment', *Quarterly Journal of Economics*, February 1937. Reprinted in *CWJMK*, vol. XIV: 109–23.

——— (1937b) 'Alternative theories of the rate of interest', *Economic Journal*, June 1937. Reprinted in *CWJMK*, vol. XIV: 201–15.

——— (1937c) 'The "ex-ante" theory of the rate of interest', *Economic Journal*, December 1937. Reprinted in *CWJMK*, vol. XIV: 215–23.

——— (1938) 'Mr Keynes and finance', *Economic Journal*, June 1938. Reprinted in *CWJMK*, vol. XIV: 229–34.

——— (1939) 'The process of capital formation', *Economic Journal*, September 1939. Reprinted in *CWJMK*, vol. XIV: 278–85.

——— (1979) *The General Theory and After: A Supplement*, *CWJMK*, vol. XXIX.

Kindleberger, C.P. (1978) *Manias, Panics, and Crashes: a History of Financial Crises*, London: Macmillan.

——— (1987) 'Financial deregulation and economic performance: an attempt to relate European financial history to current LDC issues', *Journal of Development Economics* 27: 339–53.

King, M. (1985) 'The economics of saving: a survey of recent contributions', in K.J. Arrow and S. Honkapohja (eds) *Frontiers of Economics*, Oxford: Basil Blackwell.

Kornai, J. (1971) *Anti-Equilibrium on Economic Systems: Theory and the Tasks of Research*, Amsterdam: North Holland.

Kregel, J.A. (1984–5) 'Constraints on the expansion of output and employment: real or monetary?', *Journal of Post Keynesian Economics* 7 (2): 139–52.

Kumar, R.C. (1983) 'Money in development: a monetary growth model à la McKinnon', *Southern Economic Journal* 501: 18–36.

Lal, D. (1991) 'World saving and growth in developing countries', *Discussion Paper* 91–06, University College, London.

Lavoie, M. (1985) 'Credit and money: the dynamic circuit, overdraft economics, and Post-Keynesian economics', in M. Jarsulic (ed.) *Money and Macro Policy*, Boston: Klumer-Nijhoff.

——— (1986–7) 'Systemic financial fragility', *Journal of Post Keynesian Economics* 9 (2): 258–66.

Leff, N.H. (1968) *Economic Policy and Development in Brazil 1947–1964*, London: John Wiley.

Leijonhufvud, A. (1968) *On Keynesian Economics and the Economics of Keynes: a Study in Monetary Theory*, New York: Oxford University Press.

——— (1981) *Information and Coordination: Essays in Macroeconomic Theory*, New York: Oxford University Press.

Lessa, C. (1982) *Quinze Anos de Política Econômica*, São Paulo: Brasiliense.

Lewis, M.K. (1992) 'Modern banking in theory and practice', *Revue Économique* 43 (2): 203–25.

Ludwick, A.K. (1978) *Brazil: a Handbook of Historical Statistics*, Boston, Mass.: Hall.

Malan, P.S., Bonelli, R., Abreu, M.P. and Pereira, J.E.C. (1980) *Política Econômica Externa e Industrialização no Brasil (1939–52)*, Rio de Janeiro: IPEA/INPES.

Mathieson, D.J. (1980) 'Financial Reform and Stabilization Policy in Developing Economy', *Journal of Development Economics* 7: 359–98.

Mayer, C. (1988) 'New issues in corporate finance', *European Economic Review* 32: 1167–89.

McKinnon, R.I. (1973) *Money and Capital in Economic Development*, Washington, DC: Brookings Institution.

MiniPlan (1965) 'Ministério do Planejamento e Coordenação Geral', *Mercado Brasileiro de Capitais*, Documentos EPEA, 2.

Minsky, H.P. (1982) 'The financial-instability hypothesis: capitalist processes and the behavior of the economy', in C.P. Kindleberger and J.P. Laffargue (eds) *Financial Crises*, Cambridge: Cambridge University Press.

——— (1986) *Stabilizing an Unstable Economy*, New Haven: Yale University Press.

Minsky, H.P. and Ferri, P. (1984) 'Prices, employment and profits', *Journal of Post Keynesian Economics* 6 (4): 489–99.

Molho, L. (1986) 'Interest rates, saving, and investment in developing countries: a re-examination of the McKinnon–Shaw hypothesis', *IMF Staff Papers* 33.

Moore, B.J. (1985) 'Wages, bank lending and the endogeneity of credit money', in M. Jarsulic (ed.) *Money and Macro Policy*, Boston: Klumer-Nijhoff, pp. 1–28.

——— (1988) *Horizontalists and Verticalists : The Macroeconomics of Credit Money*, Cambridge: Cambridge University Press.

——— (1989) 'A simple model of bank intermediation', *Journal of Post Keynesian Economics* 12 (1): 10–28.

Moura da Silva, A. (1979) *Intermediação Financeira no Brasil: Origens, Estrutura e Problemas*, São Paulo: FEA-IPE, Universidade de São Paulo.

Ohlin, B. (1937a) 'Some notes on the Stockholm theory of saving and investment', *Economic Journal* 47: 53–69.

——— (1937b) 'Alternative theories of the rate of interest: rejoinder', *Economic Journal* 47: 423–7.

Pagano, M. (1989) 'Endogenous market thinness and stock price', *Review of Economic Studies* 56: 269–88.

Patinkin, D. and Levhari, D. (1968) 'The role of money in a simple growth model', *American Economic Review* 58 (4): 713–53.

Pereira, J.E.C. (1974) *Financiamento Externo e Crescimento Econômico no Brasil: 1966/73*, Rio de Janeiro: IPEA/INPES.

Pereira, L.C.B. (1983) *Development and Crisis in Brazil*, Westview Special Studies on Latin America and Caribbean, Westview Press: Colorado.

Pettenati, P. (1977) 'Alternative theories of a money-capital economy: Keynes, Tobin and the neoclassics', *Oxford Economic Papers* 29 (1): 357–69.

Pollard, S. (1964) 'Fixed capital in the Industrial Revolution in Britain', *Journal of Economic History* 24 (3), September: 299–314.

Portocarrero de Castro, H.O. (1981) *As Causas Econômicas da Concentração Bancária*, Rio de Janeiro: Instituto Brasileiro de Mercado de Capitais.

Resende, A.L. (1982) 'A política brasileira de estabilisação: 1963/68', *Pesquisa e Planejamento Econômico* 12 (3): 757–806.

Richardson, D.R. (1986) 'Asimakopolus on Kalecki and Keynes on finance, investment and saving', *Cambridge Journal of Economics* 10 (2): 191–8.

Robertson, D.H. (1937a) 'Some notes on Keynes's General Theory of Employment', *Economic Journal* 47: 395–411.

——— (1937b) 'Theories of the rate of interest: rejoinder', *Economic Journal* 47: 428–36.

Robinson, J. (1972) *Economic Heresies – Some Old Fashioned Questions in Economic Theory*, London: Macmillan.

——— (1979) *The Generalisation of the General Theory and Other Essays*, London: Macmillan.

Rogers, C. (1989) *Money, Interest and Capital*, Cambridge: Cambridge University Press.

Schumpeter, J. (1934) *The Theory of Economic Development*, Cambridge, Mass.: Cambridge University Press; reprinted, 1951.

——— (1939) *Business Cycles*, New York: McGraw-Hill.

——— (1954) *History of Economic Analysis*, London: Allen.

Sen, A. (ed.) (1970) Introduction to *Growth Economics*, Harmondsworth: Penguin Books.

Serra, J. (1982) 'Ciclos e Mudanças Estruturais na Economia Brasileira no Pós-Guerra', in L.G. Belluzzo and R. Coutinho (eds) *Desenvolvimento Capitalista no Brasil: Ensaios sobre a Crise*, São Paulo: Brasiliense, pp. 56–121.

Shackle, G.L.S. (1955) *Uncertainty in Economics*, Cambridge: Cambridge University Press.

Shaw, E.S. (1973) *Financial Deepening in Economic Development*, New York: Oxford University Press.

Simonsen, M.H. (1969) 'Inflation and the money and capital markets in Brazil', in H.S. Ellis (ed.) *The Economy of Brazil*, Berkeley, Calif.: University of California Press.

——— (1991) 'Poupança e crescimento econômico', *Revista Brasileira de Economia* 45 (1): 3–39.

Sochaczewski, A.C. (1980) 'Financial and Economic Development in Brazil, 1952–1968', unpublished Ph.D. thesis, London School of Economics, July.

Solow, R. (1956) 'A contribution to the theory of economic growth', *Quarterly Journal of Economics* 70 (1): 65–94.

Stern, N. (1989) 'The economics of development: a survey', *Economic Journal* 99: 597–685.

Stiglitz, J.E. and Weiss, A. (1981) 'Credit rationing in markets with imperfect competition', *American Economic Review* 71 (5): 393–410.

——— and ——— (1988) 'Banks as social accountants and screening devices for the allocation of credit', *National Bureau of Economic Research*, Working Paper 2710.

Studart, R. (1993) 'Financial repression and economic development: towards a post-Keynesian alternative', *Review of Political Economy* 5 (3): 277–98.

Syrup, D. (1972) 'Estrutura e política de juros no Brasil – 1960–70', *Revista Brasileira de Economia* 26 (1): 117–40.

Tavares, M.C. (1972) *Da Substitutição de Importações ao Capitalismo Financeiro*, Rio de Janeiro: Zahar.

——— (1978) *Ciclo e Crise: o Movimento Recente da Industrialização Brasileira*, Department of Economics, Universidade Federal do Rio de Janeiro.

Taylor, L. (1991) *Income Distribution, Inflation, and Growth: Lectures on Structuralist Macroeconomic Theory*, Cambridge, Mass.: MIT Press.
Taylor, L. and O'Connell, S.A. (1985) 'A Minsky crisis', *Quarterly Journal of Economics* C (4): 871–85.
Terzi, A. (1986) 'The independence of finance from saving: a flow of funds interpretation', *Journal of Post Keynesian Economics* 9 (2): 188–97.
Tobin, J. (1958) 'Liquidity preference as behaviour towards risk', *Review of Economic Studies* 25 (2): 65–86.
——— (1965) 'Money and economic growth', *Econometrica* 33 (4): 671–84.
——— (1982) 'The commercial banking firm: a simple model', *Scandinavian Journal of Economics* 84 (4): 495–530.
Todaro, M.P. (1981) *Economic Development in the Third World*, 2nd edn, New York and London: Longman.
Torr, C.S.W. (1983) 'Equilibrium, expectations and information', unpublished Ph.D. thesis, Rhodes University.
Trebat, T.J. (1983) *Brazil's State-Owned Enterprises*, Cambridge: Cambridge University Press.
Wade, R. (1989) 'The role of government in overcoming market failure: Taiwan, Republic of Korea and Japan', in H. Hughes (ed.) *Achieving Industrialization in East Asia*, Cambridge: Cambridge University Press.
Weintraub, E.R. (1979) *Microfoundations: the Compatibility of Microeconomics and Macroeconomics*, Cambridge: Cambridge University Press.
——— (1982) *General Equilibrium Theory*, London: Macmillan.
Wells, J.R. (1979) 'Brazil and the post-1973 crisis and the international economy', in Rosemary Thorp and Laurence Whitehead (eds) *Inflation and Stabilization in Latin America*, London: Macmillan.
Werneck, A.O. (1969) 'As atividades empresariais do governo federal no Brasil', *Revista Brasileira de Economia* 23 (3): 89–100.
Werneck, R.F. (1985) 'Uma análise do financiamento e do investmento das empresas estatais federais no Brasil: 1980–3', *Revista Brasileira de Economia* 39 (1): 3–26.
Winnet, A. (1992) 'Some semantics of endogeneity', in V. Chick and P. Arestis (eds) *Recent Development in Post-Keynesian Economics*, London: Edward Elgar.
World Bank (1984a) *Brazil: Economic Memorandum: A World Bank Country Study*, Washington, DC: World Bank.
——— (1984b) *The World Development Report 1984*, New York: Oxford University Press.
——— (1985) *Brasil, Análise dos Sistemas Financeiros*, Rio de Janeiro: IBMEC.
——— (1989) *Financial Systems and Development*, World Development Indicators, Annual Report.
Wray, L.R. (1989) 'A Keynesian theory of banking: a comment on Dymski', *Journal of Post Keynesian Economics* 12 (1): 152–66.
——— (1992) 'Commercial banks, the central bank and endogenous money', *Journal of Post Keynesian Economics* 14 (3): 297–310.
Zini, Jr, A. (1982) 'Uma Avaliação do Setor Financeiro no Brasil da Reforma de 1965–66 a Crise dos Anos 80', unpublished M.A. Dissertation, DEPE, Universidade de Campinas.

—— (1984) 'Evolução da estrutura financeira das empresas no brasil 1969–1977', *Estudos Econômicos* 14 (1).

Zonisein, J. (1984) 'Atitudes Nacionais e Financiamentos da Indústria: A Experiência Brasileira', *Texto pare Discussão* 63, Rio de Janeiro: Instituto de Economia Industrial, Universidade Federal do Rio de Janeiro.

Zysman, J. (1983) *Governments, Markets, and Growth: Financial Systems and the Politics of Industrial Growth*, Oxford: Martin Robertson.

Index